DAGGERS, BAYONETS
AND FIGHTING KNIVES
OF
HITLER'S GERMANY

Daggers, Bayonets & Fighting Knives of Hitler's Germany

BY
MAJOR JOHN R. ANGOLIA

1st EDITION

COPYRIGHT © 1971 BY
MAJOR JOHN R. ANGOLIA

ISBN No. 0-912138-06-8

PRINTED IN THE UNITED STATES OF AMERICA
BY
D-D ASSOC., PALO ALTO, CALIFORNIA

DESIGNED AND ILLUSTRATED
BY
ROGER JAMES BENDER.

COVER PHOTO BY ED KOZLOWSKY

R. JAMES BENDER PUBLISHING P.O. BOX 1425, MOUNTAIN VIEW, CALIFORNIA 94040

ACKNOWLEDGEMENTS

Although this finalized work bears my name as author, this book is the result of many persons who have strived to put the most comprehensive reference possible into the hands of the collector. When it became known that I was about to undertake this venture, I received a great deal of encouragement, but more importantly, offers of assistance to provide much needed input in the form of information and photographs. It is the total combination of this knowledge, ideas, and exceptional photographs which have made this book what it is.

I owe a great debt of gratitude to a number of people who have devoted their time, knowledge, and trust in insuring that the most comprehensive reference of its type might be the end result. No priority can be given, since each in his own way played a key role in the completed work. The years of tutelage which I received from N. C. "Dutch" Heilman, the "Grand-daddy" of Nazi blade collecting, and Fred Davis, Jr., who has the most complete collection to my knowledge, provided me with the knowledge and the desire to undertake such a task. Phil Stober, who in my opinion is one of the finest research collectors in the business, provided the impetus to undertake the arduous task of research in seeking out the correct or best available answers. While the information may have been acquired, had it not been for Vincent and Hella Dipboye, the book still would not have been completed. Vince spent many hours over the camera and developer, while Hella made the difficult task of translation look easy. Others whom I would like to single out are:

5

Ed Anderson, Jr.	J. Scott
Roger Bender	Bob Settle
Hugh Brock	Andy Southard
Eric Campion	Griff Squire
Ed Kozlowsky	Roger Steele
Bob Kraus	Col. Clarence Stewart
George Lambertson	Kennedy W. Ward
Bob McCarthy	Ralph Weggenmann
Tony Oliver	George Wheeler
Jim Orris, Jr.	Jerry Weiblen
Gary Mahaffey	Richard Wiser
Dick Pumphrey	

and last, but not least, my friend, Fred Stephens, who should share the credit on the cover, but elected to give and not receive.

No historical reference of this type could be considered complete without utilizing the resources of the Library of Congress, the National Archives and the Imperial War Museum. The captured collections of Hermann Göring, Joachim von Ribbentrop, Adolf Wagner, Eva Braun, and Heinrich Hoffmann were graciously placed at my disposal.

I would like to express my appreciation to the many collectors who so warmly received my first book, Swords of Hitler's Third Reich, and have made my collection over the years what it is today.

JOHN R. ANGOLIA   JANUARY 1971
8117 SPRINGFIELD VILLAGE DR.
SPRINGFIELD, VIRGINIA 22152

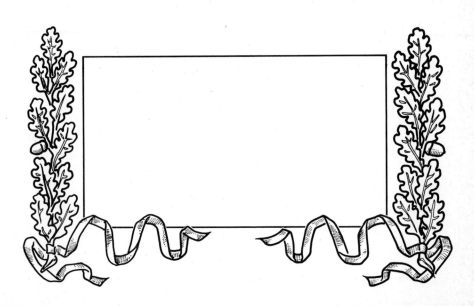

6

CONTENTS

INTRODUCTION

The venture of Adolf Hitler to become master of the world was executed with a symbolic flair. The effort being to spur his fanatical followers on to their maximum capabilities. Hitler traded the traditional brown uniform of his Nazi Party for the grey-green color of his conquering army and vowed before all Germany that he would not wear the brown uniform again until Germany was victorious over the mounting number of enemies. Fortunately for the world, the combined Allied powers did not permit Hitler to complete his symbolic transition.

The uniform change was but one symbolic act among the many that were effectively utilized by Hitler to gain growing support. In 1933, he instituted a wide range of dagger sidearms which were to reflect the intent and strength of the organizations which they represented. In many cases, the struggle for the right to wear the dagger became a means in itself. Hitler was able to get millions of people involved in his movement with such devices as uniforms and their trappings. The level of hysteria that he brought about in Germany was largely responsible for extending the war by at least one year.

Germany was on her way to total defeat when this author directed his attention to collecting German war souvenirs in 1944. Interest was spurred by the daily news coverage, the bond drives and other patriotic appeals to the war effort. Then, as the soldiers returned home, they brought with them a wide spectrum of war trophies.

It was not until 1955 that the first dagger was added to this author's general collection. There was an immediate appreciation for the craftsmanship contained in the daggers and swords of Nazi Germany. Blades of the era, more than any other category of relics, were considered to be art forms. It was this appreciation that brought about the concerted effort to acquire the wide range of patterns that were known to exist.

Due to the lack of available reference material, the collecting of blades by the general enthusiast was slow to gain momentum. The primary reference held by a few collectors was the Eickhorn Kundendienst. This initially scarce original sales catalogue was to prove a relatively reliable reference through the years. It was not until 1959 that the first in a series of dagger references was to enjoy national circulation. Armed with a degree of information, collector interest grew considerably. As with any desirable commodity, the Law of Supply and Demand was imposed, and commercial values began their rapid increase. Some daggers that sold for $18 in the mid-1950's have increased to over $300. Prices in the thousands no longer draw a surprised reaction.

The first attempt at an authoritative reference was made in 1965. It was soon to gain the reputation of being the "bible" among collectors. For the first time, an effort was made to do more than just identify the various daggers.

A degree of newly founded information and rapidly rising values caused the appearance of specimens that had previously been unheard of. Armed with the knowledge that blade collecting held some new discoveries, interest was again stimulated. The introduction of a wide range of counterfeit daggers occured in 1964 when unscrupulous dealers attempted to capitalize on the rising values. The introduction of these pieces resulted in collecting becoming a task, and in some cases a very expensive gamble rather than an enjoyable pastime. It became apparent that more information was required by the general collector.

My serious gathering of research material began in 1960 in an attempt to sift out facts from the misconceptions and half-truths that existed. This book is the culmination of those efforts.

Archives of the United States, Great Britain and Germany have been exhausted, as have the original publications and sales material produced by the manufacturing firms during the subject period. These sources provide the regulations governing wear and the specifications for the manufacture and distribution of daggers, bayonets and fighting knives. It was also found that exception existed for every rule established by regulations.

Being cognisant of the regulations, and appreciating the various exceptions to those regulations, the collector can better understand the numerous variations currently at his disposal.

It is the purpose of this reference to provide factual information relating to the sidearms (excluding swords) which were utilized by the numerous military, political and governmental formations in Nazi Germany. An effort has also been made to provide a concise history of the organizations discussed. The one area that is necessary but sorely lacking, is the production figure for each specimen produced. Most of the records maintained by the manufacturers on their production were destroyed during the closing days of the war, and no central record facility was established to maintain such accountability. While some production figures were discovered among the tons of original documents, these figures would prove to be of little value without the total production figures to be used as a base. For any gaps that may exist, others are encouraged to fill them. Perhaps time will be the answer to the questions which still exist in the most interesting and challenging of collecting fields.

———————————

Daggers of the Political Formations

SA GROUPS MASS THEIR COLORS DURING A PARTY DAY RALLY.

STORM TROOPERS
[STURMABTEILUNG (SA)]

The Sturmabteilung (SA) or Storm Troops was to achieve its zenith of power and prestige soon after the Nazis came to power in 1933. Hitler's political army, by 1934, had reached approximately 3,000,000 men in strength. The SA had grown out of necessity when, on November 4, 1921, 46 toughs were given the task of maintaining order at Hitler's rallies. Their initial security task resulted in a beer hall brawl, which was the first of a long succession of out-and-out brawls and political infighting which resulted in Hitler's rise to power. The 46 man detachment of "Brownshirts" (as they were later called) was so effective in its security mission that Hitler ordered the further expansion of the group. Hitler put the command of the SA into the capable hands of Captain Ernst Röhm, and charged him with the responsibility of developing a formidable political army. Röhm executed his orders to the letter. The strength of the SA grew to such proportions that it nearly consumed Hitler in its wake.

The man who commanded the SA, Ernst Röhm, had joined the Nazi Party during its earliest days, when Anton Drexler was its leader. After a young radical named Adolf Hitler joined the Party, it was not long before Drexler was edged out as leader. Hitler then undertook a series of political gambles in an effort to raise the infant Nazi Party from obscurity. Röhm was to prove an able organizer, especially when it came to gathering a protective security force around Hitler. Röhm had obtained the rank of captain in the Army during the First World War and, like so many others, was forced into civilian life when Germany capitulated.

15

He then became an adjutant in the quasi-military/political force of Ritter von Epp. During the infamous "Blood Purge" on November 9, 1923, Röhm walked with Hitler to the War Ministry Building in Munich where a cordon of police stopped them just outside the building. Who fired the first shot is not known, but a man standing next to Hitler fell to the street mortally wounded. Hitler panicked and fled in a nearby automobile. His lieutenant, Hermann Göring, was wounded in the thigh, and also beat a hasty retreat.... eventually fleeing to Sweden. Hitler was totally upset with the debacle and looked for a scapegoat. He removed Röhm from his command for the failure of the SA to take charge of the situation. Röhm placed himself in voluntary exile, traveling to Bolivia where he was employed as a military advisor to the Bolivian Army.

The failure of the Munich beer hall putsch, which resulted in the sacrifice of 16 SA men to the Nazi cause, caused the SA to be dissolved by the Weimar government. Two years later when the Party was once again legalized, the SA was back on the streets. During this two year period, command of the SA had been turned over to Göring. When he turned his ambitions elsewhere, Hitler gave command to another former captain, Pfeffer von Salomon. Von Salomon soon grew tired of the undisciplined group, and Hitler became increasingly displeased with von Salomon, who had proved to be totally inept for the task. He resigned his command in 1930, and Hitler took personal command of the SA. In 1931, Hitler recalled Röhm, and assigned him as Chief of Staff of the SA. Content to make the most of his position, Röhm set about to build his command to one of importance. He threw his full weight into the national elections with successful results. When Hitler came to power, Röhm saw to it that conflicting organizations were declared illegal. He formed

RÖHM AND HITLER AT THE 1933 PARTY DAY RALLY.

the SA Reserves I and II to gather in the members of the now defunct Stahl-helm and other veteran leagues. These served to add to his already mas-sive political army.

The SA had grown to be the largest of the Nazi formations, and had gathered considerable strength in doing so. Röhm envisioned the SA as his personal revolutionary army, but the power of the SA and the ambi-tions of its leaders were to consume it. Röhm's quest for personal power was not to Hitler's liking and his concern over Röhm was added to by the whisperings of Göring and Himmler. Hitler looked to the future and de-cided to cast his lot with the generals of the Army. Röhm had been aware of what was happening in August 1933, when he declared, "Any-one who thinks that the days of the SA are over must make up his mind that we are here and that we will remain". Remain they did, but with-out Röhm, as the resulting "Night of the Long Knives" on June 30, 1934, put an end to him and his ambitions. When Röhm was murdered at the age of 47, it dealt a near fatal blow to the SA. The organization was not to recover from this purge until war demands made it necessary that the SA once again achieve a degree of prominence.

SA-Obergruppenführer Viktor Lutze had become a strong opponent of Röhm, and Hitler rewarded his loyalty by appointing him Stabschef. The ranks of the SA were drastically cut back to 1,200,000, and a gen-eral reorganization took place. Lutze attempted to regain a degree of pride for his SA, and set about to build an elite force within his organ-ization. The SA-Standarte "Feldherrnhalle" was the closest group that approached the SS elite. Lutze was readily accepted in the Nazi heir-archy, and since his father-in-law was the Chief of Staff of the Army, he enjoyed good relations with the military as well. Properly leashed, the SA ceased to be a rival force to the military. Hitler's trust in Lutze al-lowed the SA to regain some degree of its earlier influence, and its strength was allowed to grow.

When Lutze was killed in an automobile accident on May 1, 1943, Hitler searched for another able Chief of Staff. It was not until August of that year that the appointment of SA-Obergruppenführer Wilhelm Schepmann was announced. Schepmann, a veteran of the World War, was a member of the Reichstag, and was formally the Police President of Dortmund, and SA Chief of Saxony. He was to retain the position of Stabs-chef until the close of the war.

The SA fulfilled many necessary functions, the most important of which was the pre-military training of all youths over 18 years of age. The war placed many manpower requirements on the SA as many of its leaders were absorbed into the fighting ranks. Approximately 80% of the SA strength was directly contributed to the war effort and its wartime strength dwindled to between 500,000 - 700,000 members. Replacement personnel for the SA were obtained by absorbing lesser organizations.

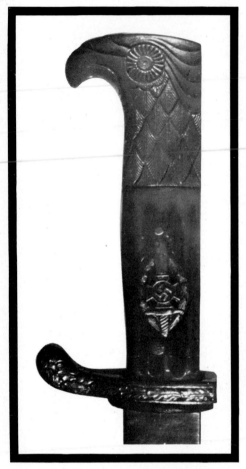

Those personnel still fit for military duty were taken into the SA from the National Socialist League for Disabled Veterans (NSKOV). SA units performed military duties in occupied countries beside regular military forces. They also augmented police and customs forces by patrolling the German frontier. These and other wartime functions greatly restored the prestige of the SA.

THE SA DAGGER

The SA recruited membership primarily from the lower middle class. It was these persons who were the most susceptible to the Nazi slogans and the various political platforms that the Party professed. Unemployment and inflation spread rapidly throughout Germany soon after the war. Especially hard hit was the working middleclass, as they found their lifesavings wiped out almost over night. It was a sincere political belief that drew the first members into the SA, not the appeal of the uniform.

THE VETERAN'S LEAGUE BAYONET WAS IDENTICAL TO THE POLICE SERVICE BAYONET WITH THE EXCEPTION OF THE NSKOV INSIGNIA.

When the SA was officially formed, their uniform consisted of a swastika armband. The brown shirt uniform was not designed until 1932, and from that time, the uniform underwent six major changes. As Germany regained some of its economic balance, the glamor of the uniform did become a major consideration in attracting new recruits.

A sidearm for the SA was inevitable as some form of defense was necessary. They had been required to fight for their lives and to protect the integrity of the Nazi Party. The early SA toughs had accomplished this with clubs, knives and guns. Many of the security force had been seen on the streets armed with bayonets of every imaginable origin.

So, it was not tradition, but necessity that gave rise to the development of a dagger sidearm. It was the fact that the SA was not armed that made them a political army. Although their status was not changed when they added a Service Dagger as a standard part of their uniform, their personal attitude was bolstered considerably.

Hitler directed that a dagger sidearm be designed for his political army, and commissioned Professor Woenne of the Solingen Industrial Trade School to design and produce a prototype. It was Hermann Göring who suggested the style which was to become the first official Nazi dagger. While the HJ Fahrtenmesser was the first blade to be produced in quantity for the Nazis, it was the SA dagger which received the first official recognition. Göring's choice stemmed from a 16th century Swiss Holbein dagger which he had seen in a Munich museum. Hitler gave his approval to the resulting prototype, and contracts for its manufacture were let. An order went out through SA channels informing its members of the availability of a dagger.

Modifications of this dagger were also made available to the members of the SS and NSKK, which had their origins with the SA. A year later, the NPEA would follow suit.

The Marine SA was authorized its own uniform in 1934, and along with it the standard SA Service Dagger. This one sub-element of the SA was an excellent example of the continuous changes which took place in the brief span of two years. Members of the SA Naval units initially wore a dagger with a black grip and black scabbard body. This was soon changed to the standard Service Dagger, but with copper or gilt plated scabbard fittings. By 1936, the Marine SA was required to wear the standard SA Service Dagger with no special mark of distinction.

During the period 1934-1944, a wide spectrum of daggers was developed for wear and/or award to the SA and its sub-elements.

1933 PATTERN SA SERVICE DAGGER

When a dress dagger was authorized for wear by all qualified members of the SA on December 15, 1933, the dagger had been placed into production without the advantage of any strict production standards or inspection criteria. Basic design specifications were made available to the Solingen blade merchants, and production began in anticipation of the many pending orders. For a brief period a wide variety of manufacturer's variations found their way into the hands of early purchasers. The very first pieces were produced without the enameled SA signet inlaid in the upper portion of the brown wood handle. This oversight was quickly corrected. **19**

A wide variety of wood was used to make the handle, including walnut, maple, pear and cherry. The early pattern national emblem, with pointed wings and elongated body, was used as a grip inlay for this handle until early 1934. The SA motto "Alles für Deutschland" (Everything for Germany) was etched in various patterns on the face of the double edge blade. Scabbards varied between the standard sheet metal steel with externally mounted nickel silver fittings to that having a copper body with nickel silver fittings. In both cases, the scabbard body was finished in a reddish-brown protective oxide.

EARLY PATTERN NATIONAL EMBLEM

The SA Service Dagger was created on December 15, 1933, when the SA Chief of Staff, SA-Obergruppenführer Krauser, issued an order (Order Nr. 1734/33) on the subject of the SA dagger. It required that each Group submit prepayment at the rate of 7.30 RM per dagger to be paid to the Munich office. Individual purchase of the dagger was prohibited, however, the SA member could obtain the dagger by making payment to his Group Central Office. The Munich office contracted for purchase of the daggers with the numerous manufacturers. The dagger was wholesaled to the SA Central Office, who in turn, made retail distribution. Group accountability was maintained by having the first two letters of the Group stamped on the reverse of the lower crossguard. In a few cases, individual accountability was maintained by means of the owner's SA serial number being stamped or engraved on the side or lower portion of the lower crossguard.

Standardization was imposed on all manufacturers late in 1933, followed by strict inspection codes. Inspections were carried out by the Reichszeugmeisterei (RZM), which was established in October 1934 to oversee standardization of all NSDAP production items. This resulted in a number of subtle and significant changes. The early pattern national emblem was replaced in 1934 with a solid nickle or silver plated national emblem with rounded wings. The scabbard with the copper base proved to be too soft and subject to denting, thus giving way to the sheet metal, steel base. A brown paint scabbard finish was offered as an option, and scabbard fittings were produced of nickel plate over steel. Significantly, the pattern of the blade motto became standardized. After 1934, the RZM inspection mark, etched on the reverse of the blade, shared that position with the manufacturer's trademark. The RZM inspection mark, with a code that included the designation of the blade manufacturer, totally replaced the trademark in 1936. The exception to these markings was the specially ordered higher quality Service Dagger. In that

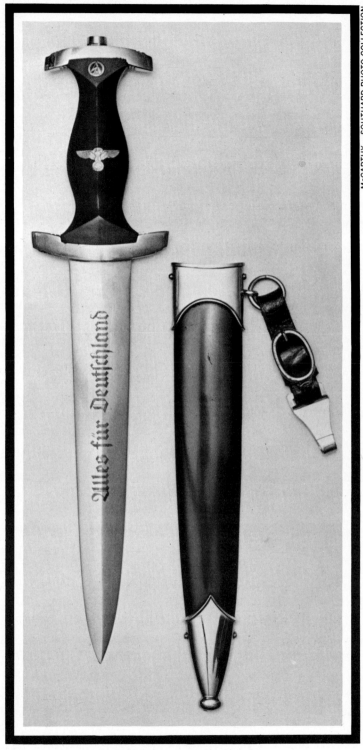

STANDARD SA SERVICE
DAGGER WITH VERY
EARLY PATTERN MOTTO
ON BLADE. THE
CHANGE IS ESPECIALLY
DISCERNIBLE IN THE
FIRST "A".

STANDARD SA SERVICE DAGGER

same year, manufacturers went to a less expensive means of production by using nickel or chrome plated zinc upper and lower crossguards. The nickle or silver plated national emblem was replaced with one stamped from aluminum. Oxidized scabbards ceased to be offered.

The 41cms dagger was authorized for wear with the Service Uniform, and was worn suspended by a short brown leather hanger that snapped to a ring on an outer belt loop. Regulations required that the dagger was to be worn with a frog or short strap attachment which caused the piece to be suspended in a vertical configuration during maneuvers or exercises. It was during these maneuvers, which required that the SA member be put through a series of simulated combat exercises, that the tip of the scabbard became dented.

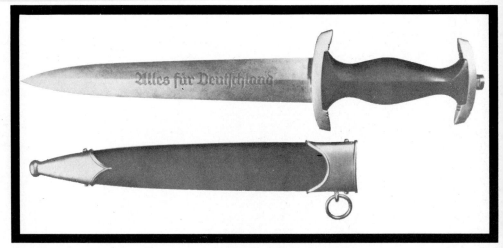

THIS UNATTRIBUTED DAGGER IS ONE POSSIBLY DESIGNATED FOR THE MARINE SA. THE HANDLE IS BLACK, AND VOID OF ANY INSIGNIA. THE SCABBARD IS PAINTED BLACK.

THE RÖHM HONOR DAGGER

SA Stabschef Röhm issued an order (Nr. 1444/34) on February 3, 1934, which authorized all SA (to include SS) leaders and subordinates who were members prior to December 31, 1931, and were members at the time of the order, to receive and wear a specially inscribed Honor Dagger. The dagger was identical in every respect to the standard Service Dagger save for the addition of Röhm's dedication on the reverse of the blade. The inscription "In herzlicher Freundschaft Ernst Röhm" (In Cordial Comradeship: Ernst Röhm) was written out by Röhm, made into a template, and transferred to the blade through an acid etching process. Röhm designated a total of 135,860 honor daggers to be distributed, with a breakout as follows:

Assigned to for subsequent award	Quantity
Staff of the Upper Group II (Stettin)	20
" " " " " III (Breslau)	20
" " " " " IV (Dresden)	35
" " " " " V (Frankfurt/M)	20
" " " " " VI (Hannover)	15
" " " " " VII (München)	25
" " " " " VIII (München)	25
Group of Berlin-Brandenburg	8,300
" " Bayerische Ostmark	3,200
" " Franken	4,100
" " Hansa	3,000
" " Hessen	5,500
" " Hochland	6,100
" " Mitte	6,000
" " Niederrhein	8,500
" " Niedersachsen	6,100
" " Nordmark	4,600
" " Nordsee	4,100
" " Oesterreich	3,200
" " Ostland (also upper Group I)	6,100
" " Ostmark	4,500
" " Pommern	5,700
" " Sachsen	7,900
" " Schlesien	8,700
" " Sudwest	7,900
" " Thuringen	4,800
" " Westmark	7,800
" " Westfalen	9,700
SS	9,900
Total	135,860

A subsequent order (Nr. 1444 II ANG) dated February 20, 1934, extended eligibility to those SA personnel who had transferred from the Hitler Youth, and had held membership in that organization prior to December 31, 1934.

Röhm's day in the sun came to an abrupt end with his murder on June 30, 1934. On the very next day, SA-Gruppenführer Obernitz, leader of SA Group "Franken", relayed orders issued by Hitler and the new SA Stabschef, Viktor Lutze. The order (Nr. 6747/34) which went out to

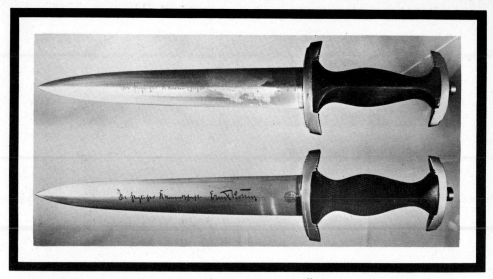

SA HONOR DAGGER DEDICATED BY SA STABSCHEF ERNST RÖHM, WITH CHECKERED WALNUT GRIP. THE STYLE OF THE EICKHORN TRADEMARK WILL EFFECTIVELY DATE A RÖHM HONOR DAGGER. WITH THE MURDER OF RÖHM, IT WAS ORDERED THAT ALL TRACES OF HIS NAME BE REMOVED. WHILE THIS WAS ACCOMPLISHED IN MANY WAYS, THE MOST COMMON MEANS WAS BY A GRINDING WHEEL, AS SHOWN IN THE EXAMPLE DAGGER ABOVE.

all SA members required that all Röhm Honor Daggers were to be disposed of. However, owners were given the option of having the Röhm inscription ground and polished, thus causing the piece to become a standard Service Dagger. A wide range of reactions was caused by the order. Those persons who continued to hold an allegience to Röhm (they were few) put their dagger in hiding and ordered a replacement piece. A dagger in a collection today that has the entire dedication is extremely scarce. The great majority who complied with the order obliterated the inscription either wholly or in part. The truly dedicated SA member, one who could not normally afford to purchase another Service Dagger, followed the order to the letter. The dagger was returned to the manufacturer or equally qualified craftsman, and the dedication was expertly ground and polished, leaving little or no trace of the original inscription.

Contrary to the practice that had been established by Röhm, Stabschef Lutze did not continue the practice of authorizing the distribution of Honor Daggers "en masse". Lutze did issue a very limited number of daggers dedicated under his signature, but they did not conform to any set pattern.

Röhm's order (1 Nr. 3707) dated February 21, 1934, permitted individual SA leaders to award or otherwise present a wide variety of daggers to deserving comrades providing the dagger maintained the identical exterior appearance of the standard Service Dagger. This single order

24

N.C. HEILMAN

HIGH QUALITY SA SERVICE DAGGER PRESENTED TO SA-STURMFÜHRER LOTHAR DE MARÉES FROM SA GROUP "THURIGEN."

25

(A) NOT AN HONOR DAGGER, BUT A HIGH QUALITY SA SERVICE DAGGER WITH ETCHED DAMASCUS BLADE. (B) SHOOTING HONOR PRIZE AWARDED BY SA LEADER ECKSTEIN OF STANDARTE R53. THE DEDICATION ON THE BLADE IS GOLD FILLED. (C) THIS SERVICE DAGGER WAS GIVEN TO OSKAR SCHMIDT ON HIS WEDDING DAY BY HIS COMRADES OF THE MARINE-STURM 15/34.

accounted for a very wide variety of SA pattern daggers. Blades with inscriptions and/or damascus steel could be had simply by putting in a special order through the Central Issue Office. From this order stemmed a series of very high quality Service Daggers that were given in recognition of outstanding deeds. While most of the recipients were in fact SA Leaders, rank had no bearing on the bestowal of this dagger. The one most often awarded was the standard Service Dagger bearing a specially etched dedication on the reverse of the blade. It was not unusual that inscriptions were also placed on the flat outer surface of the upper scabbard band.

SA HONOR DAGGER OF THE SA CHIEF OF STAFF, VICTOR LUTZE

SA Stabschef Lutze initiated a series of SA Honor Daggers, beginning in 1935, in recognition for outstanding or meritorious service by SA High Leaders. The development of this high quality, specially designed SA Honor Dagger would account for the lack of Lutze presentation daggers that were of the Röhm variety. The fact that Lutze restricted award of these daggers to SA High Leaders was the single limiting factor in the number of blades produced and eventually awarded.

The basic configuration was identical to the 1933 Pattern Service Dagger. It was worn in lieu of the Service Dagger, and on any occasion where a dagger was prescribed for wear. Like the Service Dagger, it was worn suspended by a short brown leather strap hanger that passed through the swivel ring of the upper scabbard band, and attached to a belt or pocket hook on the wearer's left side. The crossguards were cast in brass with a heavily silver plated oak leaf pattern front and back. The brown dyed wood handle did not differ from that of the standard. A silver plated tang nut secured the hilt to the blade, and was sometimes inscribed with the owner's monogram. The externally mounted silver plated scabbard fittings were grooved around the outer edge both front and back. Between the upper and lower scabbard fittings

SA HONOR DAGGER WITH DAMASCUS BLADE

was a smooth or pebbled grain dark brown leather covering over a steel scabbard body. The blade was of either the standard variety with SA motto or a beautiful damascus pattern with raised gold plated motto with gold plated oak leaves at both ends. The raised gold plated manufacturer's

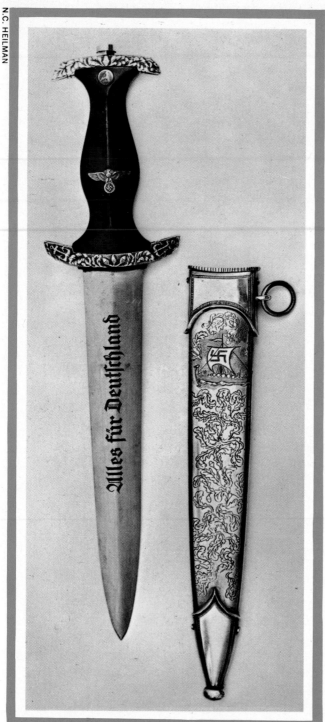

SPECIAL LUTZE DEDICATED DAGGER TO SA-STANDARTENFÜHRER HEYDRICK. NOTE THE IN-
CORPORATION OF THE ANCHORS INTO THE CROSSGUARD MOTIF. ALL METAL FITTINGS ARE
BRONZE AND THE HANDLE IS DYED BLUE WOOD.

CHAINED SA HONOR DAGGER

mark was on the upper back side of the blade. Occasionally, a raised or etched gold filled dedication was placed on the reverse of the blade.

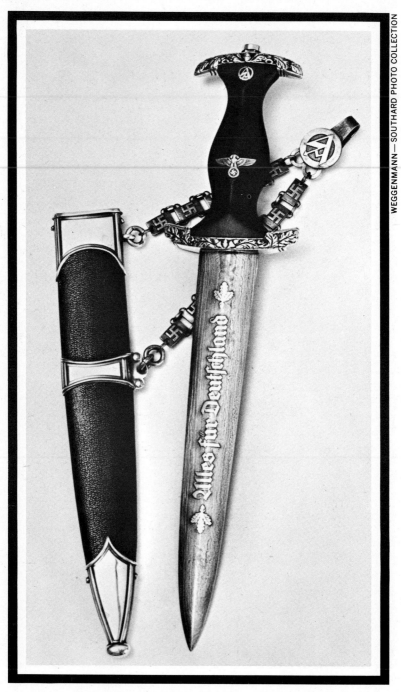

CHAINED SA HONOR DAGGER WITH DAMASCUS BLADE

In 1938, Lutze ordered that a specially designed Honor Dagger be produced for award to SA High Leaders. The dagger stemmed from the design of his personal dagger which had been produced for him in 1937. The dagger carried over the already established Honor pattern, but added a chain suspension. The chain, having five upper links and seven lower links, was joined at a snap fastener with a large SA signet on its face. The silver plated links had a raised gold squared swastika, and each was joined by two small metal links. The chain was attached to the upper and center silver plated scabbard bands by a small swivel ring. The center scabbard band came with two minor variations. One simply had a small swivel ring attached directly to the band, while the second had an ornate ramp with a small swivel ring. Date of manufacture could account for the variation as both are found having been produced by the same blade manufacturer.

SA-OBERGRUPPENFÜHRER BRÜCKNER, HITLER'S SA ADJUTANT, WEARS A SA HONOR DAGGER WITH DETACHABLE DOUBLE STRAP SUSPENSION HANGERS AT THE OPENING OF THE AUTOMOBILE SHOW, 18 FEBRUARY 1938. THE DAGGER WAS FIRST WORN BY BRÜCKNER ON 22 JANUARY OF THAT SAME YEAR WHILE ATTENDING THE ARCHITECTURE SHOW.

To allow himself greater diversity, Lutze retained the previously designed Honor Dagger to be awarded for special accomplishment rather than simply obtaining a senior position. After 1938, the 1935 Pattern Honor Dagger was modified slightly. The basic dagger retained identically the same design, while the silver plated scabbard fittings were produced with a raised oak leaf pattern front and back.

After the outbreak of the war in Europe, in 1939, modifications to the basic dagger ended. Wear of the dagger continued for the next three years until it became more expedient to wear a pistol sidearm. Blades were worn at ceremonial functions into 1944, but on an increasingly limited basis. By the middle of that same year, wear of the dagger had been phased out altogether. The dagger did not show up again in any quantity until the fall of Germany when the allied military government issued a proclamation that all weapons, to include blades, be turned in to the military constabulary.

GÖRING CHATS WITH DR. GOEBBLES AT A NUREMBERG PARTY DAY RALLY, 7 SEPTEMBER 1937. THE DAGGER SHOWN FOR WEAR IS A SPECIALLY DESIGNED HONOR DAGGER THAT WAS GIVEN TO GÖRING IN EARLY 1935, AND WAS FIRST WORN BY HIM AT THE SEPTEMBER PARTY DAY RALLY OF THAT SAME YEAR. HE WORE IT FOR THE LAST TIME IN 1938.

LIBRARY OF CONGRESS

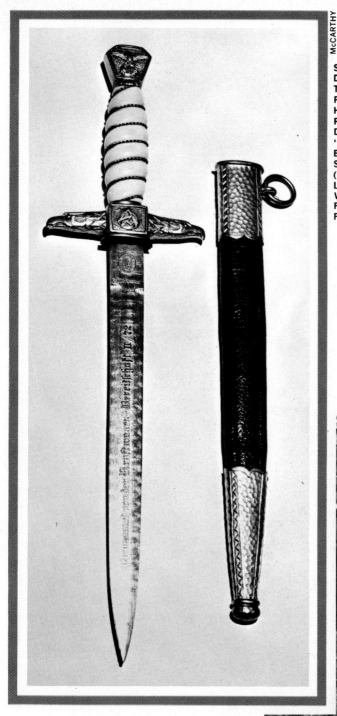

SPECIAL SA PRESENTATION DAGGER MANUFACTURED BY THE EICKHORN FIRM FOR PRESENTATION TO SELECTED HIGH GERMAN LEADERS. THE RAISED DEDICATION ON THE DAMASCUS BLADE READS, "Pg. KREISLEITER u. OBER BÜRGERMEISTER VETTER. SCHOENHOFF, OBERFÜHRER" (PARTY COMRADE DISTRICT LEADER AND LORD MAYOR VETTER. SCHOENHOFF, OBER FÜHRER). HILT AND SCABBARD FITTINGS ARE GOLD PLATED.

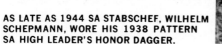

AS LATE AS 1944 SA STABSCHEF, WILHELM SCHEPMANN, WORE HIS 1938 PATTERN SA HIGH LEADER'S HONOR DAGGER.

SA-STANDARTE "FELDHERRNHALLE" COLOR GUARD HONORING GÖRING ON HIS 44th BIRTHDAY, 12 JANUARY 1937.

SA STANDARTE "FELDHERRNHALLE"

Nazi ideological doctrine set the Germans up as the "master race", but efforts were continued to establish an elite within an elite... ...witness the structure and doctrines of the SS. The SA had attempted to achieve a similar elite force, starting with the formation of the Feldjäger Korps by Göring on February 22, 1933. This corps was composed of selected SA, SS and Stahlhelm personnel with a mission to serve as an auxiliary to the police of the Berlin-Brandenburg Group. It soon came to police the internal elements of the Party, and in effect, was tasked with the mission to serve as "watch dogs" to the honor of the Party. Up until the time of his purge, Röhm designated himself as head of this politically elite organization, thus adding to the powers and prestige of its limited membership. However, when the SA was purged and its power considerably reduced, the Feldjäger Korps was made independent of the SA, and was soon dissolved.

In 1935, another attempt was made to establish a politically elite organization within the SA. The founding of a paid full-time company of SA personnel was to act as a security force for the SA Stabschef, and to perform as ceremonial troops at the various SA festivals. In an effort to establish an internal structure that was to symbolize the full embodiment of the political soldier, SA Stabschef Lutze formed the SA-Standarte "Feldherrnhalle" in 1936. The element was named after the location of the abortive Munich Putsch of 1923, which was a date of honor to the SA. The establishment of the Standarte simply meant a name change for the Stabschef's security company.

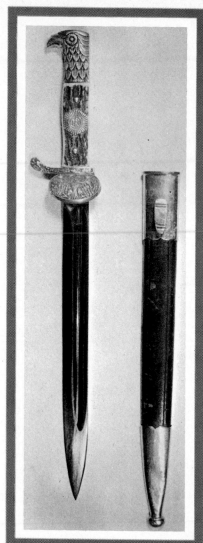

THE FELDJÄGER BAYONET

WEIMAR ERA SHIELD (LEFT) ADOPTED BY THE
FELDJÄGERKORPS UNTIL A NEW SHIELD (RIGHT)
WAS DESIGNED.

MEMBERS OF THE FELDJÄGER
SWEAR THE OATH OF ALLEGIANCE
TO HITLER, 18 JANUARY 1936.
THIS ELEMENT WAS THE PARTY
POLICE FORCE, AND WAS PHASED
OUT WHEN THE SA-STANDARTE
"FELDHERRNHALLE" WAS FORMED.

Many members of the SA, wishing to become recognized members of this elite organization, submitted their applications for membership, but few were selected. Lutze established a very strict criteria for selection, calling only for the best possible personnel. Permanent concerns to house the members were initially established at Berlin, Munich, Hattingen, Krefeld, Stettin and Stuttgart, but this eventually grew with one Sturmbann located at the headquarters of each SA group. Membership requirements grew as the organization grew. Party members between the ages of 18 and 25, having already served one year in the Hitler Youth and six months in the SA, were given the opportunity to join the "Feldherrnhalle" provided they met with all other requirements. Even as the need for membership grew, only one out of 100 was selected. Even though enlistments were for a three year period, the applicant was required to undergo a one year trial period, during which time he was required to advance or be eliminated from the Standarte. Once the candidate became a member, discipline was very severe, and the training constant. All personnel within the Standarte were sufficiently trained that in theory they could do any job put before them. The member lived full-time within the concern, and led a very stoic existence. If he was successful in his first enlistment, he was given the option of remaining with the Standarte for an additional three year enlistment.

On January 12, 1937, Hitler bestowed the position of Chief of the SA-Standarte "Feldherrnhalle" upon SA-Obergruppenführer Hermann Göring. This birthday gift from Hitler was to play a major role in the direction of the SA's most elite Standarte. The Standarte was to remain independent of any control except for direct responsibility to the SA Stabschef. The functional head of the "Feldherrnhalle" was SA-Gruppenführer Reimann, who saw to the successful completion of all staff functions within the Standarte.

As Hitler turned his aim from internal conquest to domination of the surrounding nations, the Standarte played a more active role in military functions rather than ceremonial requirements. The Standarte had long been a source of training for potential SA leaders, and it was called upon to accomplish the same task for the various military service arms. In 1939, a large segment of the "Feldherrnhalle" was transferred into the Luftwaffe paratroop units, while many of the remainder were absorbed into the 271st Infantry Regiment. This regiment was formally given the title "Feldherrnhalle" in 1942. A year later, the regiment was absorbed into the 60th Motorized Division, with that Division in turn taking on the formal title. Obviously, membership requirements such as those

SA-STABSCHEF SCHEPMANN VISITING THE PANZER-GRENADIER-DIVISION "FELDHERRNHALLE" ON AUGUST 28, 1944.

that had previously existed were curtailed, and general conscription accounted for most of the membership. The Division did not have any political semblance at all other than its name, but was a professional military arm given traditional SA affiliation. The SA headquarters entertained an idea in October 1943 of establishing a SA elite unit from the Panzer Grenadier Division "Feldherrnhalle". The OKH quickly rejected this plan. The formal title "Feldherrnhalle" continued to be used by the Luftwaffe and Heer to connote an elite unit.

THE "FELDHERRNHALLE" DAGGER

One of the precepts of the SA Standarte "Feldherrnhalle" was that the members be equal regardless of background. One of the ways this was born out was the use of a single point of standardization. All members, regardless of rank, were required to wear the "Feldherrnhalle" breast plate about his neck. This half-moon shield suspended by a chain had the gold eagle and swastika characteristic of the Standarte. In addition, all members were required to own and wear the dagger sidearm.

When the SA Standarte "Feldherrnhalle" was instituted in 1935, its members continued to wear the standard 1933 Pattern SA Service Dagger. The dagger was worn suspended by a short leather hanger attached to a belt loop on the outer belt. It was not long before subordinate personnel

SA "FELDHERRNHALLE" ENLISTED SERVICE DAGGER WORN IN VERTICAL LEATHER FROG.

adopted an especially contoured suspension frog that allowed the dagger to be worn vertically over the left hip. When this frog was utilized, the swivel ring on the upper scabbard band was removed. Leader personnel continued to wear the dagger in the diagonal suspension of the left side. A dagger especially designed for selected leaders of the "Feldherrnhalle" and for the staff of the SA Stabschef made its first appearance on December 28, 1937. SA-Gruppenführer Reimann, representing the officers of the Standarte, presented a cased dagger to SA Stabschef Viktor Lutze on the occasion of his 48th birthday. Exactly one year after his appointment as Chief of the SA-Standarte "Feldherrnhalle", Göring was also awarded a cased presentation dagger. This pattern dagger was not worn in any quantity until July 1938, when Lutze played host to Italian General Russo at Munich. General Russo was extremely impressed when he was given the gift of a special presentation "Feldherrnhalle" dagger. The dagger was worn at all formal occasions during the remainder of his visit.

The pommel, which also served as the upper crossguard, was in the design of a large sculptured national emblem with slightly downturned wings. The lower crossguard had as its central design a large SA signet. Metal fittings of the hilt were either aluminum or gold wash over aluminum. While the grip colors varied from white to brown to black, it was the brown

39

GRUPPENFÜHRER REIMANN, CHIEF OF THE SA-STANDARTE "FELDHERRNHALLE" PRESENTS
THE DAGGER TO GÖRING IN HONOR OF HIS BIRTHDAY, 12 JANUARY 1938. NOTE THAT THE
HANGERS WERE PRESENTED SEPARATELY FROM THE CASED DAGGER.

wood grip that was common to the basic dagger. It is believed that the
white grip was used only for special presentations. . . . as in the case of
Göring and General Russo. The long double edged blade was etched with
the SA motto "Alles für Deutschland" on the front, and the oval Eickhorn
trademark on the reverse. The metal scabbard was of a very basic design with two suspension bands with an oak leaf pattern. . . . very similar
to the bands found on the Army dagger. The 45cms dagger was suspended by a double strap hanger that attached to the outer service belt, or to
a hook under the left pocket flap when the dress belt was prescribed. The
presentation case had no provisions for the hangers, which were given to
the recipient separate from the cased dagger. The straps were constructed with gold metallic facings with grey outer stripes sewn to brown velvet
backs. The central portion of the straps were the round buckles bearing

40   an oak leaf design. The suspension straps were fitted with either silver

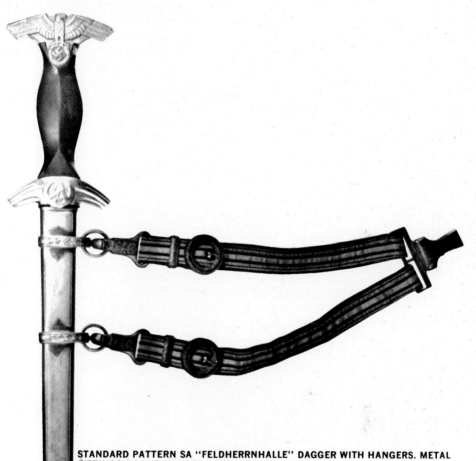

STANDARD PATTERN SA "FELDHERRNHALLE" DAGGER WITH HANGERS. METAL FITTINGS OF THE HANGER WERE FINISHED IN GOLD OR SILVER DEPENDING ON THE RANK OF THE WEARER.

STEPHENS

or gold plated metal mounts, depending on the grade or position of the recipient.

As the true intent of the Standarte began to dissolve with the absorption of its members into the armed forces, and the war was brought closer to the German homeland, ceremonial functions became less frequent. Wear of the dagger slowly diminished until it disappeared altogether.

With the exception of the unique presentation daggers, the "Feldherrnhalle" dagger is estimated to be the rarest of all the German production daggers.

GÖRING RECEIVES GENERAL RUSSO AND HIS PARTY IN BERLIN, 17 JULY 1938. STABSCHEF LUTZE WEARS THE STANDARD "FELDHERRNHALLE" DAGGER WITH THE BLACK GRIP, WHILE GENERAL RUSSO WEARS THE PRESENTATION PATTERN WITH THE WHITE GRIP.

GÖRING IS GREETED BY THE
NEW COMMANDER OF THE SA-
STANDARTE "FELDHERRNHALLE"
ON THE OCCASION OF HIS
BIRTHDAY, 12 JANUARY 1939.

VIKTOR LUTZE

Viktor Lutze, following his birth in Bevergern, Westfalen, on December 28, 1890, went on to become one of the most responsible men in Germany during the Hitler era. In spite of this achievement, he has been described in history as being a "colorless" individual. While there is no doubt that Lutze achieved his position as a result of being a dedicated Nazi and trusted supporter of Hitler, he did bring impressive credentials into the job, and gained some outstanding results.

His military background began prior to World War I. Prior to the outbreak of the War, he had served one year in the regular Army. When war was "declared", he served the Kaiser in the 369th Infantry Regiment, and was later transferred to the 15th Regiment. Among his numerous decorations, his military service earned him the Iron Cross Ist Class. Lutze was forced to leave active military service in 1919 when he received a severe eye injury. It was because of this honorable military service that he was able to establish and maintain a rapport with military leaders following the uneasy alliance between the Army and Hitler's political forces.

Forced into a civilian occupation, he became a sales administrator in Elberfeld, where he had his first contact with the NSDAP. After receiving many subtle attempts at indoctrination, he found that his own attitudes and the professed aims of the NSDAP coincided. Lutze received his Party card in 1922, and immediately pursued an active role in the Sturmabteilung. A year later, as a SA leader, Lutze played an important role in the fight to protect the coal and steel producing concerns in

45

the Ruhr area. Lutze's tenacious abilities came to Röhm's attention, whereupon he was appointed as leader of the SA Gausturm in the Ruhr Valley in 1925. In this position of increased responsibility, he directed his efforts towards the internal improvement of the SA. He formulated and submitted recommendations for the structural reorganization of the SA element at company level. The reorganization proved to be workable, and was instituted by the SA. Lutze was, in effect, the Deputy Gauleiter of the Ruhr area, and he used this position to expand his political base. Due to his organizational capabilities, Lutze began his rapid climb within the higher SA structure. In 1930, he was appointed the Supreme SA Leader of North Hanover, and in 1932, was awarded the rank of SA-Obergruppenführer with responsibility for Obergruppe West. In 1930, Lutze was appointed to the Reichstag, where he became a very active member. While in this position, he helped prepare the way for a Nazi victory in

LUTZE READING THE NAMES OF THE SA FALLEN AT THE 1935 PARTY DAY RALLY.

1933. Hitler rewarded his efforts by appointing him Superior President
and Police President of Hanover. Lutze also fell within the good graces
of Göring, who appointed him to the Prussian Stagsrat. For the remainder of 1933 and into 1934, a clandestine power struggle brewed within the
upper of the Nazi Party. This struggle culminated in a bloody purge that
left the position of SA Stabschef vacant. Hitler, as Supreme Commander
of the SA, recognized the years of loyalty that Viktor Lutze had given.
Through Hitler's personal appointment, Lutze became Stabschef of the
Nazi Party's oldest fighting group. Because of the mistrust generated
by Röhm, and what was to follow from the Blood Purge, Lutze's position
as head of the SA was a virtual anticlimax. It was necessary for him to
rebuild the senior command structure, since a large number of SA High
Leaders had been purged. More importantly, he had to restore the SA
to a position of trust in the eyes of the Führer. In spite of its former
massive membership, the SA strength had been relegated to a very minor position. Lutze began his rebuilding efforts immediately upon being
named to his high position. The SA leaders, and particularly Lutze, engaged in the fanfare that was characteristic of the Nazis. Most of their
time was devoted to heaping praise and honors on one another. The SA
was just beginning to regain its position of prominence when Lutze was
killed in an automobile accident in 1943.

During his nine year tenure as the SA Stabschef, Lutze traveled
with the Nazi inner-circles when attending the numerous state and private affairs. He was always smartly attired in his SA uniform, complete
with decorations received during his honorable military service, and a
wide variety of specialized daggers. Without exception, Lutze's daggers
were unique to his person even though they basically resembled the standard pattern daggers. How the daggers differed was obvious to the eye...
...his were approximately 25% longer than the standard counterpart, with
a general increase in size. Why they were different is not known, unless
it was to meet with the personal specifications established by Lutze himself.

1935 SA HONOR DAGGER

A specially designed SA Honor Dagger was produced and given to
SA Stabschef Lutze in 1935. This dagger was to set the pattern for the
Lutze daggers that were to follow. While the basic dagger retained the
same design as the 1933 Pattern Service Dagger, the similarity ended
there. This was the first of a succession of SA daggers that were suspended by a double metal link hanger. The length of this particular piece
was approximately 42cms....a full 5cms longer than the authorized SA
Service Dagger.

SA-STABSCHEF VIKTOR LUTZE MAKING SPEECH IN MUNICH, 24 FEBRUARY 1937. (NOTE 1935 SA HONOR DAGGER).

  The upper and lower crossguards were cast in German silver with raised oak leaves and acorns forming the ornamentation. The silver plated tang nut secured the blade in the oversized handle. Even though the length of the brown wood grip was longer, its shape remained the same as did the SA and national emblem inlays. The damascus steel blade was narrower and longer, with raised gold motto. The scabbard constituted a complete departure from previous patterns. The sheet metal steel body was covered with a fine grain, dark brown leather, and was fitted with externally mounted fittings of German silver. Unlike later patterns, the scabbard fittings appear to have been unadorned. The center scabbard band was also narrower than those that were to follow. Lutze wore his dagger suspended from a ring secured in place on his waist belt. A spring clip fastener attached to the ring served to join the double row of rectangular silver plated links. The suspension "chain" had three upper links and five lower links, all without a pattern design. The links were joined by metal rings having the same diameter as the small suspension rings on the upper and center scabbard bands. Lutze made a standard practice of wearing this dagger between 1935 and 1938. Sometime in 1936, one of the chain rings was replaced with an oversized ring. This was possibly for the purpose of looping the ring over the lower pocket button, causing the dagger to hang in a near vertical rather than diagonal configuration.

1939 LUTZE SA HONOR DAGGER

The 1935 chained Honor Dagger set the pattern for the Lutze Honor Dagger that followed in 1939. The dagger was identical in size and shape to the 1935 pattern except that all metal fittings were gold plated.

SA-STABSCHEF VIKTOR LUTZE AT HOF DER MARIANBURG, 1940, WEARING STANDARD CHAINED SA HONOR DAGGER.

Even the SA and national emblems inlaid in the brown wooden grip were gold plated. The tang nut bore a finely engraved superimposed "VL". Once again, the major departure was in the scabbard. The basic scabbard was the same, save for the impressed border around the outer edge of the upper and lower scabbard fittings. The center scabbard fitting did not have this impressed border. These fittings and the suspension chain were also gold plated. The upper and center bands were externally mounted by means of a flat head screw, while the lower fitting was externally mounted with round head screws. A new double suspension chain hanger was employed, manufactured by the Assmann Company for the Eickhorn Firm, who manufactured the blade. A round runic SA signet was affixed to the front of a spring clip that served to attach the dagger to Lutze's outer belt. The rectangular links bore a raised swastika, and were joined by oval connecting links. The upper suspension chain consisted of six links, and eight in the lower. The Assmann firm took such pride in their finished work that their firm's name was engraved in script on the lower reverse portion of the SA signet.

Lutze was so pleased with the finished design that the pattern was prescribed for the 1939 High Leader's Service Dagger following minor modifications. The dagger was worn intermittently with other special daggers from 1939 to his death in 1943.

1937 LUTZE FELDHERRNHALLE DAGGER

On December 28, 1937, SA-Gruppenführer Reimann presented his SA Stabschef with a specially made 1937 pattern SA Honor Dagger in the name of the leaders of the SA-Standarte "Feldherrnhalle" to commemorate Lutze's 47th birthday. The dagger was presented to Lutze in a flat presentation case with the dagger and scabbard recessed. The double strap hangers were separate from the case, which had no provisions for the hangers. The length and configuration were identical to the standard Model 1937 SA-Feldherrnhalle-Führerdolch, which is discussed in the previous chapter. However, the Lutze presentation was a specially constructed dagger, having all the metal fittings finished in gilt. On the front side of the damascus blade was the SA motto in raised gold letters, while the reverse bore the following dedication in raised gold gothic script: "Ihrem Stabschef in alten SA-Geist zum 28.12.37 - Das Führerkorps der Standarte Feldherrnhalle". The hangers were the standard pattern with gilt fittings.

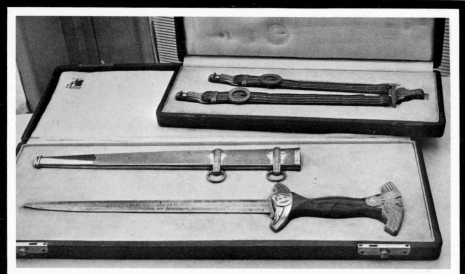

HIGH LEADERS PRESENTATION DAGGER OF THE STANDARTE FELDHERRNHALLE PRESENTED TO STABSCHEF OF THE SA VIKTOR LUTZE, ON THE OCCASION OF HIS 47th BIRTHDAY, 28 DECEMBER 1937. THE DAGGER IS GOLD PLATED, AND HAS A SOLID DAMASCUS STEEL BLADE, DEDICATED IN RELIEF GOLD-LEAFED LETTERING ON BOTH SIDES. THE OBVERSE OF THE BLADE:

    IHREM STABSCHEF IM ALTEN SA, GEIST ZUM 28.12.1937, DAS FÜHRERKORPS DER STANDARTE FELDHERRNHALLE (TO THE STABSCHEF OF ALL THE SA, 28.12.1937, FROM THE FÜHRERKORPS OF THE STANDARTE FELDHERRNHALLE)

THE REVERSE OF THE BLADE:

    ALLES FÜR DEUTSCHLAND, AND THE EICKHORN TRADEMARK, PATTERN 1935 IN GOLD-LEAF HIGH RELIEF.

LUTZE ARMY HONOR DAGGER

It appears that one of the most constant gifts that Lutze received on his birthdays after taking the reigns of the SA were specially designed presentation daggers. On his fiftieth birthday, Lutze received yet another dagger.... one of the more ornate he was to receive. It was presented by his father-in-law, Fieldmarshal von Brauchitsch, on behalf of the Army.

The Honor Dagger of the Army (Ehrendolch des Heeres) resembled the standard Army officer's dagger but only to a minor degree. The dagger was a full 6cms longer than the 40cms Model 1935 Army Dagger. All metal fittings were heavily silver plated. The pommel consisted of the standard Army pommel with oak leaves, with a finely sculptured national emblem, resembling the Navy pommel, mounted on the top. The grip was solid ivory, longer than normal and was a very broad oval rather than circular. The ridges of the grip had silver twist wire running the length of

(ABOVE) SA-STABSCHEF VIKTOR LUTZE CONGRATULATING HEER PERSONNEL IN PARIS. LUTZE WEARS HIS ARMY PRESENTATION. (RIGHT) PHOTO OF THE LUTZE ARMY HONOR DAGGER AS SHOWN IN THE "UNIFORMENMARKT." NOTE THE MANNER IN WHICH THE KNOT IS WRAPPED AS OPPOSED TO THE MANNER IN WHICH LUTZE ELECTED TO WEAR IT.

the handle. The national emblem that formed the crossguard was identical to the standard Army. On the front of the damascus blade bore the raised gold inscription "Das Deutsche Heer dem Stabschef Lutze 28. 12. 1940". On the reverse was a raised gold "Treue um Treue". The manufacturer's trademark, Alcoso, was done in a raised silver script. The scabbard was heavily plated in old silver, with the stippled portion giving the appearance of being expertly done by hand. The two scabbard suspension bands were spaced further apart than those of the standard Army scabbard.

The dagger was worn suspended from the most ornate and beautiful hanger this author has ever seen. The main motif of the hanger was a scarlet cloth shield with the design of a Wehrmacht eagle embroidered in aluminum wire. Field grey cloth strips with embroidered bars and oak leaves protruded from the top and two lower edges of the shield. The background to the oak leaves was scarlet edged in grey silk thread. Spring clips were used to attach to the two scabbard suspension rings. The upper ring was the loose swivel type, while the lower ring remained in a stationary position.

This particular Lutze presentation piece was of such singular beauty and craftsmanship that it was given detailed coverage in a 1940 edition of Uniformen-Markt .

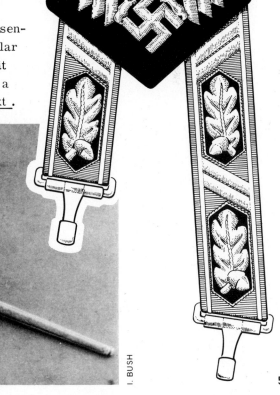

I. BUSH

SS COLORS PASSING IN REVIEW.

ELITE GUARD
[SCHUTZSTAFFEL (SS)]

The origin of the SS can be traced back to March 1923, when a small segment of the most reliable SA assumed the responsibility as Hitler's bodyguard element. Two months later, the group was officially amalgemated into the "Stosstrupp Adolf Hitler", and played an active role in the Munich beer hall putsch. From November 1923 to early 1925, members of the guard detachment were forced underground when the NSDAP was declared illegal. When they resurfaced in 1925 upon legalization, they received the designation of Schutzstaffel (Protective Detachment) or SS. By 1926, the strength had reached 250 select members. The strength was increased by only thirty personnel in the next three years. This group, under the command of Reichsführer-SS Heinrich Himmler, was relegated to a lesser position, subordinate to the SA High Command. This fact, and the ambitions of Röhm and Himmler, stirred the two elements into competition for the lead in Party mastery. Hitler sent out an order to enlarge the SS. Unemployment had already spread to the upper-middle class, which was a factor in gaining converts to the Nazis. A special black uniform was designed for the SS, and this, too, was a factor in recruitment. When Hitler gained control of the German government, SS strength had grown to 152,000.

Himmler entered into an alliance with Göring to end the competition with Röhm. Neither man had any love for the SA Stabschef, and Hitler himself was growing tired of Röhm's intrigues. A plan was conceived between the three men to eliminate the "enemies of the State"...
...real or imagined. The black uniformed men of the SS struck quickly

and efficiently on the night of June 30, 1934. Röhm's power quest was ended with a bullet, and many SA High Leaders fell victim to the SS over the span of the next few nights. Many innocent men, men who unfortunately presented obstacles to the ambitions of Göring and Himmler, also lost their lives. The unofficial count reached as high as 5,000 victims of the purge when it finally came to an end.

Hitler issued a decree in July 1934, granting an autonomous status to the loyal SS, and also directing that the SA undergo a drastic strength reduction. Though the strength of the SS remained considerably less than the SA, the SS gained the upper hand which was to last until the fall of the Nazis. Reichsführer-SS Himmler was responsible only to Hitler. His new-found status made him virtually the second most powerful man in Germany next to the Führer. Initially, there was no conflict between the SS and the military like that which had developed with the SA. The SS was charged with the internal security, while the military held to the traditional mission of the defense of the nation.

REICHSFÜHRER-SS HIMMLER

Membership in the SS remained very selective and restrictive even as the ranks grew. All members were subject to the strict codes imposed by the SS "State within a State". When the SS candidate passed a long series of tests, and had met all other membership requirements, he was sworn into the Allgemeine or General SS. He would serve with this formation until his 35th birthday, following which he would apply for transfer into the SS Reserve. When he reached his 45th birthday, and having served honorably, he entered the SS-Stammabteilung. During the entire period, the member remained under the jurisdiction of the SS.

The appeal of the uniform and the prestigious position of the SS organization drew a great many "joiners". They were persons who wanted to gain the benefits of membership without the responsibilities. This problem was compounded when numerous honorary memberships were bestowed on influential persons willing to donate to the Party treasury. This honorary membership often carried with it an equally high honorary rank.

THE SS DAGGER

On the night of November 9 of each year, each SS candidate performed the ritualistic oath of allegiance to Hitler and the SS. Following the candlelight ceremony, he was informed of his right to wear the coveted SS Service Dagger, and the responsibility to defend the honor of the SS.

The SS dagger came into being on December 15, 1934, when SA-Obergruppenführer Krauser published a notice of authorization for a Service Dagger for the SA and SS. The SS, then a subordinate element of the SA, was subject to the same regulations that governed the SA. Of the 135,860 especially dedicated Honor Daggers established by Röhm in an order dated February 3, 1934, 9,900 were allocated to the SS for distribution to authorized recipients. Röhm did not personally award these daggers, as he did not personally award the SA Honor Dagger, but delegated authority for selection and award to the commanders of each SS Group. Very strict controls were placed on the Honor Dagger, as borne out in an order found among many tons of captured war documents.

Munich, April 12, 1934

Commander in Chief of the SS
Chief of the SS-Office
II No. of Daily Record No. 5270

Subject: Honorary Daggers

1. Certificates, which authorized the holders of honorary daggers to bear those daggers, have to be issued for every holder by the competent units.

2. SS identification numbers of the holders of the SS honorary daggers must be stamped into the hilt of the dagger at the back side of the crossguard, that side on which the dedication of the Stabschef appears. Height of the numbers to be 3 to 4 millimeters.

Chief of the SS Office

Signed: Wittje
SS-Gruppenführer

When Röhm was purged, the order dated July 4, 1934, which required that the dedication be removed, was not necessary. The SS members were only too happy to remove all traces of the "traitor". As a result, few if any of the 9,900 Röhm dedicated SS Honor Daggers survived intact. As a minimum, the name portion was ground from the etched dedication on the reverse of the blade.

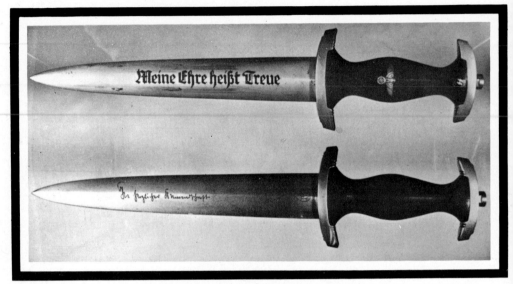

ROHM AUTHORIZED 9,900 HONOR DAGGERS TO BE AWARDED TO SELECTED SS PERSONNEL IN RECOGNITION OF MERITORIOUS SERVICE OR ACHIEVEMENT. ALL TRACES OF ROHM'S NAME WERE REMOVED FOLLOWING THE "NIGHT OF THE LONG KNIVES".

SS SERVICE DAGGER MODEL 1933

All ranks of the SS were authorized to carry a dagger sidearm, designated SS Service Dagger Model 1933, as a standard item of uniform equipment. Those that were capable were required to purchase their own dagger through the SS Administration Office. However, each SS element purchased a limited quantity to be issued to those persons unable to initially make the purchase. These daggers remained the property of the SS station, and were returned to the armorer when the member separated himself from service. It was the obligation of all officers from the rank of Lieutenant on up to purchase the Service Dagger. If an officer was unable to make the initial purchase, he was granted a loan from available SS funds, which was repaid in installments. The Reichsführer-SS, in an order signed by SS-Gruppenführer Wittje on February 17, 1934, made it perfectly clear that all SS members would have the dagger by spring.

The SS Service Dagger was identical in configuration to the SA Service Dagger, but with very noticeable changes. The brown grip was replaced with one of ebany or wood dyed black. A black enamel and silver

SS sigrunnen insigne was inlaid in the front upper portion of the grip, and a nickle or silver plated national emblem was inlaid in the center. This national emblem was later changed to aluminum. The front of the blade bore the SS motto "Meine Ehre heisst Treue" (My honor is loyalty). The reverse of the blade was etched with the manufacturer's trademark, until the RZM inspection mark caused it to be phased out. The sheet metal scabbard was finished in a protective blue oxide or black paint, and had externally mounted nickel plated fittings. As the SA Service Dagger underwent changes, the SS dagger was subject to those same changes.

The dagger was initially worn suspended by a short black leather hanger which passed through a swivel ring attached to the upper scabbard band. As of January 1, 1935, Himmler ordered that the dagger be worn in the vertical configuration, suspended by a vertical leather dagger hanger. When the Model 1936 Service Dagger was introduced, the suspension reverted back to the diagonal wear, except when worn on maneuvers or when otherwise prescribed.

THE DAGGER ILLUSTRATED WAS OBTAINED FROM A VETERAN, WHO STATES THAT THE DAGGER WAS UNCHANGED FROM THE TIME WHEN HE OBTAINED IT IN 1945. IT IS A STANDARD MODEL 1933 SS SERVICE DAGGER, BUT HAS A BROWN WOOD HANDLE WITH SA INLAY. OTHER PATTERNS HAVE BEEN ENCOUNTERED IN COLLECTIONS. IT IS POSSIBLE THAT THIS WAS TO DISTINGUISH A CHANGE IN MEMBERSHIP OR DUAL STATUS.

HERMANN FEGELEIN STANDING IN THE CENTER WITH "SEPP" DIETRICH TO HIS LEFT. ALL OFFICERS ARE WEARING THE SS SERVICE DAGGER IN THE VERTICAL HANGER EXCEPT DIETRICH, WHO OPTED TO WEAR THE DRESS BAYONET WITH KNOT.

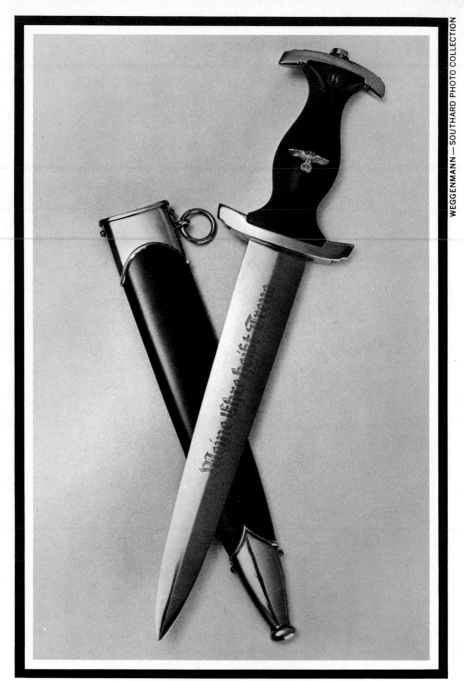

SS SERVICE DAGGER MODEL 1933

1934 SS HONOR DAGGER

Three days after the SS had successfully carried out the purge of
Röhm and his supporters, Reichsführer-SS Himmler personally presented specially dedicated SS Honor Daggers to 200 of the major participants

in the action. The dagger followed the same pattern as the SS Honor Dagger prescribed by Röhm himself, but with Himmler's name replacing Röhm's. The inscription transferred from Himmler's handwriting to the reverse of the blade read, "In herzlicher Freundschaft, H. Himmler" (In cordial friendship, H. Himmler). The daggers were produced exclusively by the Eickhorn firm for the occasion. An accountability number was stamped in the underportion of the lower crossguard. No Honor Dagger. of this type was authorized or awarded by Himmler after July 3, 1934.

MODEL 1934 SS HONOR DAGGER. REICHSFÜHRER-SS PERSONALLY AWARDED 200 OF THESE DAGGERS TO SELECTED SS PERSONNEL WHO TOOK PART IN THE 30 JUNE 1934 PURGE ACTION AGAINST RÖHM AND OTHER SA HIGH LEADERS.

SS SERVICE DAGGER MODEL 1936

A new Service Dagger was authorized for wear by specified personnel by the following order:

Berlin
August 25, 1936

Headquarters of the SS
SS Order summary 7-8
Nr. 15

Subject: SS Service Dagger with new hanger

The Reichsführer of the SS has approved the new hanger for the Service Dagger. It will be referred to as the Service Dagger, Model 1936. The old style dagger will be known as the Service Dagger, Model 1933. Every SS member who has been designated as an official "SS Man", in accordance with SS order Nr. A/9434 of November 9, 1935, will be permitted to wear the new Service Dagger, Model 1936, with chain hanger. All units will insure that this order is complied with.

The SS dagger, Model 1936, can be purchased only through the SS administration office. The price for the dagger is 12.15 RM. Consolidated orders for new daggers will be submitted by units on the first of each month. Individual orders will not be accepted and will not be answered. Delivery of the daggers will be filled as received and within manufacturer's production capabilities.

Signed: H. Himmler

SS SERVICE DAGGER MODEL 1936.

The order referenced SS Order Nr. A/9434, dated November 9, 1935, which outlined the criteria for being designated as an SS Man. It prescribed that all officers who had been an officer as of November 9, 1935, or any member who belonged to the SS for three or more years as of January 30, 1936, were so classified. It also included all SS members who had joined the SS in 1933, 1934 or 1935, but only after completion of three years service. The Model 1933 Service Dagger was then limited to wear by enlisted SS personnel, except for those persons who fell within the criteria for authorization for wear of the new model dagger. Since the Model 1936 Service Dagger was not restricted to officer personnel, SS leaders sometimes distinguished their dagger by wearing a 42 cms aluminum portepee wrapped about the black grip.

The dagger was basically the same as its predecessor, with the exception of the addition of a double chain suspension hanger and a center scabbard suspension band. Fittings of the dagger were initially nickel-silver and later, nickel plated, zinc die casting. The externally mounted scabbard fittings were first nickel-silver which were later changed to nickel plated steel. The scabbard body was finished in a blue oxide or black paint. The center scabbard band was designed with a series of linked swastikas. This and the upper scabbard band had fixed ramps for connection to the chain hangers. The nickel plated steel chain hanger consisted of two upper links (and a spacer link), while the lower chain had four links.... each alternating with the characteristic skull and crossbones and the SS sigrunnen. The chains were joined at a metal belt fastener. The superimposed SS inspection stamp was placed on the reverse of one of the chain links.

Regulations prescribed that the dagger be worn attached to an outer belt hook, from a ring under the left pocket flap or from a strap under the coat. At no time could the dagger be covered.

For some unexplained reason, it would appear that stocks of the Model 1936 Service Dagger were not maintained at a very high level, or made readily available to the newly appointed SS leaders after initial orders were placed. In a single issue of "Das Schwarz Korps", the official publication of the SS, dated 1939, numerous advertisements were placed in the "Want Ad" section requesting purchase of the chained dagger.

Regulations prescribed that the Service Dagger, SS sword (with black scabbard and metal fittings), or the bayonet could be worn with the SS uniform.[1] However, this regulation was suspended late in 1943. There

----

[1]Organisationsbuch der NSDAP (1937 and 1943 editions), Zentral-verlag der NSDAP, München.

NAZI OFFICIALS VISIT A GERMAN UNIVERSITY IN ITALY DURING THE PERIOD 1-11 APRIL 1939. THE SS OFFICER IN THE FOREGROUND WEARS THE MODEL 1936 SS SERVICE DAGGER IN THE MANNER PRESCRIBED BY REGULATIONS FOR THIS PARTICULAR UNIFORM.

was a growing concern over self-defense and the blade sidearm was not sufficient to do the job. SS headquarters became increasingly aware of the violations of uniform regulations that resulted from a wartime attitude. Regulations had always been detailed and strict, but compliance was another matter. Himmler attempted to reestablish the prescribed manner of dagger wear when he published the following directive:

May 18, 1943

Concerning: Wearing of the SS Service Daggers.

It is forbidden for SS Leaders and Police Officers to wear the SS Service Dagger with breeches without buckled belt.

Every SS Leader and Police Officer who goes against this existing order will have disciplinary action taken, and punished with three days of close house arrest.

SS Leaders and Police Officers will, by darkness, have long pants and buckled up (i. e. with belt) with pistol in the event of an air attack.

Signed: H. Himmler

Existing regulations allowed for the dagger to be worn without a belt, fastened under the left pocket flap of the tunic or overcoat when the straight pants were worn. However, the above directive limited wear of the Service Dagger to daylight duty hours when the service uniform with breeches was worn. By late 1943, wear of the dagger was suspended altogether due to the increasing demands of the war at the homefront.

AFTER 1935, HIMMLER AU-
THORIZED THE AWARD OF A
SPECIALLY DESIGNED SS
HONOR DAGGER IN RECOGNI-
TION FOR SPECIAL ACHIEVE-
MENT. IT WAS NORMALLY
AWARDED TO HIGH RANKING
LEADERS. WHEN OBTAINED
FOR AWARD, IT COULD BE
PURCHASED WITH A STANDARD
BLADE OR ONE OF FINE DAMAS-
CUS HAVING THE RAISED
GOLD SS MOTTO ON THE
FRONT WITH RAISED OAK
LEAVES AT EACH END. THE
HILT FITTINGS WERE CAST IN
SILVER, AND HAD A RAISED
OAK LEAF PATTERN. THE
SCABBARD MOUNTS WERE
MADE FROM SILVER, AND WERE
EITHER PLAIN WITH AN OUT-
LINE AROUND THE EDGE, OR
WITH RAISED OAK LEAVES
BOTH FRONT AND BACK. SS
HONOR DAGGERS COULD NOT
BE PRIVATELY PURCHASED,
AND LIKE THE RÖHM AND HIM-
MLER HONOR DAGGERS, A
CERTIFICATE OF AWARD WAS
REQUIRED.

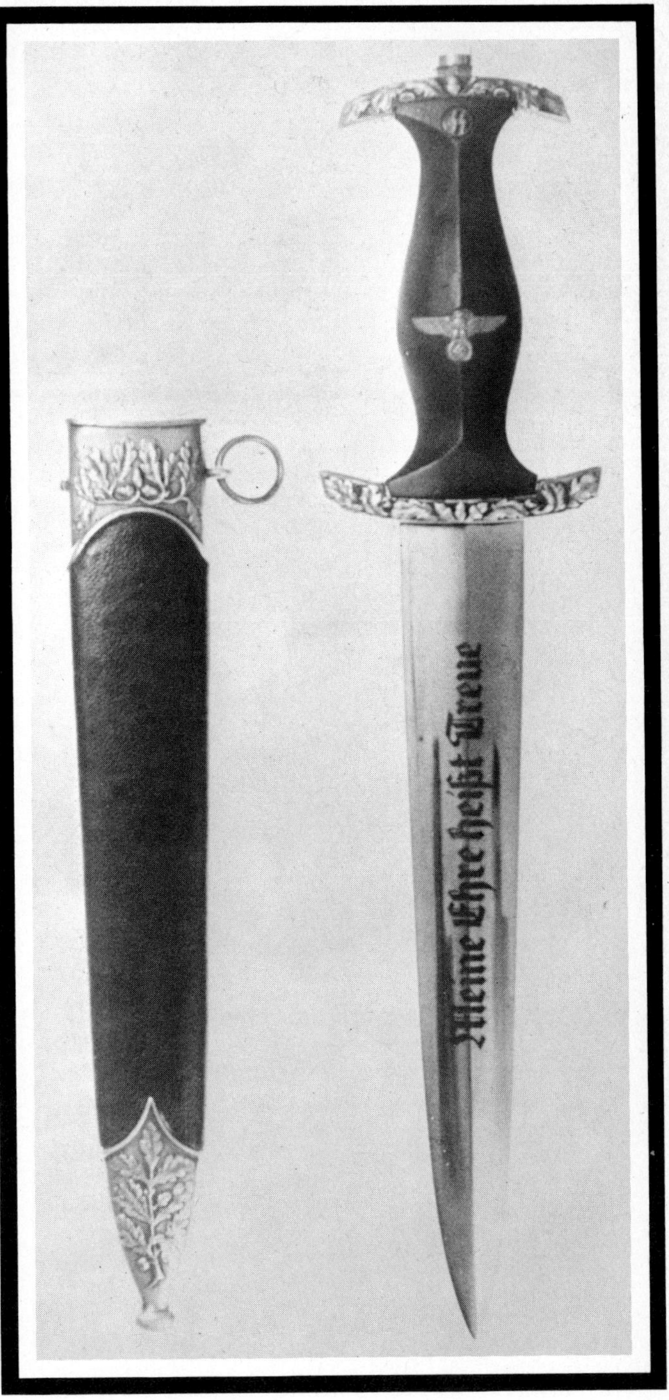

SS PROTOTYPE DAGGERS

Even after a new Service Dagger was introduced, a search for another design continued.

May 24, 1940

Fritz Weitzel
SS-Obergruppenführer

Dear Reichsführer:

Despite the war, I have long been occupied with the design of a SS dagger, and place it before you for your approval.

Because of this, I have had a discussion with Gruppenführer Wolff, and advised him that the design was finished.

Now I have succeeded, and place before you the first pattern example that is handmade, artistic, tasteful and almost without error as one can be.

Dear Reichsführer, I hope that this design has made pleasure with you, and now beg for your criticism.

The finishing firm is the

Fa. Peter Daniel Krebs, Inh. Werner Krebs,
Fabrik blanker Waffen
Solingen, Beethovenstr. 66,

Heil Hitler

Signed: Weitzel
SS-Obergruppenführer

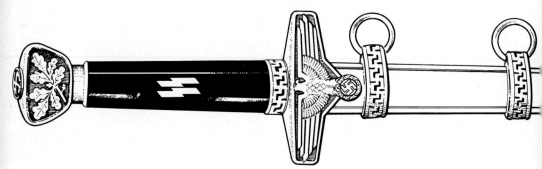

KREBS SS PROTOTYPE DAGGER

Himmler's reply through his adjutant was polite, but it demonstrated that such efforts to change the dagger design were futile. With the following reply, the Reichsführer made his position known:

June, 1940

Dear Weitzel!

The Reichsführer-SS sincerely thanks you through me for your letter of May 24, 1940, and for the pattern example of the SS dagger.

The Reichsführer-SS has carefully inspected the design; he in no case wishes to make such a decision during the war and has therefore instructed me to have the design and your letter of May 24 again laid before him after the war. I therefore keep, with your agreement, your design and will show it again to the RF-SS at a suitable time after the war. During the war by the provisions of the RF-SS, continued wearing of the dagger or the old sword with long pants is authorized.

With the best wishes and
Heil Hitler!

In a subsequent in-house message, it is interesting to note that the prototype dagger had been passed around for inspection. However, when Weitzel made an inquiry as to the status of the piece, it could not be found. No trace of the handworked SS prototype dagger has ever been established since that time.

Members of the Waffen-SS (armed segment of the SS) did not have a distinctive dagger, but were authorized to wear the standard Service Dagger.

The dagger extended to the foreign SS Legions, and became an authorized part of their dress uniform as well. In the case of the Norwegian SS, a modification was made to the SS signet inlay to conform to a design of their own making (see below). To be authorized to wear the dagger, a member of the Waffen-SS was still required to meet the criteria as established in SS Order Nr. A9434, which

NORWEGIAN SS SIGNET INLAY

automatically disqualified a great many personnel. However, esprit of the Waffen-SS gave rise to a request for a dagger pattern of their own. On September 16, 1941, a Waffen-SS messenger hand-carried two prototype daggers and three design drawings to the Reichsführer-SS for his consideration. One dagger was complete with hanger and portepee, and was put before Himmler in a deluxe case. The second dagger followed the prescribed lines of the submitted designs, which were themselves to two-thirds scale. The only information as to the description of the proposed design was a comment that was made in the accompanying message... "In the original presented SS dagger (pattern II) is one after a new style copying the established lines". Himmler had already delayed a decision on the Weitzel prototype, and was to do the same with this request. The Waffen-SS was not to get a dagger of its own.

A WAFFEN-SS OFFICER, HOME ON LEAVE, WEARS HIS MODEL 1936 SERVICE DAGGER WRAPPED WITH THE 42cms ALUMINUM PORTEPEE.

LEADERS OF THE WAFFEN-SS ON FOREIGN SOIL. NOTE THE UNUSUAL DAGGER OF THE BELT OF THE OFFICER IN THE SECOND RANK.

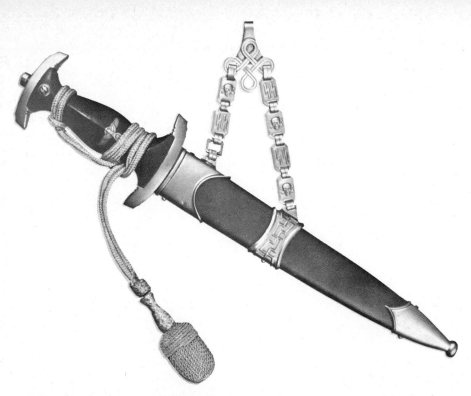

MODEL 1936 SS SERVICE DAGGER. SS OFFICER PERSONNEL WERE AUTHORIZED TO WEAR A PORTEPEE TO DISTINGUISH THE DAGGER FROM THAT WORN BY AUTHORIZED ENLISTED RECIPIENTS.

NSKK KORPSFÜHRER HÜHNLEIN CONGRATULATING GÖRING ON HIS BIRTHDAY, 12 JANUARY 1938. NOTE THAT THE GRIP OF HIS HIGH LEADER'S DAGGER IS VOID OF ANY GRIP INLAYS.

NATIONAL SOCIALIST MOTOR CORPS
[NATIONALSOZIALISTICHES KRAFTFAHR-KORPS (NSKK)]

As the political struggle increased across Germany, the Nazis mobilized their forces to cover even the remotest corner of each Gau. Private automobiles, which were on the increase all over Germany, were pressed into service along with rental trucks. These were used to transport speakers that extolled the Nazi movement, and the large army of political agitators who put down any opposition. This makeshift element became formalized as the official transportation structure of the NSDAP on April 1, 1930, and was given the designation National Socialist Motor Corps (Nationalsozialistisches Kraftfahr-Korps - NSKK).

The SA had formed a motor section within its own ranks to meet its internal transportation needs. This section served to augment the NSKK when excessive demands were placed on the latter organization. The primary purpose of both groups was to meet all transportation requirements of the Party. By 1933, the NSKK had grown to 30,000 members. A year later, it increased still further with the absorption of the Motor-SA into its own ranks, thus giving the NSKK sole authority over transportation requirements within the Party. The NSKK continued to expand until it reached its highest membership peak in 1938 of approximately 500,000 members. This ranked the NSKK as the third largest Party formation behind the SA and the SS.

A dynamic and avowed Nazi, Obergruppenführer Adolf Hühnlein, assumed the position of NSKK Korpsführer from SA Stabschef, Captain

NSKK KORPSFÜHRER ADOLF HÜHNLEIN

Pfeffer von Salomon, who had temporarily held the dual positions as head of the SA and NSKK. Hühnlein, who had been a major on the German General Staff, fell under Hitler's spell during the infancy of the Nazi movement. He became one of Hitler's earliest supporters, taking part in the abortive Munich Putsch on November 9, 1923. He stood trial with Hitler for these activities, and was sentenced to a six month jail term. Hitler rewarded his steadfast support by appointing him to the top position of the NSKK. In effect, however, Hitler retained the supreme position in his capacity as Party leader and Führer. Hitler saw to it that he personally was awarded NSKK membership card No. 1 upon the formalization of the Corps.

Prior to the war years, the NSKK directed their efforts towards road safety and generally making the people "motor-minded". Their prescribed mission, following a Führer Decree on January 27, 1939, was the training of members of the Party and the RAD in their motoring responsibility, and the training of instructors who were to instruct motoring, technical aspects and political philosophies as relates to motoring. Members of the organization pursued their mission with dedicated enthusiasm. They sponsored state competitive sporting events for race cars and cycles, in addition to numerous motor rallies. The Nazis attempted to garner publicity at all of the international sporting events that Germany participated in. For example, the driver who set the world auto speed record in an "Auto Union", was in the racing uniform of the NSKK at the time of the event.

After the outbreak of the war, the functions of the NSKK altered considerably. The organization played a more prominent role in the activities of the Party and the conduct of the war. When Hitler found himself in need of finances to support his war effort, he hit upon a scheme to bilk the German public. Hitler promised the German workers an economic Volkswagen or "People's Car" once the war was won. However, the workers were required to make weekly payments to the government treasury in their bid to purchase the economic automobile. The NSKK fully endorsed the Volkswagen, thus luring even more unsuspecting workers into

THE NSKK MOTOR SCHOOL FOR TANK DRIVERS.

the scheme.   Not a single car was delivered by the Hitler regime to the hard-pressed workers.

Demands of the war considerably changed the intent of the NSKK. Once it became obvious that the Blitzkrieg had run its course, the German military settled down to fighting a give-and-take war.   The NSKK played a critical role in the mobilization of forces, the movement of men and supplies, and the training of drivers and mechanics.   As the war progressed, vehicles of the Party were placed under full control of the military, and qualified NSKK members were required to exchange their uniforms for the combat uniform of a military arm.   All tasks were not restricted to either two or four wheeled vehicles. Requirements of the war made it necessary for the NSKK to undertake the training of its drivers

NSKK KORPSFÜHRER HÜHNLEIN CONFERS THE "DEUTSCHE MOTORSPORTABZEICHEN"

for assault boats and other water vessels, principally in connection with the needs of the Army engineers. In doing so, the NSKK developed motor-boat units of its own, and went on to build an impressive Rhine Flotilla. These surface vessels were absorbed into the Navy late in 1942, along with the NSKK personnel.

In all, approximately 80% of the NSKK membership had been mo-bilized by the end of the war in one fashion or another. They played a prominent role in their direct support to the military effort. In addition to their direct efforts, Korpsführer Hühnlein and von Schirach founded and supervised the training of the Motor-Hitler Youth. This resulted in 200,000 vehicular trained youth as a manpower pool to be drawn upon for military service. It is not surprising that Hitler showed his gratitude by

ON STAFFELFÜHRER CARACCIOLA AT THE GERMAN AUTO SHOW, BERLIN, 1938.

making Hühnlein a Generalleutant in the Army. Hühnlein continued to faithfully serve Hitler until his death in 1942. Hitler appointed NSKK-Obergruppenführer Erwin Kraus as the successor to Hühnlein.

DAGGERS OF THE NSKK

The NSKK was initially subjected to wearing the 1933 **pattern dag**ger that had been designed for the SA. The Corps did not make the transition to the black scabbard until May 19, 1936, when Korpsführer Hühnlein ordered that all scabbards would be painted black. Until other patterns were designed specifically for the NSKK, the scabbard color remained the only distinguishing feature between the SA and NSKK daggers.

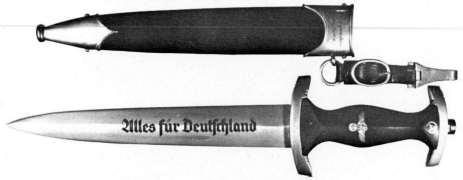

STANDARD MODEL 1933 NSKK SERVICE DAGGER

When the SS made the transition to a new pattern dagger in 1936, Hühnlein saw to it that the NSKK followed suit. The resulting piece designed for the NSKK was the Model 1936 NSKK Dienstdolch or Service Dagger. This dagger retained the same basic dagger design as the 1933 Pattern Service Dagger, but with the addition of a double chain suspension hanger to the scabbard. For some yet unexplained reason, variations are encountered with hangers having four upper and five lower links, while others are found with three upper and five lower links. The chain hanger was made up of links with a raised insigne. . . . alternating the emblem of the NSKK with the "sun-wheel" swastika. The RZM and NSKK inspection marks are found on the reverse side of the chain links. A shield of oak leaves joined the short upper and the long lower suspension chains. This type hanger required that a center suspension band be added to the black painted scabbard. The chain and scabbard fittings were constructed of nickel plated steel. Crossguards of the standard Model 1936 Service Dagger were made of solid nickel, which were later changed to nickel plate over die-cast zinc. However, the small but elite Marine-NSKK wore this same pattern dagger, but with the dagger,

MODEL 1936 NSKK SERVICE DAGGER. CONTRARY TO POPULAR BELIEF, THIS IS NOT A HIGH LEADER'S DAGGER SINCE IT WAS AUTHORIZED FOR ALL MEMBERS OF THE NSKK AFTER 1936.

hanger and scabbard fittings being a distinct copper plate. The national emblem inlay in the grip was either nickel, silver plate, or aluminum in both the nickel or copper plated daggers.

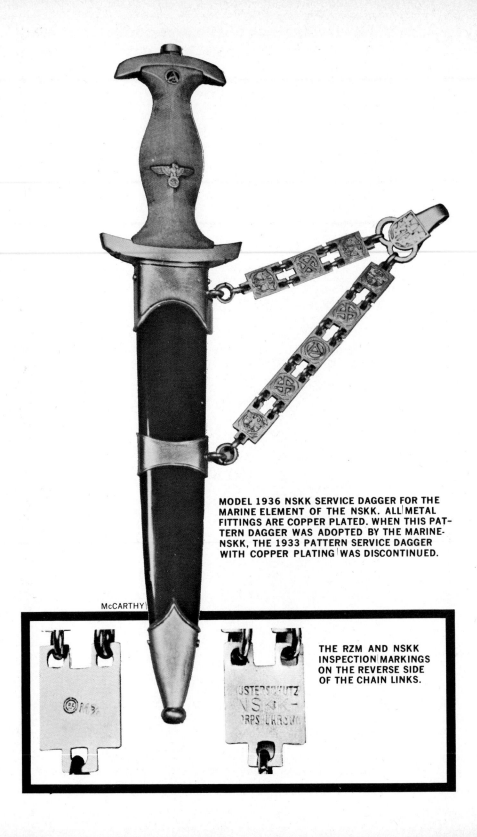

MODEL 1936 NSKK SERVICE DAGGER FOR THE
MARINE ELEMENT OF THE NSKK. ALL METAL
FITTINGS ARE COPPER PLATED. WHEN THIS PAT-
TERN DAGGER WAS ADOPTED BY THE MARINE-
NSKK, THE 1933 PATTERN SERVICE DAGGER
WITH COPPER PLATING WAS DISCONTINUED.

McCARTHY

THE RZM AND NSKK
INSPECTION MARKINGS
ON THE REVERSE SIDE
OF THE CHAIN LINKS.

Regulations prescribing wear of the standard Model 1936 and the Naval model Service Daggers, as taken from the "Organizationsbuch der NSDAP" (1937 and 1943 editions), are as follows:

The NSKK wears the Service Dagger with the black scabbard:

1. With the dress uniform, worn vertically with the handle strap-fastener (Dolchfeststellriemen) or dagger frog (Tasche) on the left hip.

2. With the service uniform, the same as No. 1 or with a double chain hanger worn from the belt.

3. With walking-out dress uniform, worn without the belt, with double chain hanger on the underbelt under the tunic, or through the slit under the left pocket flap.

   When ordered, the dagger is not worn for the country and drive duty.

   The dagger is not worn with the ski uniform.

4. The NSKK dagger is worn by Motorboat Division with yellow metal fittings on double chain hanger.

   With the dress and service uniform, hooked on the belt.

   With the walking-out dress uniform, when no belt is worn, with double chain hanger on the underbelt under the tunic, or thru the slit under the left pocket flap.

As these regulations would indicate, the chained pattern dagger was prescribed for wear by all ranks, and not limited solely to officers. Therefore, the designation "High Leader's" dagger is incorrect. The 1933 Pattern Service Dagger with the black scabbard remained in circulation after the introduction of the Model 1936, as regulations allowed for optional wear between the two daggers with specified uniforms. However, with the adoption of the 1936 Pattern Service Dagger, the earlier Model 1933 Motorboat daggers (those with the copper plated fittings) were discontinued.

Hühnlein also made provisions for a special Honor Dagger or NSKK-Ehrendolch that was to be bestowed by himself in recognition for special or meritorious achievement. The piece was of the same basic design as the Model 1936, but of more ornate workmanship. The crossguards were cast in brass with a high relief oak leaf design, and heavily silver plated. The silver plated scabbard fittings were also of an ornate pattern. The scabbard body was covered with a fine grain black leather.

In 1938, a distinctively designed dagger was approved for wear by leaders holding the rank of Brigadeführer and above. This rank limitation would account for the extremely limited number produced, and even more limited reference to the dagger. The 1938 Pattern Dagger was designated NSKK Höhere-Führerdolch or High Leader's Dagger. The dagger was purchased by the NSKK by special order from the manufacturer, and bestowed upon selected recipients. Research has been able to uncover

McCARTHY

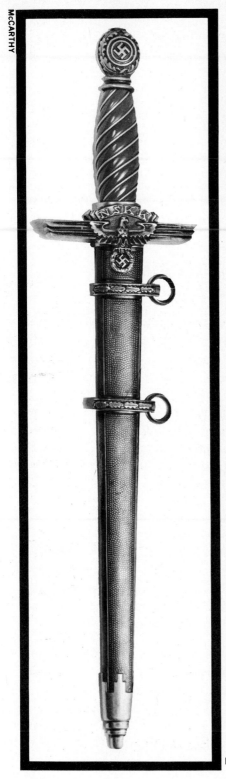

80

NSKK HIGH LEADER'S DAGGER.

three daggers worn by NSKK High Leaders after 1938, each bearing a marked similarity. In each specimen, the crossguard was in the design of an eagle with outstreched wings with the NSKK banner overhead. In two of the three, the wings had a pronounced downward curve. The scabbard appears to be nearly identical in all three cases. In at least two of the three specimens, there was a complete departure from the standard shape of the wooden handle. Research has indicated a virtual absence of information concerning the High Leader's Dagger, except for the photographs illustrated here.

(BELOW) NAZI LEADERS ATTEND A GATHERING IN HONOR OF THE FÜHRER'S BIRTHDAY, 20 APRIL 1940. AMONG THOSE SHOWN ARE RIBBENTROP, TODT, WAGNER, AND HÜHNLEIN. NOTE THAT THE HANDLE OF THE NSKK HIGH LEADER'S DAGGER IS ALSO VOID OF ANY GRIP INLAYS. THIS PATTERN COMBINES THE OLD STYLE UPPER CROSSGUARD WITH THE NEW STYLE LOWER CROSSGUARD. THE DAGGER IMMEDIATELY IN THE FOREGROUND IS A "FELD-HERRNHALLE."

LIBRARY OF CONGRESS

LABOR CORPS EMBLEM

REICHS LABOR SERVICE
[REICHSARBEITSDIENST (RAD)]

The Reichs Labor Service was formed by its leader, Konstantin Hierl. From its conception, the primary purpose of the organization was to combat the excessive unemployment and embroil the German youth in the Nazi movement. Hierl saw to the fact that the 1928 Nazi Party program included the intention to institute obligatory labor service throughout Germany once the Nazis achieved political domination in the Reichstag. The basic principles and the need for such an obligatory service were further defined by Hierl in 1930. Brüning's Weimar government attempted to preempt Hitler by passing an emergency decree in June 1931, which created a voluntary labor service. This service was on a par with the Civilian Conservation Corps that was to be instituted by President Roosevelt in the United States in an effort to combat the unemployment problem.

The labor problem, among other things, reached such a state that the Brüning government went down to defeat to Hitler's well organized political campaign that used this issue as its major platform. Once Hitler was Chancellor, he removed all vestages of a voluntary service by passing a law making service in the RAD the obligation of all German youth. This period of service was between graduation from school and the calling up for military service.

The Labor Corps was a para-military formation which concentrated heavily on the preparation of the male youth for his eventual military service. The Corps members lead a regimented life, evenly balanced

83

between the performance of labor services and extensive military-type training. The RAD was supported by funds from the Unemployment Insurance Fund, the Fund for the Relief of Economic Distress, and Party dues which most of the Corps members themselves were required to pay. Each member cost the German people approximately two Marks per day to maintain. One-eighth of that cost went to the Corps members as a minimal stipend. [1] The value of the services that the RAD performed far outweighed the demands for supporting funds that were levied against the German economy. The Labor Corps participated in a great many projects.... all designed to improve the German land. Land reclamation through controlled irrigation, forestry work and agricultural projects accounted for the bulk of the tasks given to the RAD. Following construction of a series of dikes, approximately 345,000 hectars were converted to fertile and productive land during the period 1933-36.[2] (One hectar is equal to 2.471 acres.) By 1938, a firm 70% of the RAD's efforts were directed towards land reclamation. By the end of that year, Germany was deriving major economic benefits from the 35 labor districts that had been formed. For control purposes, these districts were further subdivided into six to eight Labor Service Groups. The strength of the Corps was initially in direct relation with that of the military services. By 1938, the strength had grown to 230,000 members to include personnel of the administrative elements.

Corps leaders were competitively selected from among the ranks, and were subjected to extensive training and schooling at the various RAD centers. Hierl also drew extensively upon the ex-officers of the military .... especially for the higher professional leadership positions within the RAD. The non-professional advanced through the ranks by a series of educational progressions and advanced to the next higher school. This started with the Troop Leader School, moved on to the Field-Master School, Regional School and finally the Reich Training Center. In addition to the varied technical training that the prospective leaders received, they also underwent extensive political and philosophical orientation.

Service in the RAD did not exempt the youth from military service. On the contrary, it served as a training formation for the military services. At the same time it performed a major service for the German nation and allowed the Nazi machine to exert a more inclusive hold on the youth. When war broke out, Hierl had successfully fought to keep his RAD

---

[1] Cesare Santoro, Hitler's Germany - as seen by a Foreigner, (Berlin: Internationaler Verlag, 1938).

[2] Ibid.

intact in spite of the reintroduction of conscription. As the military forces moved across the borders in their march to conquest, male members of the RAD moved with them. They took with them the concept of a labor service in support of a nation. As a result, in May 1941, a labor service was established in Holland. Quisling had his Norwegian Nazi Party emulate Hierl's RAD, boasting a Labor Service totalling 20,000 members in 1942. Similar services were also established in the Balkan nations of Bulgaria, Rumania, Croatia, Slovakia and Hungary.

FEMALE YOUTH AND THE RAD

While the female members of the RAD were in no way concerned with the pre-military induction training, they did play a very prominent role in the advancement of the precepts of the Labor Corps. On January 1, 1934, Hierl entrusted the formation of a Women's Labor Service to Frau Scholtz-Klink. She undertook this task with the zeal of a dedicated Nazi. By April 1936, the Women's Labor Service was fully absorbed and subordinated to the Reichs Labor Service. Prior to 1941, both male and female youths were only required to perform six months of obligatory service, but in that year, Hitler ordered that this period of service be extended to a full year.

Unlike their male counter-parts, the brunt of female efforts were directed at helping overburdened mothers, building the member's character, and engaging in light field work. Throughout the 13 RADwJ districts in Germany, over 600 camps had been built to accomodate the female members. Requirements of the war caused a shift in the use of female labor. Their efforts were primarily diverted to work in factories and munitions plants, service in hospitals and schools, and working with transportation and utility services. By 1943, approximately 226,000 females were thus employed, removing these burdens from the male working class. Manpower shortages towards the end of the war required that female volunteers be absorbed into military services.... to include the Waffen-SS.

As with all other organizations within Germany, the blade sidearm was solely a male prerogative. Thus, the female members of the Corps were not concerned with the RAD traditions that were relative to the hewer.

REICHSARBEITSFÜHRER KONSTANTIN HIERL

Hierl, born in Bavaria in 1875, had an outstanding career even before he embarked on his new career as leader of the Reichs Labor Service. He served as a General Staff officer in the Imperial Army and the

REICHSARBEITSFÜHRER KONSTANTIN HIERL

Reichswehr, achieving the rank of Colonel. One of his most noted talents was that of writing, with the publication of a number of military regulations and five volumes of history to his credit. He became embroiled in politics while still a member of the Reichswehr, and became very active in political discussions and meetings. He made a very favorable impression on Hitler as early as 1920, however, Hitler was not initially able to garner Hierl's support. Hierl retired from the Reichswehr in 1924 and cast his lot with General Ludendorff rather than Hitler. It was not until 1927 that Hierl shifted his allegience to Hitler by joining the Nazi Party. He was to prove an able organizer, and laid the foundation for the highly effective Reichs Labor Service. After January 30, 1933, Hierl was appointed Secretary of State for Labor Service, and was placed directly under Reichsminister of Labor, Franz Seldte. Shortly thereafter, Hierl was named directly to Hitler's cabinet. On July 1, 1934, Hitler appointed Labor Leader Hierl as Reichs Commissioner for Voluntary Labor Service. Supervisory control was removed from the Reichs Minister of Labor and placed in the hands of the Reichs Minister of Interior. By doing so, the shift in supervisory authority gave Hierl total control over the Labor Service. It was not long before Reichsarbeitsführer Hierl headed up an autonomous organization, responsible directly to Hitler.

THE HEWER TRADITION

Reichsarbeitsführer Hierl not only was an able organizer, but a flamboyant leader. He sought out ways to add to the prestige of his organization, and provide an esprit to its members. Shortly after his appointment as head of the RAD, Hierl laid down the provisions for the designing and institution of a distinctive uniform for all members of the Corps. In the autumn of 1933, a special earth-brown uniform complete with its distinctive insigne of organization and rank was approved and became a standard item of issue. As an additional embellishment, leaders of the RAD in the grades of Feldmeister and Amtswalter on up to the Reichsarbeitsführer were authorized to wear a distinctively designed hewer sidearm.

The hewer was not made available for general distribution until the early months of 1934. During the initial period of blade manufacture, production was accomplished with little or no inspection or standardization save for the very basic design specifications that had been established. This brief period was to account for a number of minor variations that were to be developed within the hewer line. However, inspection criteria was imposed on manufacturers late in 1934, and the subsequent blades were to bear the RAD inspection mark. This inspection brought about the desired standardization of design throughout the field of manufacturers.

The basic design of the RAD hewer implied ruggedness....in keeping with the character of the Labor Service. As would be indicated by the sharpened blades, a few of the hewers were undoubtedly utilized in the field. However, the hewer was intended to be worn as a dress sidearm, and its construction would not allow for any sustained or heavy blows to be struck with the blade.

The forged steel bolo-type blade bore the etched Gothic lettered motto "Arbeit adelt"(Labor Enobles) on the obverse. The single edged blade had a groove running along the flat upper edge. On the reverse side of the blade, near the crossguard, were the manufacturer's mark and the RAD patent/inspection mark. In some cases, organizational issue numbers were stamped or etched into the pieces to provide for accountability. The metal parts of the hilt were either nickel-silver or nickel plated steel. The stag horn grip plates were retained by two screws. A few early hewers had the stag horn grip extending fully over the "beak" of the pommel, but this was eliminated through standardization. The black enamel steel scabbard had upper and lower nickel plated steel fittings externally mounted by means of screws. These fittings

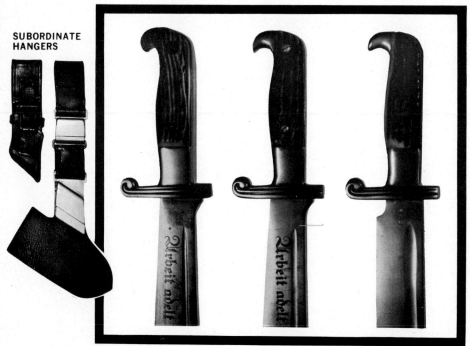

SUBORDINATE HANGERS

RAD HEWERS FROM LEFT TO RIGHT: FULL STAG GRIP; STANDARD PATTERN; "FAT MAN" PATTERN. THE MOTTO OF THE LATTER IS ON THE REVERSE SIDE OF THE BLADE.

had a design motif, with the lower fitting having the insigne of the RAD engraved on the obverse. The overall length measured 40cms, and the weight was an impressive 19 ounces.

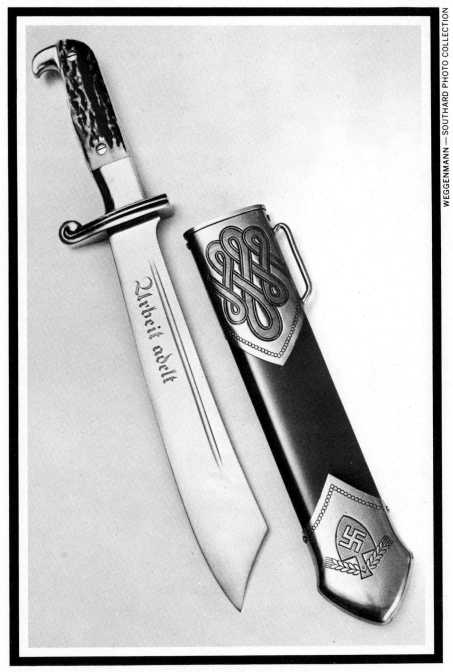

STANDARD PATTERN RAD HEWER

"FAT MAN" HEWER

Yet a third design is encountered for which little information is available. The RAD inspection mark would indicate that the pattern design was an acceptable one. Since the representative pieces only bear the Krebs trademark, it is possible that the pattern was a patented design, and boasted only limited distribution. The design was identical in every respect to the basic design of the 1934 hewer with the exception of the blade and the very thick stag horn grip plates, which has earned the piece the contemporary nickname of "Fat Man". The blade, however, was the major point of departure from the basic design. The etched motto was placed on the reverse of the blade, which resembled more the meat cleaver rather than the bolo-shaped blade.

The hewer was suspended from the outer belt by a large black leather hanger that was to undergo two pattern changes. The first was a strap and buckle, while the final pattern incorporated a large metal gate ramp fastener that snapped on the hanger bar of the scabbard rather than passing through it as with the first design. The large bullet-shaped leather extension was to serve as a protective shield between the wearer and the sharp pointed edge of the upper scabbard fitting. It was not uncommon to cut this extension from the hanger.

With the introduction of the 1937 hewer, the 1934 pattern was then authorized for wear by subordinate ranks. Even after the introduction of the leader's model, Reichsarbeitsführer Hierl continued to carry a 1934 pattern hewer for a brief period. His personal hewer was modified to be worn with the double strap hanger that was designed specifically for the 1937 pattern hewer.

The Reichs Labor Service Hewing Knife Model 1937 was designed and introduced in 1937. It replaced the 1934 pattern hewer that had previously been worn by RAD leaders. This piece was in no way intended for any field use. It was lighter in weight and considerably more ornate, thus making it more appropriate in meeting the needs as a dress sidearm.

The weight was trimmed to a mere 9 ounces, while the overall length was 39cms. Metal parts of the hilt were initially silver plate, while subsequent production pieces were constructed from natural finished aluminum. The pommel was changed from the hint of an eagle's head as on the 1934 pattern to a detailed sculptured eagle head. A spiral ferrule led down to a crossguard bearing the spade and wheat stalk insigne of the RAD on the langet. The two piece plastic handle was secured to the grip by means of a single screw on the obverse of the grip. The handle was normally ivory colored, but a dark orange handle option was offered by a few firms.

REICHSARBEITSFÜHRER HIERL WITH HITLER AT A PARTY DAY RALLY, 7 SEPTEMBER 1938. NOTE THE FIRST ISSUE HEWING KNIFE FITTED FOR DOUBLE STRAP DETACHABLE HANGERS.

1937 PATTERN HEWER

The forged steel blade still resembled the bolo-shaped pattern previously established, but the blade was narrower and thinner than its forerunner. The RAD motto was etched on the obverse. The scabbard was silver plated sheet metal with a design pattern engraved on the upper and lower sections. This design pattern did not extend to the back side of the scabbard. The center section of the scabbard body resembled a pebbled effect. This center section was oxidized, giving it a blue/grey appearance. Most pieces found in collections today have this oxidation polished off.

The leader's hewer was worn suspended from under the left pocket flap by means of a double brown leather suspension strap with dull metal fittings. Depending on the patent design, the hangers are found with smooth or pebbled leather finish, sliding gate ramp catches, and smooth or pebbled rectangular buckles. It was not uncommon to back the straps with wool or similar material to protect clothing from wear.

Neither the 1934 or 1937 model hewers were worn with a porte-pee.

As the greater majority of the RAD membership were drawn into war service, extensive wear of the hewer gradually declined. For those members in service on the front or in an occupied country, its wear was prohibited.

WISER

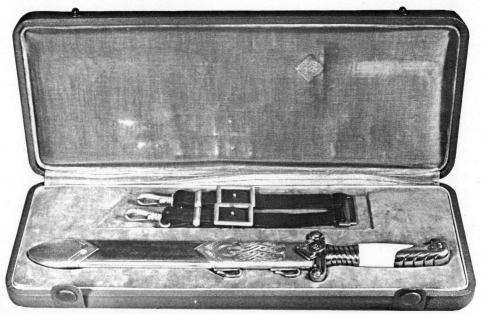

CASED RAD LEADER'S HEWER WITH SUSPENSION HANGERS

A YOUTHFUL SEAMAN IN THE MARINE-H.J.

HITLER YOUTH
[HITLER JUGEND (HJ)]

℗℗Corrupt the youth and control the country" has always been
the watchword for would-be dictators. Hitler employed his charismatic
personality during the very early stages of his struggle to gain dominance
within Germany. He attempted to exert his influence over any element
of German society that might gain him the least bit of political recognition and eventual control. The greatest concerted effort was directed
against the largest population segment....those persons 25 years of age
or younger. As early as 1922, the then infant SA maintained authority
over the Youth League of the NSDAP. It was from this small beginning
that the controls over the German youth were to have their start. By
1926 (the year normally attributed as the official organization of the Hitler Youth), the Party had extended its influence to a faction of the aristocratic youth. This was by the founding of the National Socialistic Student Association (Studentenbund) for college and university students and
the National Socialistic League of Pupils (NS Schulerbund). It was from
the university level organization that Hitler drew upon the talents of a
fiery young (aged 24) leader named Baldur von Schirach. In October,
1931, von Schirach was appointed Reich Youth Leader of the National
Socialists with his control extending over some 20,000 youths.

Prior to 1933, virtually all youth groups were associated with a
single over-all national group, the Reich Committee of German Youth
Associations. However, in April 1933, von Schirach brought about a
successful coup over the organization....a coup made easy because of

95

the solidarity of the youth groups, which allowed them to fall in unison rather than separately. With this coup, von Schirach emerged on June 17, 1933, as Youth Leader over all segments of the youth organization. A year earlier, von Schirach had set out on the road to an autonomous organization by removing the youth organization from any SA control. His efforts were crowned in 1934 when the Hitler Youth was designated a government sponsored organization. The Reich Youth Law of December 1, 1936, divested the youth of any semblance of independence, and gave the Führer total authority to unite all German youth under Party control. All non-Nazi youth organizations were either absorbed into the Hitler Youth or were declared illegal. Hitler elevated von Schirach to a position equivalent to that of ministry rank, with responsibility to none other than Hitler himself. Another of Hitler's early associates, Artur Axmann, succeeded von Schirach in the post of Reichsjugendführer.

Membership for all ages between ten and eighteen became obligatory with the Youth Service Decree of April 1939. By April of the previous year, leadership positions were held by 562,000 men and women, of which 30,000 were paid professional Youth Leaders. Successful expansion of the Hitler Youth is demonstrated in the following strength chart[1]:

	End of 1932	End of 1933	End of 1938	Beginning of 1939
Deutsches Jungvolk (DJ) Boys from 10-14 years	28,691	1,130,521	2,064,538	2,137,594
Hitler Jugend (HJ) Boys from 14-17 years	55,365	368,288	1,663,305	1,723,886
Jungmädel (JM) Girls from 10-14 years	4,556	394,482	1,855,119	1,923,419
Bund Deutscher Mädel (BDM) Girls from 14-21 years	19,244	243,750	1,448,264	1,502,571
Totals	107,856	2,137,041	7,031,226	7,287,470

The Hitler Youth membership, by 1942, had grown to over ten million dues paying members. These strength relationships are provided to give some idea as to the number of potential blade sales that existed within this one organization as compared with other blade bearing organizations.

As Germany progressed into full war mobilization, the youth became a reservoir for manpower. Their training became more oriented

---

[1] Alfred Vagts, Hitler's Second Army, (Washington, D.C.: Infantry Journal, 1943).

to military requirements. Within the Hitler Youth structure a series of schools were established to further political teachings and to develop leaders for the SA, SS, Police and NSDAP. Those students showing exceptional leadership capability, and tentatively selected for professional leadership roles, were educated in the Academy for Youth Leadership at Brunswich. Members of the Youth were required to serve one year in the Reichs Labor Service, whereupon the majority went on to serve in one of the military branches. However, the potential leader continued on in his select education. If the designee passed all his required examinations, physical tests, etc., he began his service as a professional Youth Leader, having a minimum service obligation of twelve years.

BLADES OF THE HITLER YOUTH

The mark of success following the numerous proficiency tests was the authorization for a candidate to carry the Fahrtenmesser or "hike knife". This knife was carried with pride, and was utilized much in the same manner as the Boy Scout Knife of today. While the Pimpf candidate was authorized to wear the uniform without straps, he was not authorized to wear the knife until he earned the distinction "Pimpfenprobe". After all tests were successfully passed, the District Leader would make the determination for award of the knife. Approval was granted when the District Leader so annotated the Pimpf's "Leistungsbuch" or achievement book. When the Pimpf graduated to candidate for the Hitler Youth, he was required to undergo this six month trial period, during which time he was required to pay dues, but was not extended the privilege of wearing the uniform or the knife. As with the Pimpf, authority for the wear of the knife came from the District Leader. Even when approval for wear was granted, purchase of the knife was not mandatory. Manufacturer's codes would indicate that the Fahrtenmesser was the first of the Nazi originated blades, coming into existence in early 1933. Considering the membership of the Youth, and the lack of restrictions on sales, the knife boasted the greatest distribution.... exceeding even the SA. Even though it only cost 2.88RM ($1.60), this constituted 1/8 of the average weekly salary, which was a limiting factor in the purchase of the knife by the total membership. The basic pattern measured 25cms in overall length. The hilt was a nickel plate over alloy, with twin slab checkered plastic grips secured by two nickel plated rivets. Centered in the front portion of the grip is the red, black and silver diamond insigne of the Hitler Youth inset between the two rivets. The crossguard consists of a single upswept quillon. The blade was single edged, usually with a pronounced ricasso which sometimes bore the RZM mark and date. Examples manufactured between 1933 and August 1938 bore the etched inscription in German script "Blut und Ehre" (Blood and Honor). Sometimes centered in the backside of the blade was the manufacturer's mark and/or RZM mark. After August 1938, the motto on the blade was discontinued. The scabbard was made of sheet metal steel with the finish in metallic blue or stove black enamel. Retaining springs were fitted inside the scabbard, and secured by two rivets. The knife was suspended from the outer belt by means of a black or brown leather belt loop riveted to the back of the scabbard. Following the introduction of controls by the RZM, the Fahrtenmesser came under strict standardization in September 1935. Heretofore, the knife was subject to minor variations in blade length, configuration and shape of the pommel. Prior to the introduction of the Führerdolch, this knife was worn by all ranks with the summer service uniform. However, after 1937, wear of the Fahrtenmesser was restricted to ranks of Hauptgefolgschastsführer and below, and could only be worn when the Youth uniform was officially worn.

(ABOVE) STANDARD YOUTH KNIFE WITH MOTTO

(LEFT) REICHSJUGENDFÜHRER BALDUR VON SCHIRACH, WEARING THE HJ-FAHRTENMESSER, WORKS TO ADJUST HIS CAR'S ENGINE.

АЬЛГЬ И ЧЕСТЬ

RUSSIAN YOUTH KNIFE

(ABOVE LEFT) DUTCH YOUTH KNIFE (ABOVE RIGHT) LEADER OF THE LEVANTE.

A special honor knife, the HJ-Ehrenfahrtenmesser, was designated for award to members of the Youth who had excelled in competition and accomplishment. This pattern bore a strong resemblance to the standard hike knife yet differed in a number of respects, especially in the configuration of the hilt. The hilt was longer and thinner, bearing engraved ornation in the form of foliage and oak leaves surrounded either the HJ diamond or HJ flag. The blade bore a stylized etched motto in black block letters surrounded by oak leaves. A variation of this piece is recorded as having a swastika within a circle etched in the pommel or a HJ flag surrounded by oak leaves. The blade bears the SS motto "Meine Ehre heisst Treue" in black block letters within a foliage panel. The grips of the Ehrenfahrtenmesser were made of black checkered wood secured by two nickel plated rivets, with no inlay. The scabbard was basically identical to the Fahrtenmesser.

TWO VARIATIONS OF HJ HONOR KNIVES

A third piece falling into this basic pattern, but measuring only 20cms in overall length, was a knife attributed to the German Youth, and designated the DJ-Fahrtenmesser. Since the standard Fahrtenmesser was designated for wear by both the HJ and DJ, it is doubtful that this piece can be attributed solely to the DJ. No confirming evidence has been found to correctly attribute this knife or determine the purpose for wear. This configuration of the DJ knife was a reduced version of the standard piece. The handle was made up of twin black checkered plastic slabs without inlay, and retained in place by two rivets. The metal portion of the hilt was aluminum. The thin blade had a pronounced point and

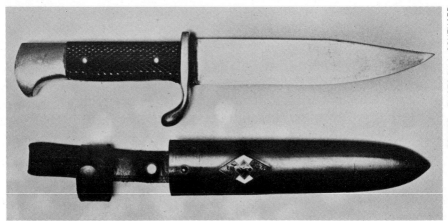

UNATTRIBUTED YOUTH KNIFE

no ricasso. There have been no examples of this piece encountered with an etched blade, or any other blade markings for that matter. The enamed diamond shaped Youth insigne was affixed to the upper face of the scabbard. The scabbard was constructed of sheet metal steel, and finished in stove black enamel. A black leather belt loop was riveted to the reverse of the scabbard.

A special 34.5cms dress bayonet was authorized for wear by members of the Wachgefolgschast or "Watch Followers," an elite element of the Hitler Youth. This nickel plated dress bayonet bore the standard configuration, but had the Hitler Youth diamond insigne inlaid in the center

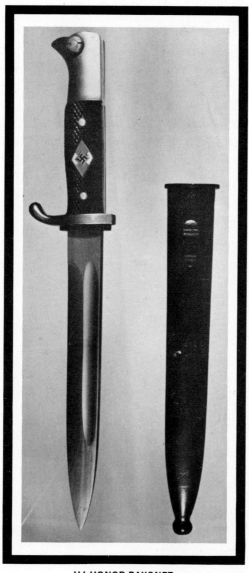

HJ HONOR BAYONET

front of the black checkered plastic handle. The scabbard was the standard black sheet metal steel version and was suspended by a black leather frog. The special Youth member was entitled to wear a leather and aluminum portepee affixed to the belt frog. Due to the limited membership of this element, specimens of this piece are relatively rare.

A Hitler Youth Leader's Dagger, specifically designed for wear by the professional Youth-Leader, was authorized in 1937 following Hitler's personal approval. This dagger of simple yet beautiful design was limited to Leaders between the ranks of Stammführer to Stabsführer, and also worn by the Reichsjugendführer. The dagger measured 34cms in overall length. The handle was constructed of wood bound in silver wire. The hilt fittings were either aluminum or silver plated, with the pommel having a raised diamond insigne with swastika. Depending on the manufacturer, the pommel served one of two functions. . . . either decorative or functional. In the case of the decorative pommel, the blade was secured into the handle by means of a locknut screwed to the blade tang, with the pommel placed over the top of the handle as a decorative cap. The functional pommel served as the screw to secure the blade to the hilt. This type pommel was secured in place by means of a small lock screw on the side flat portion of the pommel. The decorative type pommel was retained in place by either one or two pins. The flat gradually upturned crossguard

THE REICHSJUGENDFÜHRER PAYS A VISIT TO MEMBERS OF THE MASSIVE HITLER YOUTH ORGANIZATION.

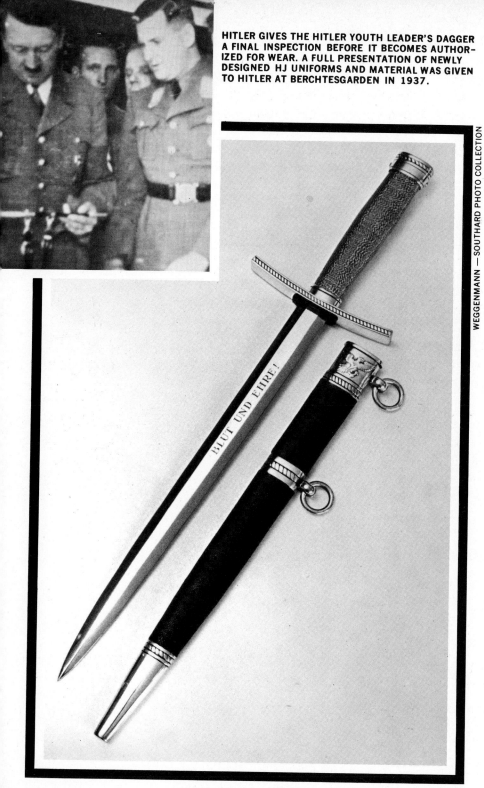

HITLER GIVES THE HITLER YOUTH LEADER'S DAGGER A FINAL INSPECTION BEFORE IT BECOMES AUTHORIZED FOR WEAR. A FULL PRESENTATION OF NEWLY DESIGNED HJ UNIFORMS AND MATERIAL WAS GIVEN TO HITLER AT BERCHTESGARDEN IN 1937.

WEGGENMANN — SOUTHARD PHOTO COLLECTION

YOUTH LEADER'S DAGGER

bore no other design than a simple pattern running along the edge. The blade was identical in design to the Army blade, but was shorter and narrower. The Youth motto "Blut und Ehre" was etched in block letters on the flat obverse portion of the blade. The letters were filled with black, which was often removed by polishing or normal scabbard wear. Only the RZM mark and the manufacturer's code was etched into the flat portion of the reverse blade. The scabbard was totally metal based, constructed of silver plated aluminum or steel. The upper suspension band was designed with the Youth eagle in relief. The scabbard was wrapped in a dark-blue (giving the appearance of being black) leather above and below the center suspension band. Few of the daggers had scabbards without the leather wrap. In this case, the scabbard was uniformly silver plated. This latter piece was worn with white suspension hangers. The detachable double

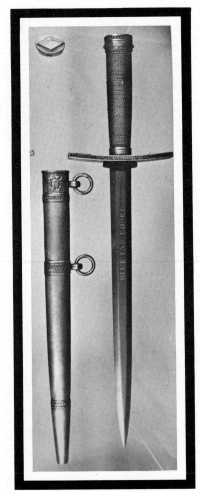

THE YOUTH LEADER'S DAGGER AT THE RIGHT IS BELIEVED TO HAVE BEEN USED BY MEMBERS OF THE HJ HONOR DETACHMENT.

NATIONAL ARCHIVES

strap hangers affixed to the swivel ring at the upper and center scabbard suspension bands. The HJ-Führerdolch could not be purchased from a retailer as it was obtained only through RZM channels, and awarded rather than sold to the Youth Leader. When the dagger was bestowed upon the Youth Leader, he received, in addition to the dagger, an official certificate of award. The Führerdolch was presented in either a blue or red leather case that bore the Hitler Youth Leader's eagle clutching the diamond insigne impressed in silver and centered between the two leather retaining straps on the upper lid. The dagger was in a recessed pocket within the case. Separated from the dagger by a spacer lid were the double strap hangers held in place by two straps. The standard hangers were black leather with plain aluminum or silver plated fittings. However, a special hanger having double white suspension straps was worn on ceremonial occassions.

FOREIGN MINISTER RIBBENTROP RECEIVES A GATHERING OF YOUTH LEADERS. NOTE THAT BOTH PATTERNS OF THE DAGGER AND HANGERS ARE BEING WORN.

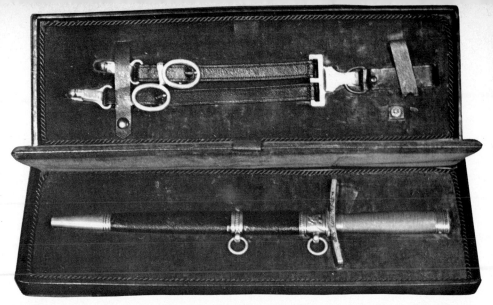

ALL HITLER YOUTH LEADER DAGGERS WERE PRESENTED IN A RED OR BLUE LEATHER OR LEATHERETTE CASE. THE CASE MEASURED 5"x15¼"x2¼". A SPACER PANEL SEPARATED THE DAGGER FROM THE HANGERS. THE CASE, WHICH HAD A SILVER EAGLE AND SWASTIKA EMBOSSED IN THE TOP, WAS SECURED BY TWO WIDE STRAPS.

A gold plated HJ-Führerdolch has been attributed to the professional Youth Leader of the Marine HJ. However, the dagger awarded to the
Marine Youth Leader was of identical specifications to the standard dagger, and was not gold plated.

While wear of the various Youth blades continued briefly after 1942,
production was discontinued in October of that year.

MARINE-HJ STUDENTS, UNDER THE SUPERVISION OF A MARINE-HJ LEADER GIVE A DEMON-
STRATION TO A DELEGATION OF JAPANESE YOUTH.

NATIONAL ARCHIVES

NPEA LEADERS ON AN INSPECTION TOUR AT ONE OF THE SCHOOLS. NOTE THAT THE SA DAGGER WORN AT THE RIGHT IS OF THE VERY EARLY PATTERN AS DISTINGUISHED BY THE ELONGATED NATIONAL EMBLEM INLAY.

LEADERSHIP SCHOOLS OF THE NSDAP
[NATIONALPOLITISCHE ERZIEHUNGSANSTALT]

H itler, dissatisfied with virtual total domination of every aspect of German life, exerted his control over every level of education. This chapter does not deal with the normal educational facilities that were placed under the supervision of Reichsminister of Education, Bernhard Rust, but those special institutions originated by the Nazis for the purpose of training potential leaders and Nazi elite. Three new types of schools found their way into existence following Hitler's move into the Chancellory.... the National Political Educational Establishment, the Adolf Hitler Schools and the Order Castles.

The first three National Political Educational Establishments (Nationalpolitische Erziehungsanstalt.... NPEA or NAPOLA) were established by Bernhard Rust on April 20, 1933. These schools were nothing more than a reinstitution of the old Prussian military academies, but with the purpose of systematically turning out leaders for the SA, SS, Police and RAD. The need for such leaders was so increased after the outbreak of the war that the number of schools exceeded forty in 1945. Of these schools three were specifically designated for developing Nazi indoctrinated females for leadership positions in the Reichs Labor Service. Schools were also established in Austria, Sudetenland and Alsace-Lorraine. Supervision of the school system was placed in the hands of the SS, with an SS-Obergruppenführer (General) overseeing the entire system.

By 1938, the fifteen schools within the system were producing a total of 400 graduates annually. Even with the rapid expansion of the school system in 1939, enrollment in that peak year was limited to 4,500 students, with a faculty and administrative staff of 500. Leaders and instructors for the school system were themselves taken from the ranks of the SA and SS. The everyday existence of the instructors and students centered around the school curriculum, which dealt largely with physical training and political indoctrination.

For a student to be selected for attendance at one of the NAPOLA's, he or she had to be a member of the Hitler Youth, and demonstrate leadership potential by excelling in the numerous physical competitions and tests to determine the extent of political indoctrination. Once in the school these tests were intensified, with a continuous weeding out process between the dormant and the overt leader. A student would normally enter the program at age ten, and if he met all the requirements to be retained, he would spend eight years being molded as a leader for one of the armed elements of the NSDAP. Following his graduation, he was given the opportunity of going on to a college or university, but most elected to enter the political arm for which they had been trained.

The Adolf Hitler Schools were established in 1937 to provide the necessary leadership for all elements of the NSDAP and state positions. Selection for these schools was limited to boys only, entering at the age of twelve, and remaining in the system for six years. The criteria for selection was a bit more broad yet restricted to members of the Stamm-HJ, and like the NPEA, instruction was largely physical and political. Membership was rather limited since only ten schools were established, and centrally located in Bavaria. Instructors, who were drawn from the SA/SS/HJ, as well as students were required to live full-time at the school. A successful graduate had the options of entering a university, of assuming a leadership role in one of the many NSDAP formations, of becoming an officer in one of the military services or of playing a prominent role in one of the bureaucratic positions in state government. In any event, a graduate's success was assured by his close affiliation with the Nazi Party.

In keeping with the selective educational programs, a third institute, the Order Castle, was established (or rather reinstituted since it had its origin in the thirteenth century). While the NPEA and the Order Castle had as their mission the development and training of the Nazi elite, it was the latter that was the more selective of the two. Only one fourth of the graduates of the NPEA were permitted admittance into the higher educational institute of the Order Castle. Although four Order Castles were established, the student did not spend his entire five years at just one of the schools, but was rotated between the four in a predetermined plan.

HIGH RANKING MILITARY AND POLITICAL DIGNITARIES ON AN INSPECTION TOUR ARE GIVEN A DEMONSTRATION BY NPEA STUDENTS. THE NPEA LEADER AT CENTER-RIGHT WEARS THE NPEA DAGGER WITH FROG.

Prior to entry into the system, the student candidate must have completed his one year obligation with the Reichs Labor Service, his two years with a military arm, and still be faced with a waiting period of between one and three years, during which time he must serve in some capacity within the Nazi framework.

The first year of training, designed to develop the trainees' ideological preparation, specialized in the fields of "race" biology and related "sciences". The second year concentrated on the physical development of the student, with programs to include mountain climbing, parachuting and marksmanship. As the student progressed, training became more intense, with the third phase lasting a year and a half. This phase was an intensified period of both physical and political training designed to further develop the skills of the potential leader. The fourth and final phase also was one and a half years, and dealt specifically with the more complex political questions that faced the German diplomatic and military leaders. The Order Castle at Marienburg was selected for the final stage of training. This Castle was one of the original

Castles stemming from the thirteenth century "Order of the German Knights." The selection of this location for the final stage allowed for the coupling of intensified political training with the teutonic military tradition of the middle centuries.

DAGGERS OF THE LEADERSHIP SCHOOLS

There exists a series of daggers that are normally attributed to the NPEA. However, the variations within this particular series are so extensive, it leads one to the possible conclusion that the daggers were absorbed within the entire educational structure of the NSDAP rather than limited to the singular system of the NPEA. Since the NPEA dagger is readily identifiable, it is with this dagger that we will first deal.

Even though the NPEA was established in 1933, it was not until the fall of 1935 that students were authorized to wear a dagger sidearm. The NPEA-Kurzteilnehmer Dienstdolch or Service Dagger was first worn by instructor staff members. It soon became a part of regulation dress for the student or Jungemannen of the NPEA when the Service Dress Uniform was worn. The dagger was always worn in the vertical configuration, suspended from the outer belt by means of a brown or black leather bayonet-type frog. The scabbard was the main distinguishing feature of the dagger, constructed of steel, and painted olive-drab or brown. Unlike the standard political forms, the scabbard did not have externally mounted fittings. It did have a bayonet type carrying hook to fasten to the belt frog. The basic dagger was of the same simple design as used throughout the political formations. The overall length measured 35cms. Metal fittings of the hilt were constructed initially of nickel and later of aluminum. It was not uncommon for either the upper or lower crossguard to have the name and/or number of the student's institute stamped or engraved to allow for identification. This is a good indication that the various daggers were purchased and retained by the institutions rather than by the individual wearer. The brown wood handle was void of any insignia inlays. The hilt was secured to the blade by means of a tang button. The obverse of the blade bore the organizational motto "Mehr Sein als Scheinen" (Be more than you appear to be), while the reverse of the blade normally bore the name of the distributor. Of all the specimens encountered, an extremely limited number were found to have the manufacturer's trademark (Eickhorn in each case). It would appear that the firm of Karl Burgsmuller of Berlin, not a manufacturer of daggers, had sole distribution rights for this particular series of daggers.

The NPEA-Leiter Dienstdolch was identical to the aforementioned, with the exception that the scabbard varied considerably. The Staff Leader's Service Dagger was suspended by means of a chain hanger that was

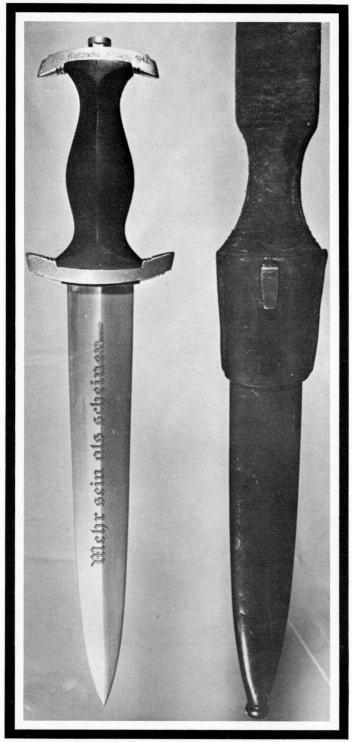

NPEA STUDENT'S DAGGER. THE UPPER CROSSGUARD IS ENGRAVED "NPEA KLOTZSCHE
KRIEGS J. 1942." THE WOOD HANDLE AND LEATHER FROG ARE BROWN, WHILE THE
SCABBARD PAINT IS OLIVE DRAB.

113

similar to that found on the Railway Protection Leader's dagger, but having only five upper and seven lower nickel links. As a result of the chain suspension, the scabbard had a center band. A swivel ring was attached to the upper and center scabbard bands, and attached to the chain hangers. The steel body of the scabbard was painted either olive-drab or brown, and was fitted with nickel plated fittings identical to those found on the 1936 pattern NSKK Service Dagger.

The NPEA-Leiter Dienstdolch Modell 1936, as would indicate, was introduced for wear by Staff Leaders in 1936. The dagger was identical to those previously described with the exception of the addition of a silver plated or nickel national emblem centered and inlaid in the face of the brown wood handle. The configuration of the scabbard varied somewhat from the earlier model in that the center suspension band was wider, and the suspension swivel rings were replaced by stationary ramps. The same type of chain suspension was used, but was crudely attached rather than being an integral part of the scabbard.

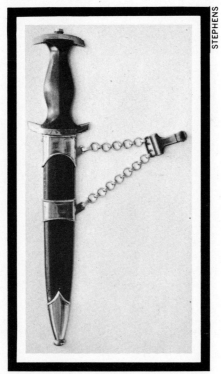

STEPHENS

NPEA LEADER'S DAGGER WITH FIXED RAMP
SCABBARD FITTINGS. THE GRIP IS WITH-
OUT INLAY.

PEA LEADER'S DAGGER WITH SWIVEL RING
TTACHMENTS TO THE CHAIN HANGER.

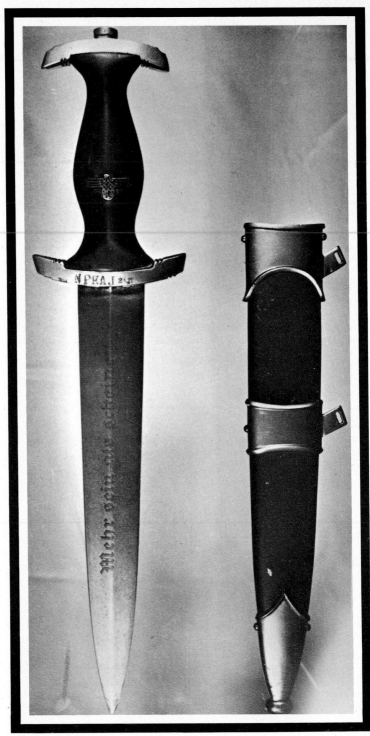

NPEA LEADER'S DAGGER WITH FIXED RAMP SCABBARD FITTINGS. THE INLAY IN THE GRIP IS A FLEMISH NAZI INSIGNIA. THE STAMPING ON THE LOWER ALUMINUM CROSSGUARD IS THE DESIGNATION OF THE SCHOOL.

No attempt will be made to offer an explanation for the other design variations encountered, but evidence would indicate that they fall somewhere within the framework of the educational system. The presence or lack of the national emblem in the same pattern dagger, in addition to the fact that the "S" within the motto is found in two patterns, would indicate that these are more than just manufacturer's variations. In addition to those already described, the following specimens have been encountered, but are unattributed:

1. NPEA-Kurzteilnehmer Dienstdolch with national emblem inlay, with a blued bayonet type scabbard.
2. NPEA-Kurzteilnehmer Dienstdolch, black handle with national emblem inlay, with a blued bayonet type scabbard.
3. NPEA-Kurzteilnehmer Dienstdolch, black handle with national emblem and SS inlays, with blued bayonet stype scabbard.
4. NPEA-Leiter Dienstdolch, without national emblem inlay.

Even though specimens have been encountered, externally mounted scabbard fittings, such as those found on the standard unchained political patterns of the SA, SS, etc., were not authorized for the NPEA-Kurzteilnehmer Dienstdolch. It can be assumed that an interchange of scabbards has taken place at some point in time.

Through observation it has been found that this is the only series of daggers within the political series that characteristically made use of a felt buffer pad placed between the lower portion of the crossguard and the scabbard throat. The primary purpose of this pad was to eliminate metal to metal contact.

Due to the very limited number and attendance of the institutions, it can be assumed that dagger production to meet the requirements was extremely limited. The NPEA series, and especially those patterns having chain suspensions, is considered to be among the rarest of the Nazi era daggers.

NOTE:

In a letter dated January 31, 1945, SA-Sturmführer Cammann, NPEA-Reichsenau, sent an inquiry through Oberlandesrat Müller to Reichsleiter Bormann concerning the question of calling in all daggers for possible issue to the Volksturm or other similar use. There is no record of the response.

THE LUFTSPORTS OFFICER TO THE LEFT WEARS THE FLIEGERDOLCH, WHILE THE ENLISTED MEMBER WEARS THE 1936 PATTERN KNIFE.

GERMAN AIR SPORTS FORMATION
[DEUTSCHER LUFTSPORT-VERBAND (DLV)]

In an attempt to stimulate the air-mindedness of the German people, the numerous civilian aero clubs of the Deutschen Luftfahrt-Verbandes were incorporated into the newly formed Deutscher Luftsport-Verband on March 25, 1933. The early formation of aero clubs evolved from independent flying units formed by aviation enthusiasts.... the most notable being SA and SS men who banded together to form local Fliegersturme units. The Versailles Treaty imposed very strict limitations on the use and production of all forms of motor-driven aircraft. Production was restricted to civilian requirements necessary to the very existence of air transportation. Production of military type aircraft, even for defensive purposes, was strictly forbidden. Under no circumstances did the world powers at the League of Nations wish any resurgence of German air strength.

World War I brought considerable attention to the relatively new flying machine, and exposed the numerous uses that could be derived from aircraft. During the air engagements of the war, air aces were born from noblemen and farmers alike. Once the freedom of the skies had been tasted, interest in flying gripped the German nation. Restrictions on flying motor-driven aircraft were circumvented by a mass migration to gliders, which were free of all restrictions. Germans became masters at building precision airframes that allowed the glider enthusiasts to soar to new heights and greater distances. Hitler's desire to throw off the shackles of the Versailles Treaty, especially in the field of aviation, was supported by the growing number of aviators. Motor-driven aircraft were absorbed largely into general civilian usage, and especially into the numerous sports clubs under the auspices of the DLV.

A HALT ALONG THE PARADE ROUTE, MEMBERS OF THE LUFTSPORTSVERBAND EACH WEAR THE KNIFE DESIGNED FOR THEIR ORGANIZATION. THIS SAME PIECE WAS LATER ADOPTED BY THE NSFK.

With the establishment of the Deutscher Luftsport-Verband in 1933, three principal groups made up its organization: (1) flyers of motor-driven aircraft, (2) flyers of gliders, and (3) flyers of balloons. Heading up the DLV was Bruno Loerzer, a retired captain and old friend of Hermann Göring. While the organization did not fall under direct Nazi political control, it did fall under the heavy hand of Göring acting in the capacity of Reichsminister of Aviation and Honorary President of the DLV. A noticeable Nazi influence found its way into the DLV through the controls administered by Göring, and the general membership, which consisted of numerous Nazi Party members. Upon the formulation of the DLV, Göring prescribed that the uniform to be worn by members of the DLV was to follow the same pattern as worn by personnel of his suppressed Luftwaffe. With Hitler's official decree of March 5, 1935, establishing the new German Luftwaffe in contradiction to the Versailles Treaty, the uniform style underwent a change from that of the previous two years.

To add to the uniform trappings, a Nazi inspired sidearm was designed, approved and adopted in 1934. All ranks within the DLV initially had the approval for wear of the newly established Fliegermesser or Flyer's Knife. It was worn suspended from the outer belt when the service uniform was worn. The basic Flyer's Knife had an overall prescribed length of 34cms. This length resulted in its classification as a knife rather than a dagger. The ribbed screw-on pommel and the downward sloping crossguard were silver plate over a nickel base. A black enamel swastika on a silver circle was inset into the center of the crossguard both front and back. The grip was without adornment, being constructed of a blue colored leather over a wood base. The short double edged blade bore only the markings of the manufacturer's trademark on the reverse side. The metal fittings externally mounted by screws on the scabbard were also silver plate over nickel. The blue leather was carried over to the scabbard, and covered the steel scabbard body. The knife was suspended by the use of a short brown or black leather hanger attached to a single suspension swivel ring on the upper scabbard band by an oval rivet plate. A slight variation on this same design was adopted following the introduction of a newly designed officer's pattern established in 1934. The 1936 modification added .5cms to the overall length. Knife and scabbard fittings were constructed from a dull brushed aluminum. A blue enamel was sprayed over a die-impressed aluminum that simulated the rough grain of leather. A gold or black colored swastika was inscribed in the center of both sides of the crossguard. Since both the 1934 and 1936 designs were carried over to the Nationalsozialistische Fliegerkorps (NSFK) in 1937, as that organization's officially adopted sidearm, illustrations of these pieces will be referred to in the chapter dealing with that subject. The DLV Fliegermesser can be distinguished from the later NSFK Fliegermesser by an inscribed insigne on the scabbard throat (see inset).

DLV SCABBARD THROAT MARKING

The Fliegerdolch (Flyer's Dagger), which was introduced in 1934, was prescribed for wear by officers of the DLV. This dagger was the forerunner of the Fliegerdolch adopted for general wear within the ranks of the Luftwaffe by flying personnel. The overall length was an amazing 55cms. The grip was blue leather wrap over wood, and had no provisions for wire wrapping. However, there were a series of sharp ridges running at a slight diagonal from high left to low right. The circular pommel and the down swept crossguard were constructed of nickel. **121**

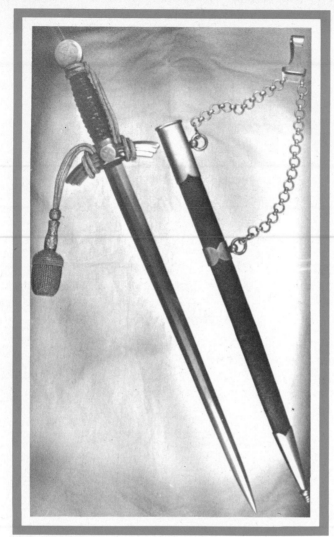

**LUFTSPORTS OFFICER WEAR-
ING EARLY PATTERN LUFT-
SPORTS DAGGER WHILE IN
ATTENDANCE AT GÖRING'S
BIRTHDAY, 12 JANUARY
1935.**

**THIS LEADER'S DAGGER WAS DESIGNED SPECIFICALLY FOR THE OFFICERS OF THE LUFT-
SPORTSVERBAND. IT IS THE FORERUNNER TO THE FLIEGERDOLCH ADOPTED IN 1934 BY
THE LUFTWAFFE.**

Both bore a brass swastika of the pinwheel design inset on both sides.
The swastika did not have a recessed outline, and was on a flat rather
than a convex plane. The scabbard followed through with the blue leather
motif, but was void of any metal underbody. Scabbard fittings were
nickel, and had suspension swivel rings on both the upper and center
bands. The tip of the lower scabbard fitting was longer than the standard 1934 Fliegerdolch, and had four ridges rather than two. The double
chain hanger, constructed of nickel, had nine upper rings and four
teen lower rings.... longer in both cases than the standard Fliegerdolch
which was soon to evolve. The standard 42cms aluminum cord with acorn
was worn when a portepee was required.

ENLARGEMENT OF THE UPPER SCAB-BARD BAND OF THE PRESENTATION LUFTSPORTS DAGGER. IT READS "TO THE FURTHERANCE OF THE GERMAN LUFTSPORTS, DIRECTOR P. SPECK, LUFTSPORTS-ORTSGRUPPE BERLIN VI 1936."

PRESENTATION LUFTSPORTS LEADER'S DAGGER—IDENTICAL IN DESIGN TO THE LUFTWAFFE FLIEGERDOLCH. HOWEVER, THERE IS NO METAL BASE TO THE SCABBARD, AND THE SCABBARD FITTINGS ARE MOUNTED IN A DIFFERENT MANNER.

By mid-1935, the early pattern Fliegerdolch was removed from wear in deference to the standard pattern 1934 Fliegerdolch that had evolved for wear by members of the Luftwaffe. The Deutscher Luftsport-Verband ceased to exist after April 17, 1937. However, the Fliegermesser designed for wear by the members of the DLV was carried over to the NSFK.

NSFK STANDARD BEARER

NATIONAL SOCIALIST FLYING CORPS
[NATIONALSOZIALISTISCHES FLIEGERKORPS (NSFK)]

On April 17, 1937, a transition was made from the civilian organizations of the Luftsportsverband to a state-controlled organization entitled the "National Socialistic Flying Corps" (Nationalsozialistisches Fliegerkorps...NSFK). Unlike other paramilitary organizations that fell under Nazi control, the NSFK was not considered to be a full part of the Gliederung or Party organizational structure per se. While the NSFK enjoyed the status of a state-registered corporation, indirect Party control was still exerted. With General Friedrich Christiansen, an active duty Luftwaffe officer, at its head, principal control was exerted by the Luftwaffe rather than the political hierarchy. Considering Göring's dual status, this situation posed little or no problem to the Nazis.

Göring considered the organization an extension of his Luftwaffe. Since virtually every restriction imposed against aircraft manufacture and development of a German air arm had already been broken by 1936, Göring proceeded at full speed to increase the number of inductees into the infant Luftwaffe. He also expanded and improved training as well as facilities, and insured a reservoir of capable replacement personnel. It was through the NSFK that he partially intended to meet these needs.

Air-minded members of the Aviation Hitler Youth, between the ages of 11-13, were taught basic aviation concepts through model building. As they progressed in age, they were graduated into the more technical skills of piloting gliders (which after 1942 gained them award of the silver glider pilot's badge) and eventually motor-driven aircraft. Many of these youths went on to become pilots in the Luftwaffe.

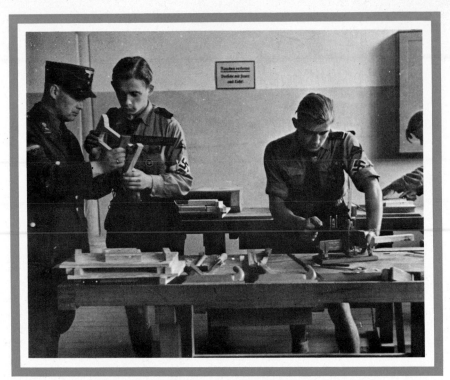

PRE-MILITARY TRAINING FOR THE FLIEGER-HITLER-JUGEND.

Membership in the NSFK was highly restrictive. No persons that held active membership in any of the major Nazi organizations such as the SS, SA, NSKK, etc., were permitted to join. The Hitler Youth, because of its state affiliation, was the exception to this membership rule. Though membership was voluntary, the NSFK became a holding organization (a reserve component so to speak) for trained pilots and technical personnel discharged from the Luftwaffe. At the outbreak of World War II, membership continued to climb. In addition to those functions already mentioned, the NSFK had as its prime function the maintenance of training schools to produce pilots, radio operators, glider troops and parachutists for the Luftwaffe. By 1943, the NSFK maintained sixteen glider schools throughout Germany, and assisted in the functions of three National Glider Schools.

When General Christiansen became Chief of Luftwaffe Personnel, leadership of the NSFK was turned over to Generaloberst Alfred Keller. It was he who retained control of the NSFK as Korpsführer to the end of the war.

With the 1937 reorganization, the uniform underwent yet another change. The major holdover from the earlier Luftsport-Verband was the

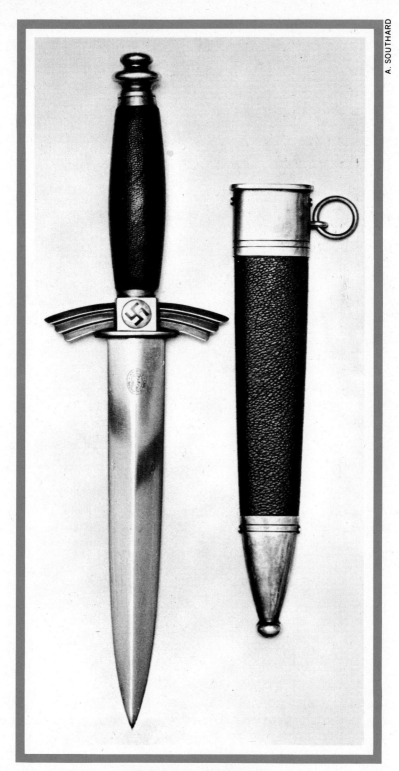

MODEL 1934 FLIEGERMESSER

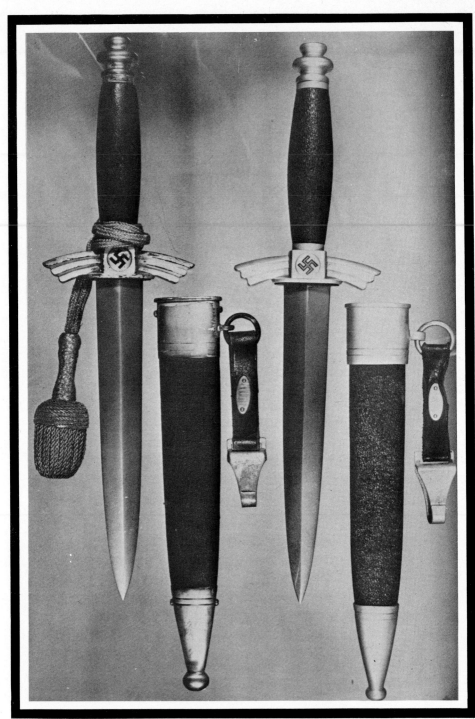

THE DAGGER TO THE LEFT WAS INTRODUCED IN 1934 FOR WEAR BY MEMBERS OF THE LUFTSPORTSVERBAND. ITS GRIP AND SCABBARD WAS COVERED WITH A BLUE LEATHER WHILE THE ONE TO THE RIGHT, ADOPTED IN 1936 FOR THAT SAME ORGANIZATION, IS FINISHED WITH BLUE PAINT OVER AN ALUMINUM CRACKLE FINISH. THIS SAME PATTERN DAGGER WAS ADOPTED BY THE NSFK WHEN IT RECEIVED ITS CHARTER ON 17 APRIL 1937.

Fliegermesser which had been designed for that organization. While the first design 1934 Fliegerdolch had been completely phased out, the second design was adopted by the Luftwaffe as its basic dagger sidearm. The use of the second design 1934 Fliegerdolch by the Luftwaffe precluded its continued use by the DLV on a broad basis. Thus the design was not considered for selection when the NSFK came into being. The Fliegermesser was designated as the official sidearm of the NSFK in 1937. Previous members of the Luftsport-Verband merely retained their old blade upon making the transition into the newly formed NSFK. After 1937, stricter controls were instituted for the sale and distribution of the Fliegermesser. Sale of the Fliegermesser thru retail sales distribution was not authorized. However, the knife could be obtained by purchasing it through

NSFK SCABBARD THROAT MARKING

a centrally controlled agency within the NSFK. Upon manufacture, a die-stamp of the NSFK insigne (see inset) replaced the DLV insigne on the throat of the scabbard.

Relatively speaking, there were far fewer of the 1936 design Fliegermessers due to the very restrictive and rather limited membership of the NSFK (excluding the Aviation Hitler Youth, which numbered 101,000 at the end of 1938). Towards the end of the war, the wear of the NSFK Fliegermesser like other dagger sidearms was phased out.

Daggers of the Civil and National Governmental Agencies

THE DIPLOMATIC DAGGER, WORN BY FOREIGN MINISTER RIBBENTROP, MAKES ITS DEBUT IN ROME IN 1938.

DIPLOMATIC AND CAREER OFFICIALS
[DIPLOMATEN UND STAATSBEAMTE]

$\mathbb{D}$ue to the fact that the facing of the eagle's head on the cross-guard is the only distinguishing feature between the Diplomatic Official's Dagger and the Government Official's Dagger, the two basically distinct functions of internal and external administration and policy will be discussed in a single chapter. Foreign Minister Joachim von Ribbentrop helped to create a problem for himself when he placed the two functions under a single roof, with the Diplomatic Corps directly responsible to him, and the Government Officials sharing responsibility through the Ministry of Interior. Up to the end of the war, von Ribbentrop was attempting to settle the question of a distinctive uniform for each office....as quite often, it was only the sleeve insignia which distinguished the two functionaries.

GERMAN POLICY AND THE FOREIGN MINISTRY

It has been said that war reflects the failures of diplomats in pursuit of a successful foreign policy. This is based on the assumption that war was not part of the grand diplomatic strategy to begin with....as was the case with Hitler's foreign policy. German foreign policy remained little changed from its inception during the First Reich. Kaiser Wilhelm gave that policy an avowed direction...."World domination or decline". Coming out of WWI as the vanquished simply meant a temporary setback in Germany's drive to world domination. With the legal overthrow of the Weimar Republic, Hitler embarked on the road of world conquest in the fashion that he had spelled out in great detail in his book, "Mein Kampf" (My Struggle). Hitler made it fully clear that Germany was in a state of struggle, and that peace could not be achieved until all opposition (both internal and external) had either been quieted or eliminated. In achieving his end, historical events would have German foreign policy divided into four broad segments: 1933-1936, Germany attempts to achieve equal rights in concert with world powers; 1936-1938, unification of all German-speaking peoples under the absolute control of the German government; 1938-1940, demands for increased living space; 1940-1945, an attempt at world domination through military aggression.

The Nazis used the failure of the Second Reich to lay the claim of the "stab-in-the-back". In the eyes of the Germans, the dictates of the Versailles Treaty had been exceptionally harsh from an economic standpoint, excessively restrictive from a defensive posture, and denied Germany the necessary living space to accomodate its expanding population. To a limited degree, the Germans had just cause for their attitude. The attitude of the German people, stemming from both real and imagined causes, allowed Hitler to get a grip on Germany and guide it along a path to self-destruction.

Hitler was to use the most unlikely of allies to gain his objectives. He joined into a secret agreement with Russia, his staunchest enemy, which allowed him to send personnel to Russia for training, and develop equipment for testing on her terrain and air. When Hitler's legions crossed into Russia on their ill-fated attempt at conquest, their initial march was rapid and direct, as many of the officers had been there years earlier learning the terrain and the Russian weaknesses. By agreement, the fate of Poland was sealed in the terms drawn up between the two dictitorial powers. As Ambassador to England, Joachim von Ribbentrop(a former champaign salesman whose star rose rapidly as a result of being a dedicated Nazi) laid the groundwork for future agreements between Prime Minister Chamberlain and Hitler. The series of pacts, pledges, and agreements that were to follow were all designed to guarantee Germany a relatively free hand in the pursuit of expansionism.

When Ribbentrop succeeded von Neurath as Foreign Minister, he immediately commenced a constant flow of heads of state to Hitler. Following Mussolini's visit to Berlin in 1937, Hitler accepted his invitation for a visit to Rome. Hitler, flanked by von Ribbentrop and Himmler (not to mention a virtual army of diplomatic officials and high-ranking Nazis), went to Rome to court the support of Mussolini. Hitler had greatly overestimated the value of Italian support in his grand strategy. In sealing the fate of the two countries, Mussolini allowed himself to become overly impressed with the pomp and ceremony of the Nazis, and thus became deeply embroiled in Hitler's intrigues. During the visit, an exchange of

HITLER WEARING A SPECIAL PRESENTATION FASCIST DAGGER IN ROME, MAY 1938.

honors was accorded Hitler when Mussolini presented him with a beautiful Fascist dagger. At a subsequent meeting, when he signed the "Pact of Steel" in Berlin on May 22, 1939, Mussolini bestowed the Order of Annunziata on von Ribbentrop.

As Ribbentrop gathered these diplomatic agreements, he knew full well that they were to be systematically discarded when it was to Hitler's best interest.

GOVERNMENT OR CAREER OFFICIALS

Shortly after his appointment as Hitler's Foreign Minister in 1938, von Ribbentrop instituted a series of internal changes in the structure of the Foreign Ministry. What evolved were two distinct functionaries serving under the same roof, but serving two different masters. Since the government officials' duties were totally unrelated to foreign affairs, and were specifically concerned with internal government administration, they were subordinate to the Gauleiters and ultimately to the Minister of Interior, Himmler. This situation was created following a law passed on January 30, 1934, promulgating the reconstruction of Germany. This law called for the abolition of the various state elective bodies, the transferral of sovereign power to Hitler, the subordination of the state governments to that of the Government of the German Reich, and control of the various Reich Governors being placed in the hands of the Minister of In-

135

terior.   On March 29, 1936, 99% of the German electorate voted an affirmation of Hitler's policies.

Following the outbreak of war, the question arises as to why government officials were found in the remote villages of Russia, Greece, France and other occupied countries.   The logical progression in Hitler's scheme of conquest was that when the Wehrmacht had crossed the borders of a country that had fallen prey, that country in effect became a state added to the Greater German Reich.   As such, it ceased to exist as a foreign power, and had no right to diplomatic recognition.   As an "Ausland" state, it was administered in part by government officials.

DIPLOMATIC OFFICIAL'S DRESS DAGGER

The Diplomatic Official's Dagger was worn for the first time during Hitler's visit to Rome in May 1938, when he was accompanied by von Ribbentrop and a large entourage of diplomatic officials.   Ribbentrop's officials mixed well with the Italian diplomats, making quite an impression with their gold and silver daggers contrasting with the grey or black service uniform.   During the evening functions when the mess dress uniform was worn, the dagger was replaced with the silver Diplomatic Official's Sword, which was symbolic of strength with diplomacy.   The diplomats, heaped in their pomp and ceremony, were resplendent in their uniforms.

FOREIGN MINISTER RIBBENTROP CONFERS WITH MUSSOLINI'S SON-IN-LAW, COUNT GALEAZZO CIANO, ROME 1938.

However, not all members of the Foreign Ministry were authorized to wear the dagger as it was approved on a very select basis. This resulted in very limited distribution, causing it to be one of the rarer daggers on todays collector market.

The metal hilt fittings of the Diplomatic Official's Dagger were cast in German silver with a finished appearance which was referred to as "old silver"... a finish intended to give a burnish or tarnished effect. However, the highest grades of officials had their superior rank distinguished by a dagger finished with a gold plate. The eagle head pommel and backstrap were cast in a single piece. Recessed in the crown of the pommel was a tang button that secured the blade in the hilt. This tang button was a nut having two round holes, and was tightened by means of a spanner wrench.

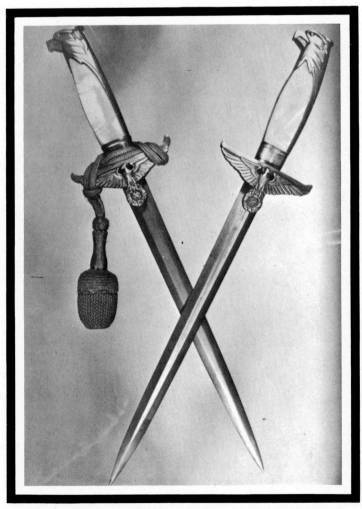

A SILVER PLATED DIPLOMATIC DAGGER (RIGHT) IS COMPARED WITH A GOLD PLATED GOVERNMENT OFFICIAL'S DAGGER (LEFT).

Slabs of celluloid simulating mother-of-pearl were placed over a wood base to adorn the handle. The national emblem with slightly upturned wing tips formed the design of the crossguard. The head of the eagle faced to its left, exactly opposite from the direction of the eagle head pommel. The blade and scabbard were identical to the Army dagger...
...with the exception of the scabbard bands, which were formed from two rows of overlapping oak leaves. All metal parts (with the exception of the scabbard) and the wood base of the grip bore identical numbers stamped in them, which is assumed were intended as assembly numbers.

The 38.5 cms dagger was worn suspended on the left side from either an external belt or sash, or from an underbelt or cross strap with the double strap hangers passing under the flap of the lower left pocket. The bright metal fittings of the hanger were identical to the Luftwaffe fittings worn with the 1937 pattern dagger. Hangers worn with the gold finished dagger had gold wash fittings of identical design. Both sets of hangers employed a silver facing sewn to black velvet in the make-up of the suspension straps. The 42cms silver portepee with a smaller than normal acorn was characteristically worn with the silver dagger, while a gold portepee was worn with the gold dagger. The hangers and portepees described above were also worn with the Government Official's daggers.

GOVERNMENT OFFICIAL'S DRESS DAGGER

The career service uniform dagger of the Government Official made its appearance in 1938, but was not approved for wear until March 30, 1939.[1] Selected officials were authorized to wear either the German silver or gold plated dagger depending on rank. The Government Official's Dagger was identical in every respect to the Diplomatic Official's Dagger with the exception that the head of the eagle crossguard faced to its right (the same direction as the

THE REICHSPROTECTOR OF THE SUDETENLAND, FREIHERR VON NEURATH, REVIEWS A PARADE IN PRAGUE FOLLOWING THE ANNEXATION OF THE SUDETENLAND IN OCTOBER 1938 (NOTE GOVERNMENT OFFICIAL'S DAGGER).

[1]Uniform-Markt, 1939.

GOVERNMENT OFFICIAL'S DAGGER WITH 42cms ALUMINUM PORTEPEE.

GOVERNMENT OFFICIAL'S DAGGER

pommel eagle) rather than to the left was with the Diplomatic Official's Dagger. The conditions and manner of wear were the same for both.

The main distinguishing feature of the two daggers was, therefore, the direction the eagle's head faced on the crossguard. The confusion that has existed between the proper identification of the two daggers can be directly attributed to the Eickhorn Kundendienst dated 1939, and subsequent catalogue publications. It can only be assumed that the printer reversed the photo negatives or captions, with the error going undetected or unchanged. The May 1940, Alcoso catalogue corrects the confusion by specifically spelling out the direction of the eagle's head on the Diplomatic Official's Dagger. The F. W. Höller sales catalogue correctly illustrated the Government Official's Dagger the previous year. These two sources have gone unheeded in deference to the Eickhorn catalogue. The latter's error has been perpetuated by authors over the years.

A seldom seen dagger was the "Eischereiaufsichtsbeamte Dolch" or Fishery Control Official's Dagger worn by high ranking government officials assigned to the state hatcheries.[2] The dagger was introduced in 1940, and replaced the naval officer's sword that was a part of the uniform trappings at the time. It was identical to the Government Official's Dagger with the exception that the scabbard was black. The limited rank and file of this particular agency would account for the rarity of this dagger.

In 1941, a dagger was proposed for the officials of the Ministry of Occupied Eastern Territories.[3] The piece was of a completely new design. It is believed that the dagger was placed into limited production, but was never completed due to the turn of events in the war. Hanger fittings with an exact design that corresponds with the scabbard suspension bands are in the author's collection.

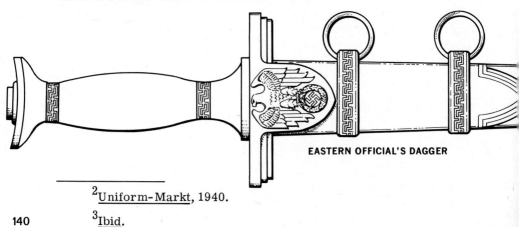

EASTERN OFFICIAL'S DAGGER

[2] Uniform-Markt, 1940.

[3] Ibid.

REICHSMINISTER OF OCCUPIED EASTERN TERRITORIES ALFRED ROSENBERG VISITING A GER-
MAN SCHOOL IN THE UKRAINE ON AUGUST 19, 1943.

In late 1939, selected subordinates in the lower diplomatic ranks were authorized to wear a specially designed dress sidearm.[4] It was designed solely as a dress sidearm as it had no provision to fit it to a rifle. The pommel and grip were of the same design as the dagger worn by higher ranking officials. The crossguard departed from the dagger design as it was relatively unembelished. The single edged blade was of a standard bayonet design. A choice of a black painted steel scabbard or brown leather with nickel plated fittings was open to the wearer. The sidearm was worn suspended over the left hip by means of a brown leather frog attached to an outer belt.

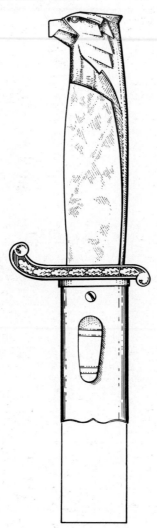

[4]Alcoso Sales Catalogue, May 1940.

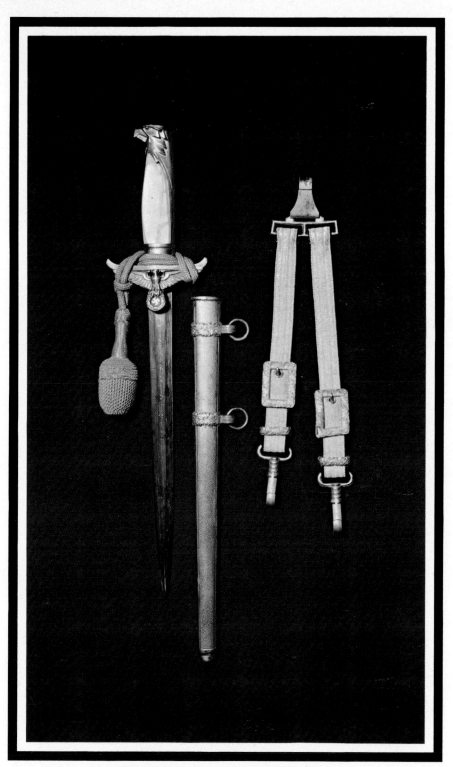

GOVERNMENT OFFICIAL'S DAGGER IN GOLD

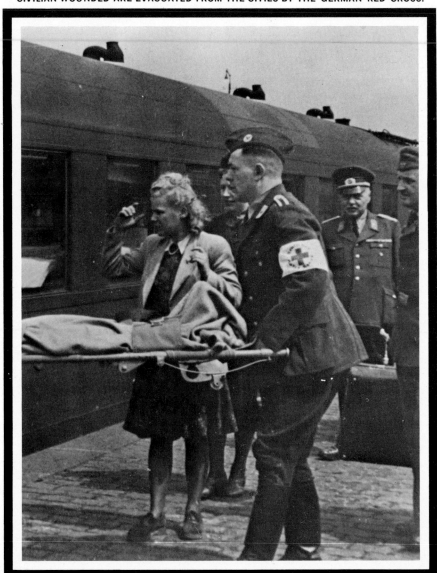

THE GERMAN RED CROSS
[DEUTSCHES ROTES KREUZ]

The principal institutions providing private welfare assistance within Germany were the National Socialist People's Welfare Organization, the Protestant Home Mission, the Catholic Caritas Union, and the German Red Cross. These organizations worked closely together to cope with internal civil disasters, and provide general aid to the needy. One of the greatest contributions to stem from their alliance was the National Winter Help (Winterhilfswerk des Deutschen Volkes, or WHW). Of these organizations, the German Red Cross was the most prominent. When Hitler became Chancellor, the Red Cross ceased to exist as an independent agency, and became directly subordinate to the Minister of the Interior. With the nationalization of the Red Cross, the slow process of Nazification began. In addition to its normal services, Hitler used the agency extensively throughout the country to administer aid stations at the numerous military and political rallies.

Most of the agency's membership were volunteers supervised by a cadre of paid, full-time leaders. Unlike many of the volunteer organizations, all members, both male and female, were authorized to wear the uniform regardless of their status.

RED CROSS LEADER'S DAGGER

A dress dagger was introduced in 1938 for wear by male members of the Red Cross in ranks of Wachtführer on up. Circumstances of wear were very limited, and restricted to the service uniform. The overall design was basic and simple. The unadorned pommel served as a counter-weight, and a housing for the tang fasteners. Recessed in the pommel were two lock-nuts, which secured the blade in the grip. The recess was covered by a screw cap, which was in no way intended to be used to tighten the blade in the grip. The only part to have any outward design was the crossguard. The obverse of the guard was predominently an oval with an eagle with a swastika on its chest and clutching the cross insigne of the International Red Cross. The reverse of the guard was a large plain oval that sometimes bore an engraved dedication or a stamped district marking. Noticeable variations in the thickness of the crossguard have been encountered, which were probably due to variations in specifications of the manufacturers. The handle was normally white plastic with a series of parallel ridges. The white plastic often discolored to a pale yellow, and sometimes light orange. The metal hilt fittings were finished in a dull nickel plate, while the steel blade was finished in a high polish. The blade bore no external markings, however, markings have been found on the blade tang. The pebbled scabbard was also finished in a dull nickel plate. Scabbards are found with two minor variation holes in the suspension ramps.... rectangular and round. Overall length of the dagger was 37.5cms. A 42cms aluminum portepee was usually worn wrapped about the lower portion of the handle. It is this writer's opinion that the Red Cross Leader's dagger was worn by two main groups.... those primarily concerned with functions specifically related to the Red Cross, and those concerned with welfare matters. While the dagger remained the same, there were two distinct double strap hangers provided to bear out the distinction. The Red Cross hangers had a dull aluminum facing with red stripes at its edges sewn to a mouse grey velvet backing. All metal fittings were finished in dull aluminum, with the buckle being an unadorned oval. Those hangers believed to have been used by the social welfare had a dull aluminum facing with the purple stripes at its edges sewn to mouse grey velvet. The aluminum fittings were pebbled, and the buckles were rectangular. This latter hanger is sometimes erroneously attributed to the Government Officials.

RED CROSS HEWER

Subordinates in the grades of Helfer to Haupthelfer were also authorized to wear a sidearm following its introduction in 1938. The hewer was issued to all male members, and was worn with the service uniform suspended over the left hip by a black leather frog. The overall length was 40cms, and was rather massive in design. In spite of its rather sturdy appearance, the piece was not intended to undergo any sustained blows. The design basically met the needs of a hospital corps knife. The blunt point disqualified the piece as being designated a weapon under

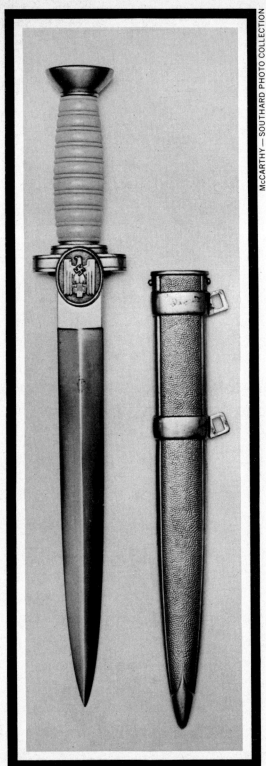

**RED CROSS
LEADER'S
DAGGER
WITH 42cms
PORTEPEE**

**RED CROSS
HANGERS**

**SOCIAL WELFARE
HANGERS**

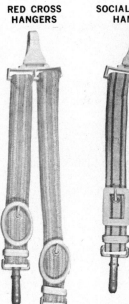

RED CROSS LEADER'S DAGGER

147

the provisions of the Geneva Convention. Its weight allowed it to be used as a utility tool, though not for any sustained heavy-duty use. The saw-back was used in preparing splints, removing casts, etc. The metal portions of the hilt were basically the same as the leader's dagger except for the wider crossguard. The metal portion of the handle was cast in a single piece, and was finished in either dull nickel or bright silver plate. Since the hewer was an issue piece, issue designators were more likely to be stamped on the reverse crossguard. The two piece slab grips, smooth on the back and checkered on the front, were made of plastic, and retained by two screws. The blade was brightly polished with no external markings with the possible exception of the patent pending (Ges. Geschützt) found under the langet. However, the tang of the hewer has also been found with a manufacturer's proof. The steel scabbard was finished in black paint, and had either integral or externally mounted scabbard fittings finished in dull nickel or bright silver plate.

After the outbreak of the war, Red Cross leaders who served in the field in support of the Armed Forces relinquished the right to wear the dagger sidearm due to the restrictions imposed by the Geneva Convention. Wear of the hewer was also phased out shortly thereafter.

148   REVERSE LANGET OF A RED CROSS HEWER SHOWING ORGANIZATIONAL MARKS STAMPED IN.

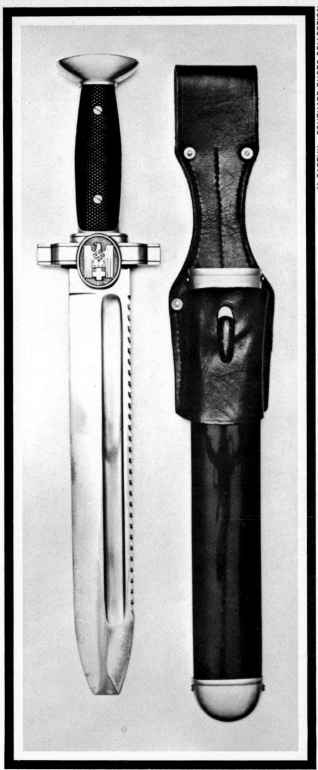

RED CROSS HEWER

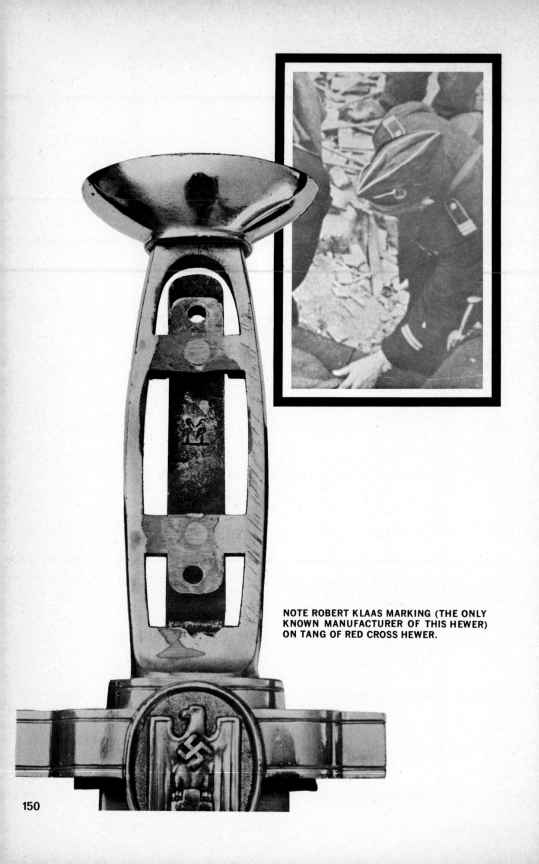

NOTE ROBERT KLAAS MARKING (THE ONLY KNOWN MANUFACTURER OF THIS HEWER) ON TANG OF RED CROSS HEWER.

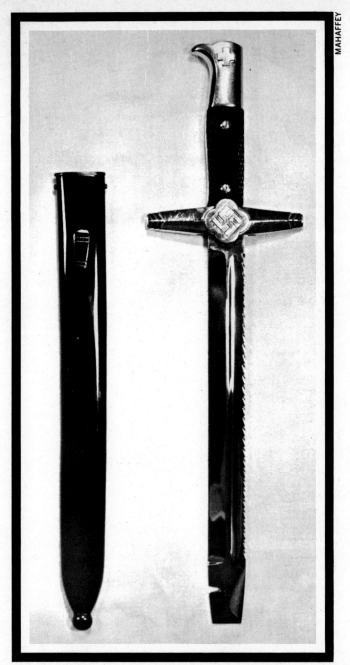

THIS HAND-CRAFTED PROTOTYPE BAYONET WAS DESIGNED SPECIFICALLY FOR ENLISTED PERSONNEL OF THE GERMAN RED CROSS. IT MEASURES 42 cms IN OVERALL LENGTH, WITH A 26 cms BLADE. THE BLADE IS A LONGER BUT NARROWER VERSION OF THE HEWING KNIFE, AND HAS A SLOT NEAR THE BLUNTED TIP. THE HILT FITTINGS ARE NICKEL PLATE, WITH THE OBVERSE OF THE POMMEL HAVING A SMALL RED CROSS INSIGNIA. THERE IS NO IN-SIGNIA ON THE REVERSE OF THE POMMEL. THE FRONT OF THE CROSSGUARD HAS A LARGE SWASTIKA, WHILE THE BACK HAS A LARGE RED CROSS INSIGNIA. THE MANUFACTURER'S PROOF, ROBERT KLAAS, APPEARS ON THE RICASSO. THIS IS THE ONLY PIECE OF ITS TYPE KNOWN TO HAVE BEEN MADE.

151

A BERLIN POLICEMAN INSPECTING A SHELL CRATER FOLLOWING A BRITISH AIR RAID, OCTOBER 24, 1940.

POLICE
[POLIZEI]

Police service in Germany during the Weimar Republic (1920–1933) reflected the ineffectiveness of the Weimar government. Since there was no national police force, each state had independent control over its police. The Reichsminister of the Interior exerted token control by maintaining approval authority over financial grants to the states. However, in the final analysis, it was the state and not the national government that was responsible for the control of law and order.

Due to this lack of centralized control, the reaction of the individual states to the Nazi movement varied....depending on the degree of infiltration by Nazi supporters. While some states legally banned the Nazi Party, a few states were either subtly sympathetic or totally unconcerned with the radical movement that was soon to disrupt the state and national scene. Hitler and his heirarchy recognized the need to exert a rigid control over a uniform police force. The process of gaining total control was slow and pains-taking. It was recognized throughout Germany that the police structure was badly in need of reform. Under the guise of structural reform, police leaders and subordinates who were in opposition to the Nazis were either purged or relegated to positions where they could not influence the "counter-revolutionary movement".

The Nazis had a major breakthrough when Göring was appointed Minister of Interior in the State of Prussia....Germany's largest and most influential state. The Nazis wasted no time in penetrating the

153

Prussian Police. Infiltration was so successful that a major reorganization was soon effected. The existing Prussian political police, the Staatspolizei, were transformed into the Geheime Staatspolizei (Gestapo or Secret State Police), which served as Göring's political enforcement arm. The initial purpose of the Gestapo was the removal of opposition to Göring within the Prussian State. However, as Göring rose to power with the Nazis, the organization applied its trade throughout the entire country.

Shortly after the Weimar Republic was politically defeated, Hitler implemented his intended restructuring of all police forces to further achieve his own aims. In 1934, authority over all police forces was transferred from the individual states to the Reich Government. The Hitler government continued reorganization for a total unified control. Hitler finally achieved national control in 1936 when he established the position of Chef der Deutschen Polizei. Reichsführer-SS Himmler was given the honor of this new position. He vigorously set about to absorb the police into the structural control of the SS. Since Himmler simultaneously held the positions of Reichsführer-SS and Commander-in-Chief of the Police, he needed only to circumvent the Reichsminister of the Interior, Wilhelm Frick, who was technically the highest official in the Police hierarchy. Himmler had this stumbling block removed when he was appointed Minister of Interior in 1943 following Frick's dismissal. Prior to that time, Himmler received little or no opposition from Frick, which allowed him to set his own course in the reorganization of the police.

Two main categories evolved from the complete reorganization that followed.... the Ordnungspolizei (Regular Police) and the Sicherheitspolizei (Security Police). The Ordnungspolizei (Orpo), in addition to the uniformed police functions, was responsible for the great majority of administrative matters that were related to police matters. The Orpo exercised direct administrative responsibility over the following subordinate elements:

(a) Schutzpolizei des Reichs (Reich Protection Police)

(b) Schutzpolizei der Gemeinden (Municipal Protection Police), having responsibility in towns with 2,000 or more population.

(c) Gendarmerie (Rural Police) having responsibility in towns with less than 2,000 population.

(d) Kolonialpolizei (Colonial Police)

(e) Wasserschutzpolizei (Water Protection Police)

(f) Feuerschutzpolizei (Fire Protection Police)

(g) Technische Hilfspolizeien (Technical Auxiliary Police Service) consisting of:

1. Feuerwehren (Fire Brigades)
2. Luftschutzpolizei (Air Raid Protection Police)
3. Technische Nothilfe (TN - Technical Emergency Corps)

(h) Verwaltungspolizei (Administrative Police)

(i) Hilfpolizeien (Auxiliary Police Force)

(j) Sonderpolizeien (Special Police Branches), consisting of:

1. Bahnpolizei (Railway Police)
2. Postschutz (Postal Protection Police)
3. Zollschutz (Customs Police)
4. Bergpolizei (Police for supervision of mines)

The foundation of any successful dictatorship is strengthened by an active and effective security police. Hitler's regime was no different in that it relied heavily on its security police to ferret out and eliminate the "enemies of the state". To best achieve this end, Himmler formed the Sicherheitspolizei (Sipo) and the Kriminalpolizei (Kripo), and appointed SS-Gruppenführer Reinhard Heydrich Chef der Sicherheitspolizei. When Heydrich was assassinated in 1942, he was replaced by Ernst Kaltenbrunner. Kaltenbrunner was to go to his death following the guilty verdict of the Nuremberg tribunal for his notorious actions during the remaining war years. Not only did the Sipo and Kripo establish an intensive intelligence gathering capability, but they responded to this intelligence with the swift and often brutal hand characteristic of the security police. It is not surprising that this powerful and elite organization required that all its members be both professional policemen and members of the SS.

In 1937, the Gestapo assumed control over the Frontier Police, and immediately formed a specialized branch of that police....the Grenzpolizei. SS influence was such that the Grenzpolizei were required to wear the SS uniform. Their primary function was the control of frontiers determined by the Reichs Government as falling within their domain.

Utilization of the uniformed police forces was extended far beyond their normal functions as Germany found herself more deeply embroiled in war. At the beginning of the war, the OKW had organized the Geheime Feldpolizei (Secret Field Police....not to be confused with the already existing Feldgendarmerie, which was the equivilent of the military police). Even though this was a military organization, personnel were drawn primarily from the Kripo and Orpo, and was controlled by the Gestapo.

THE POLICE BAYONET

During the Weimar Republic, members of the uniformed police were authorized to wear a bayonet sidearm, the Model 98/05 bayonet. A police general order allowed police armorers to render a major modification to the bayonet.[1] The blade was shortened to approximately 14 inches, narrowed by 6mm, and nickel plated. The grip underwent the greatest change; the wooden handle was replaced with stag horn grips, which were retained in place by two rivets. The pommel and cross-guard were designed with an oakleaf pattern, while the clamshell was designed with the Weimar eagle. A six-sided national badge was centered on the surface of the front grip. The metal scabbard was replaced by a leather scabbard with nickel plated fittings, and was narrowed to conform with the narrower blade. Early models were either nickel plated or German silver, while later models were produced of aluminum.

When the various state police forces were unified under national control, the bayonet was to prove unsatisfactory to the new government. Since many bayonets were produced with the extremely long blade that was characteristic of the period, it was very unwieldy. Issue bayonets

A POLICE CHOIR GIVES A CONCERT AT CONCERT HALL, BERLIN, TO COMMEMORATE POLICE DAY, FEBRUARY 17, 1941. NOTE THAT ALL MEMBERS OF THE CHOIR ARE WEARING THE STANDARD MODEL 98 BAYONET RATHER THAN THE POLICE SERVICE OR DRESS BAYONET.

---

[1] Waffentechnischen Leiffaden für Die Ordnungspolizei, Karl Fischer, 1941.

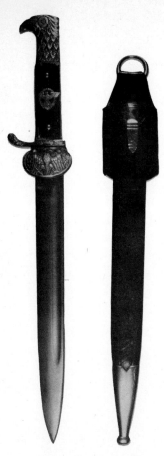

**CLAMSHELL POLICE BAYONET
WITH 25 cms BLADE**

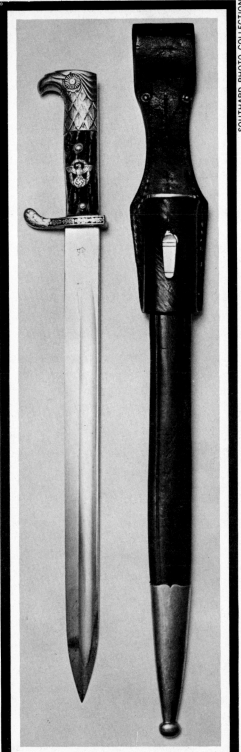

**POLICE SERVICE BAYONET
WITHOUT SLOT.**

157

were recalled to police ordnance depots, and were subjected to still further modifications. The clamshell was removed from the service bayonet, although they were found on the dress sidearms as late as 1938. When the grip was shortened, the rivets had to be moved, which required that the old holes be filled in. The new national police insignia, normally made of aluminum, replaced the defunct Weimar insignia. The blades of the service bayonets were shortened to a uniform length, new issue numbers stamped into the reverse guard and on other surfaces, and reissued for wear by both officers and subordinates on uniform status. The service bayonet was produced with and without a bayonet lug.

Officers and senior subordinates had the option of purchasing an extra-quality dress sidearm. The overall sidearm was smaller in size. Both the handle and blade were shorter and narrower, but retained the same design as the service bayonet. The scabbard fittings were nickel plated, but the hilt was produced from nickel plated steel or aluminum. In some cases, a sheet metal steel scabbard replaced the leather scabbard body. On rare occassions, the dress sidearm was purchased with an etched dedication on the blade.

UNSLOTED DRESS SIDEARM   SLOTED SERVICE BAYONET

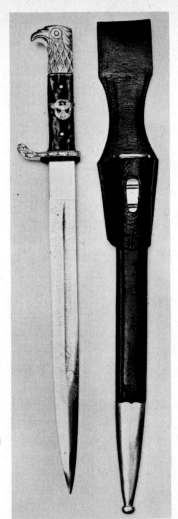

EXTRA-QUALITY DRESS SIDEARM WITH ETCHED DEDICATION

OBVERSE

Zur Erinnerung
1938–1939

REVERSE

Schutz-Polizei
Wiesbaden-Biebrich

SQUIRE—PHOTOS BY A. SOUTHARD

Both the service and dress bayonets were worn suspended by a leather frog attached to an outer belt on the left side. The black leather frog was for Municipal Police and the brown leather frog was for Rural Police. The characteristic silver, red and black knot was often attached to the frog for ornamentation.

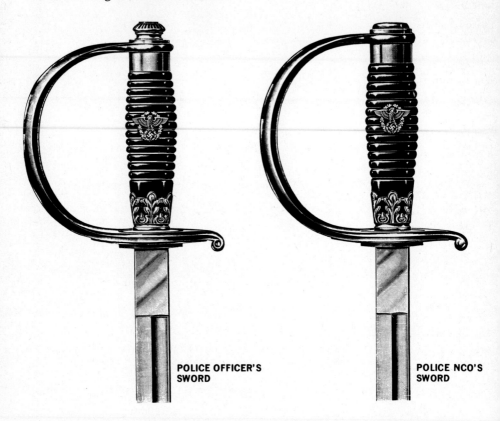

POLICE OFFICER'S
SWORD

POLICE NCO'S
SWORD

By 1938, officer personnel had totally replaced the bayonet with the Police Leader's Sword. It is curious that, while over half the subordinate elements of the police had their own specially designed dagger, the Reich, Municipal and Rural Police never succumbed to the dagger "race". Or maybe they did? There are indications that the police were not totally immune to the dagger fever. A honor dagger designated for "Paul Stroop, SS Pf. u. H. H. Pf. Warschau" was referenced in the <u>Ehrenbuch der Deutschen Polizei</u>, dated 1943. The dagger was designed with a double edged damascus blade, a specially designed crossguard and a pommel designed in the shape of the national police insignia. Further details are not available. Considering that the piece was specifically designated, it is doubtful that it was made in any quantity.

The matter of a sidearm ceased to be a problem when, in 1944, the pistol totally replaced the wear of any blade.

NEWLY CONSECRATED POLICE FLAGS AT THE 1937 PARTY DAY RALLY.

BLADE SIDEARMS OF THE POLICE

There are the following types of edged weapons:

- (a) Short edged weapons (bayonets), some of which can be affixed to rifles.
- (b) Long edged weapons (sabers and swords). Sabers have a slightly curved blade, while sword blades are straight.

The Police are equipped with the following edged weapons:

- (a) S. 84/98; S. 98/05; Police bayonet, affixable (P. S. a.);
- (b) Police bayonet, not affixable (P. S. n.);
- (c) Police bayonet, special type (P. S. S.);
- (d) Saber for mounted personnel (S. f. B.);
- (e) SS- Police sword (Officer and NCO swords).

BAYONETS (S. 84/98, S. 98/05)

The S. 98/05 has a broader blade and outswept guard with button end. The grips are made of walnut with rounded edges. The face of the grip is smooth, with the exception of the S. 98/05 which is grooved. The scabbard of the S. 98/05 has an upper scabbard band with a carrying hook hard soldered to the outer portion.

POLICE BAYONET, FIXABLE AND NOT FIXABLE

The police bayonets were shortened from 59cms to 48cms in the years 1938 and 1939. The description of the S. 84/98 and S. 98/05 basically applies to the police bayonets with the following exceptions:

- (a) The blade has a rounded back.
- (b) The grip and guard are made of new silver, chiselled and nickelled. Those made to fit rifles are made to the same dimensions as the S. 98/05 in regard to the bayonet adaption. Instead of wood grips, Hirschhorn (stag) grips are used. The outside grip has the police insigne (Polizeihoheitszeichen) affixed.
- (c) The sheath is black; for Gendarmerie officials some are brown. Fittings are of new silver sheeting and nickelled.

POLICE BAYONET, SPECIAL TYPE (P. S. S.)

The P. S. S. is a modified S. 98/05....the blade and sheath are about 6mm narrower than the S. 98/05. The pommel and guard are chiselled. The blade and grip are nickelled. Stag grips replace the wooden ones, and the police insigne is affixed to the outer grip plate.

CARE

Rust on zaponierte parts means paint is bad. Report this immediately. Bayonets not issued belong with the rifles, and are to be affixed on the rifles or left next to them. Blades are to be left 300mm out of the scabbard to prevent weakening the scabbard springs.

WEAR OF SIDEARMS

Honor Sidearms: Only officially presented Honor Sidearms of the same type as the official sidearm may be worn on and off duty. If the Honor Sidearm differs from the official sidearm by only an inscription or organization etched on the blade or engraved on the grip, it may be worn.

Personal Sidearms: Personal sidearms must be of the same type as official ones. The white metal parts may be nickeled, chromed or polished (bright).

EQUIPPING WITH SIDEARM

The police bayonet or S. 94/98 or S. 98/05 is worn by all Wachtmeisters not entitled to wear the sword or saber. Officers and NCO's wear the S. 84/98 when the combat uniform is worn, or unmounted for police action. The police bayonet, S. 84/98 or S. 98/05 is worn by the unmounted Meister of Gendarmerie with the service uniform. Officers and officials of the motor service (including motorized Gendarmerie and motorized traffic units) carry no sidearm except the pistol when on motor duty.

DELIVERY OF SIDEARMS

1. From state resources without payment for use (item of issue):
    (a) Bayonets for all officers and police officials required to carry same for duty.

MANNER OF WEAR

Bayonets are carried in bayonet frog on the outer belt with all uniforms.

MEMBERS OF THE FACTORY FIRE PROTECTION POLICE WEARING THE STANDARD FIRE DEPARTMENT BAYONET WITH RECURVE GUARD. THE KNOT AFFIXED TO THE FROG HAS THE ALTERNATING SILVER AND PINK KNOT-BASE.

FIRE DEPARTMENT
[FEUERWEHR]

The various German states were responsible for their own fire protection, and each maintained their own independent fire department. It was composed of a small paid cadre, bolstered by a volunteer force. One of the first acts of the Nazi Party was to restructure the police system to provide for better internal controls throughout Germany. The reorganization provided the opportunity of making fire protection elements more efficient and effective. At the same time, it allowed the Nazis to place dedicated Party members into key positions in order that they might further extend their influence. The fire departments were in effect nationalized when control was taken from the state governments and placed in the hands of the Minister of Interior. He in turn relegated the fire departments to a subordinate position within the police structure.

Destruction by fire was the single largest threat to big cities following the introduction of massive air raids by the Allies. However, as the intensity of the raids grew, fire protection placed such a drain on German resources that all fire fighting assets were strained to the limit. In order to cope with this problem, yet another reorganization took place in September 1939, with the creation of the Fire Protection Police (Feuerschutzpolizei - Fschupo). Existing fire brigades were ordered into this organization, and a general expansion was required throughout the towns and villages. Volunteer fire brigades still existed in towns where there were no elements of the Fire Protection Police, or when it was necessary to augment these forces.

SIDEARMS OF THE FIRE DEPARTMENT

The Fire Department was one of the few organizations that did not have to enter into the search for a distinct organizational dagger. Leaders of the Royal Prussian Fire Departments had long been armed with a dress dagger, having adopted this sidearm in the last decade of the 19th century. This same pattern dagger was to remain with the Fire Department even though Germany underwent a series of governmental changes. From the time of its conception to the time the dagger went out of use during the war years, it underwent only slight design modifications. The design of the dagger that was to be used during the Nazi period had its origin during the era of the Weimar Republic. During the Weimar period, the flaming ball pommel, that was used since the time the dagger was adopted by the Royal Prussian Fire Department, was replaced with a pommel of contemporary design. The crossguard as well underwent a minor design change. In all other respects, the features remained the same. Due to its longevity, it becomes difficult to properly identify the period to which this particular design dagger can be attributed. Only the trademark on the blade will identify the period of manufacture.

The official's dagger was worn with the service uniform suspended on the left side by two leather strap hangers attached to an outer belt. It was worn interchangeably with the Fire Department sword up until the time the dagger was abolished following the outbreak of war. The piece was rather long, normally measuring 48cms. It was one of the very few daggers that did not incorporate a swastika into its design. All metal fittings of the dagger and scabbard were either silver or gold plated. The pommel largely served as a counter-weight, since once the dagger was assembled the tang ending of the blade was braised into the pommel. The handle was constructed of wood with a thin black leather cover. A double wire wrap ran from low right to high left, and followed the ridges in the grip. The reverse of the crossguard did not have a pattern design, while the front incorporated the fireman's helmet and crossed axes. The double edged blade had the identical fire department motif lightly etched on both sides. The base scabbard was black leather with upper, center and lower metal scabbard fittings. A swivel ring was attached to the upper and center fittings to provide for suspension.

Subordinate personnel of the Fire Department were authorized to wear a nickel plated bayonet termed "Faschinenmesser". It differed from the M84/98 bayonet only in that it was not slotted to fit a rifle, and had a recurve crossguard. Subordinates in the grade of Feuerwehrmann to Brandmeister were authorized the long (40cms) blade, while those in

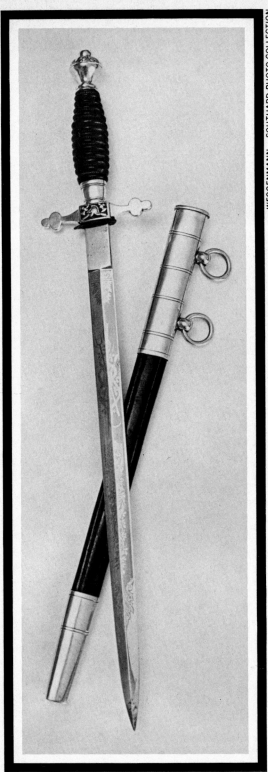

**FIRE DEPARTMENT
OFFICIAL'S DAGGER**

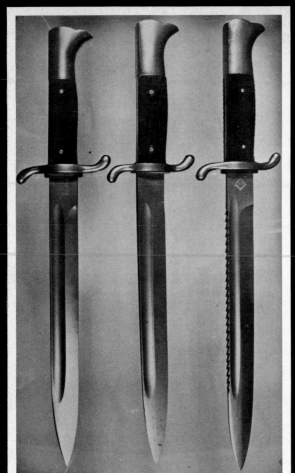

THREE SPECIMENS OF THE 40 cms
JUNIOR SUBORDINATE DRESS BAYONET.

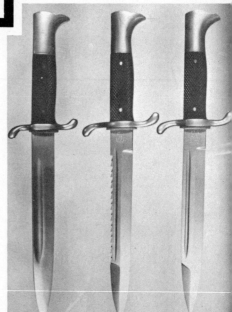

THREE SPECIMENS OF THE 35 cms
SENIOR SUBORDINATE DRESS BAYONET.

**FIRE PROTECTION POLICE SENIOR SUBORDINATE'S 35cms
SAWTOOTH DRESS BAYONET, WITH BRONZE INSIGNIA.**

the grade of Oberbrandmeister on up were authorized the short (35cms) blade. Both levels of subordinates were given the option of having the blade with or without the sawtooth back. On rare occassions, the bayonet was purchased with a dedication inscription or pattern on the blade. The sidearm was worn suspended by a black leather bayonet frog from an outer belt. It was a usual practice to wear a Fire Department portepee attached to the frog for ornamentation.

Still another bayonet was worn, possibly by senior subordinates of the Feuerschutzpolizei, that was identical to the short bladed sidearm. However, the hilt fittings were unplated, and a bronze Fire Department insigne was fitted on the center surface of the black checkered plastic handle. This particular pattern bayonet was mounted with a blade having a false edge and a sawtooth back. The scabbard, like the standard, was a black painted sheet metal steel.

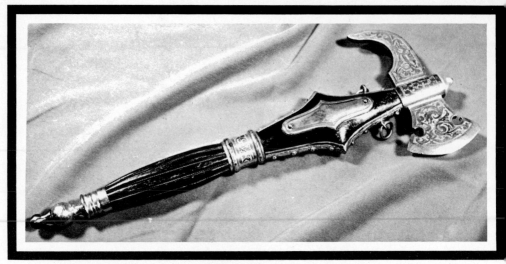

FIRE DEPARTMENT OFFICIAL'S CEREMONIAL DRESS AX WITH ORNATELY CHISELED ENGRAVING ON THE AX HEAD AND HANDLE RING.

The one sidearm that was both ornamental and functional was the fire ax. The ax retained basically the same design regardless of function.... a broad chopping edge and a curved point. Fire fighters used the ax in the performance of their duties to break through barriers and remove debris. It was worn in a black leather case on the left side of the belt when not in use. A more ornamental variety was used for ceremonial functions. This pattern was worn suspended by two leather strap hangers which snapped to a swivel ring on each side of the handle. The ceremonial ax normally had very ornately etched or engraved head and side plates.

As members of the Fire Department were not armed, they retained the right to wear the dress bayonets or sword right up to the close of the war. The ax gave way to the purely functional use as a fire fighting implement rather than a show piece. As the war progressed, dagger wear had given way to the sword. By the close of 1943, the official's dagger was no longer produced.

FIRE PROTECTION POLICE VIGOROUSLY FIGHT A FIRE FOLLOWING ONE OF
MANY ALLIED BOMBING RAIDS.

A LUFTSCHUTZ MEMBER DURING TRAINING AGAINST INCENDIARY BOMBING.

GERMAN AIR PROTECTION LEAGUE
[REICHSLUFTSCHUTZBUND (RLB)]

The Allied bombing raids on Germany were not so much out of retaliation for raids such as that conducted against Coventry, but were a direct attack against the German economy. The raids constituted a general attack against the civilian consumer/producer as well as those commodities produced. The total German civilian losses from air raids at the close of WWI were 746 killed. However, in a single air raid during WWII, at Dresden, the Allied fire bombings took the lives of an estimated 135, 000 civilians.[1] By comparison, this dreadful loss of life was almost twice that which resulted from the atomic detonation at Hiroshima. The German civilian casualties could have been considerably worse had the government not gained some insight from the raids on Germany at the close of the Great War.

Air raid protection measures were developed and adopted to provide a defense for the civilian population. The first German air raid protection group, the Deutsche Luftschutz, was established in 1922 with Herr Krohne at its head. Another similar organization, the Deutsche Luftschutzliga, was a competitive and distinctive organization also functioning in support of the public. To provide a more efficient service, both elements were united in December 1932, and formed the Deutsches Luftschutzverband (German Air Protection League) under Krohne's leadership. Göring did not waste any time following Hitler's rise to power to transform the League into the Reichsluftschutzbund (RLB), with General

---

[1]David Irving, The Destruction of Dresden, (New York: 1964).

Grimme appointed as President. Göring, on April 29, 1933, proclaimed the RLB to be the official air raid protection (ARP) service of the state. All other competitive services were either absorbed into the RLB or dissolved. The great task of protecting the people and the cities from hostile attacks resulted in the development of these basic duties for the RLB:

(1) Provide an air raid warning service.
(2) Provide security following an air raid, and act in the capacity of an air raid warden.
(3) Provide plant protection and thus allow for the continuation of work.
(4) Safeguard human lives.

Air raid protection extended to every population center in Germany regardless of size or remoteness. A system, similar to that of volunteer fire departments, provided the necessary manpower. Membership in the RLB at the end of 1938 was approximately thirteen million men. Few were carried on the rolls as paid full-time officials of the RLB, since most of the membership were volunteers.

Following the British air raid on Cologne in 1942, the Luftschutz-polizei was formed to supplement the RLB. This highly professional section was integrated into the Protection Police (Schupo), and was responsible for the administrative as well as technical aspects of ARP. Professional ARP personnel were drawn into this newly formed element from the Rescue and Repair Service (Sicherheits-und Hilfsdienst), which was initially under the auspices of the Luftwaffe, and augmented by the Technical Emergency Corps. Regardless of the degree of unity, the Schupo

ON-LOOKING OF BOMB DAMAGE IN 1944 BY OFFICIALS.

retained ultimate control over matters dealing with ARP. Due to the emphasis placed on ARP, the RLB grew to approximately twenty million men in 1942. Lt. Gen. von Rogues was appointed President of the League, while Gen. Grimme was designated Honorary President.

Primary emphasis for preparedness was placed on individual dwellings. However, measures were all but uniform, and did not meet with the desires of the Führer, especially after the Allied bombings of major German cities became more frequent. The hastily passed Luftschutzgesetz or Air Raid Precautions Act of August 31, 1943, provided for a detailed and systematic preparedness of individual dwellings, subject to continuous inspections by RLB authorities. While civilian air raid casualties were extremely high, the precautionary measures taken by the RLB could be directly attributed to saving untold German lives.

VON ROGUES, PRESIDENT OF THE RLB

Aside from the tremendous impact on civilian morale, there is no evidence that the true intent of the saturation bombings ever was achieved.[2] While the civilian economy was affected to a degree, there was never a point at which the German authorities were forced to transfer from war production in order to prevent disintegration on the home front. The bombings, by 1944, had failed to achieve the effect of preventing the conversion of consumer goods to the war effort. One positive consideration of the bombings is that ARP requirements caused a considerable drain on the replacement manpower that could have been available to the military forces. This drain in manpower did have considerable effect on the progress of the war.

DAGGERS OF THE REICHSLUFTSCHUTZBUND

Daggers for the subordinate and leader grades were introduced in the summer of 1936. Owing to the extremely large membership of the RLB,

---

[2] J. Kenneth Galbraith, The Effects of Strategic Bombing on the German War Economy (survey), 1945.

one would think the daggers would have been numerous. However, wear of the dagger was limited only to those leaders and subordinates on paid full-time duty with the RLB. Being on uniform status did not necessarily guarantee one would be authorized a dagger since it was bestowed by special act. For this reason, the dagger was acquired through official RLB channels rather than through normal retail outlets. In 1938, the leader's dagger underwent a slight design modification followed by an official insigne change later in the year. This would account for the two grip insignia variations on the RLB daggers.

Selected subordinates in grades 5 - 10 were authorized to wear the subordinate's dagger with their service uniform. The 36cms dagger was worn attached to an outer waist belt by means of a single short black leather strap riveted to a swivel device attached to the scabbard. All of the nickel plated metal fittings served to contrast with the black handle and scabbard. The slightly oval ridged pommel screwed to the tang, securing the blade to the hilt. To the front surface of the dark wood or ebony grip was affixed the silver and enamel RLB insigne. The crossguard was formed from a stylized national emblem. The highly polished double edged steel blade bore no markings other than the manufacturer's trademark. The steel scabbard was painted black with a nickel plated lower fitting externally mounted by means of inset screws. The complete design of this pattern dagger remained unchanged when the grip insigne made its transition.

BROCK

McCARTHY

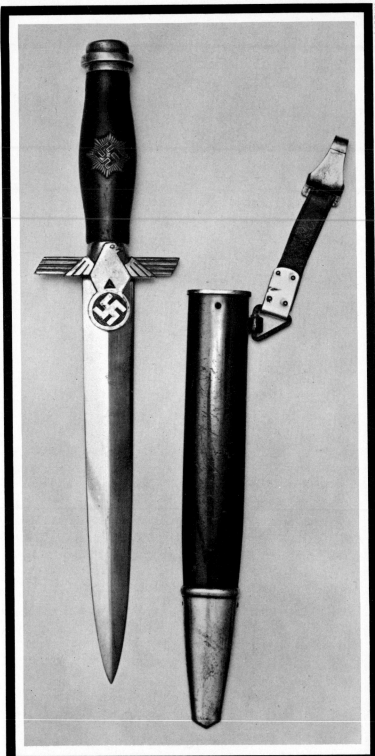

**1938 PATTERN
LUFTSCHUTZ
SUBORDINATE'S
DAGGER**

LUFTSCHUTZ LEADER MAKING COLLECTION FOR WINTER RELIEF, JANUARY 24, 1941.

The pattern worn by leaders in the grades 1 - 4 was slightly longer than the subordinate dagger, measuring an overall length of 38.5 cms. While the basic design of the two grades of daggers was the same, there were noticible differences to tell the two apart. The pommel was a broad semi-flat ribbed oval, and the wing span of the national emblem forming the crossguard was longer. The handle and scabbard were covered with either a black or dark blue leather. From 1936 to 1938, the scabbard had two externally mounted nickel plated fittings, and was suspended by means of a single short black leather hanger riveted to the suspension ring on the upper scabbard fitting. The grip insigne on this first pattern was the black enamel RLB monogram with a small black enamel swastika below, both on a silver plated sunburst. In 1938, a center scabbard band was added, and a double strap hanger provided for the suspension. Later in the year, the grip insigne was officially changed to the black enamel swastika on a silver plated sunburst. The hangers were of dark blue or black leather with white metal fittings similar to those of the Army dagger hangers.

The President and Vice-President of the League wore the same design daggers, however, all metal fittings (to include those of the hanger) were finished in a dull gold plate.

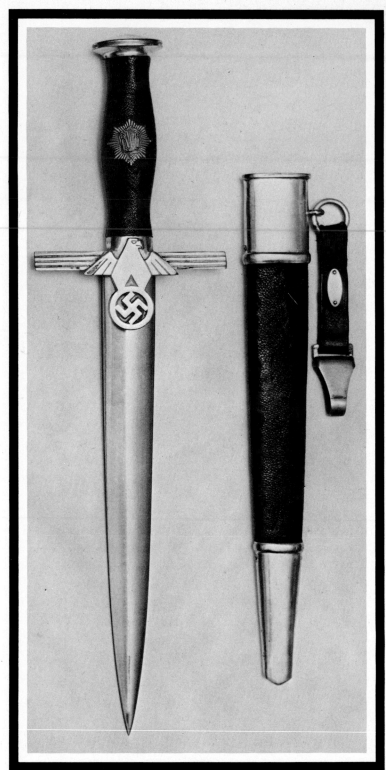

McCARTHY

McCARTHY

TECHNICAL EMERGENCY CORPS
[TECHNISCHE NOTHILFE (TeNo)]

An organization, made up from "old army engineer" mercenaries, was formed in 1918 for standby duty in the event of a general strike which threatened Germany. The organization was titled the Technical Emergency Corps (Technische Nothilfe - TN or TeNo) on September 30, 1919. The Corps then became a solely voluntary organization under the control of the Reichsminister of the Interior. With the exception of a cadre of salaried leaders, it was to retain this status up to the end of WWII. Besides performing a national service, the Corps held a certain prestige for its members. By the end of the 1930's, TeNo membership stood at approximately 200,000. The Corps continued strictly as a voluntary registered society until it received legal state status on March 25, 1939. The need for such an organization, which was brought about by the war, caused the membership to grow. After 1940, leaders in the TeNo were paid full-time members, while the remainder of the membership continued on a voluntary status.

The TeNo was absorbed into the Order Police (Orpo) in 1937, and became the engineer corps of the German Police. Leadership positions within the TeNo were partially filled by Police and SS personnel. After the outbreak of the war, Himmler's SS assumed full control of the Police, and in turn, the TeNo. Overall responsibility was still retained by the Reichsminister of the Interior. This dual relationship was born out in the title of the Chief of the TeNo, SS-Gruppenführer und Generalleutnant of Police, Weinreich. In spite of the "absolute" controls that Reichsminister of the Interior Himmler exerted over the TeNo, a close relationship necessarily existed between him and the Reichsminister of Finance, since the latter controlled the budgetary matters relating to the organization.

Duties of the TeNo broadened considerably from the time of its inception. The organization played a major role in the digging out of cities following air raids, and aiding in the restoration of necessary life-sustaining services. Due to the close relationship between air raid protection and the restoration of services, over 100,000 personnel were channeled into the TeNo to support the overtaxed Reichsluftschutzbund. The services provided by the two organizations often overlapped in a post-raid situation. As the war progressed, some of the membership were mobilized into various arms of the military service. Members of the TeNo saw service in occupied countries outside Germany, providing an extension of the life-giving services that they performed at home.

Members of the TeNo had long maintained their own distinct uniform. As with most politically oriented organizations during the period, the membership was required to purchase their own uniforms and accessories. After extensive mobilization began, members within the ranks were issued uniforms identical to that worn by the Luftwaffe, but bearing a combination of TeNo and Lutfwaffe insignia.

THE TeNo SIDEARMS

Himmler approved the introduction of two blade sidearms for the uniformed cadre of the TeNo. Leaders in the organization were authorized to purchase the TeNo-Führerdolch for general wear through official TeNo channels following its introduction in 1938. While the TeNo Leader's Dagger could only be obtained in these channels, it was the Solingen firm of Eickhorn which held the exclusive patent on this and the TeNo hewer. However, the TeNo maintained strict controls over the firm through a series of rigid inspections, which resulted in the TeNo inspection mark being placed on the reverse of each blade. Distribution of both the Führerdolch and the hewer was so limited that a serial number was stamped on the obverse of the blade to allow for strict accountability. This accountability stemmed partially from the fact that the hewer was authorized for wear only following special award. It would appear that accountability and inspection did not necessarily coincide, since one of the earliest representative pieces....a TeNo-Führerdolch bearing the serial number 0028....was completely void of any inspection mark.

The TeNo-Führerdolch was one of the largest of the dress daggers worn by leaders of the various organizations, having an overall length of

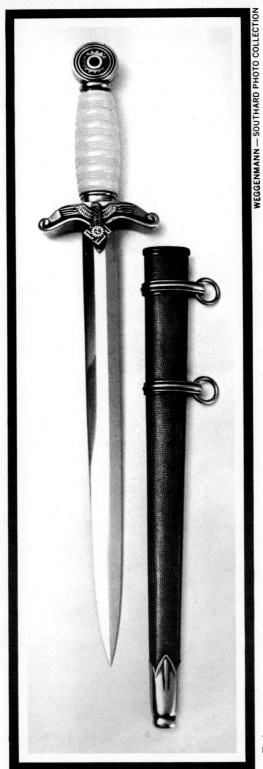

TeNo LEADER'S DAGGER

LANDESFÜHRER SIEBERT

THE REVERSE OF THE TeNo LEADER'S DAGGER BLADE BEARS THE MANUFACTURER'S MARK AND THE TeNo PATENT/INSPECTION MARK. THE SERIAL NUMBER IS ON THE OBVERSE UNDER THE LANGET.

42cms. The insigne on the crossguard was the official eagle of the organization, while that on the pommel was the symbolic cogwheel. The metal fittings were plated and finished with a black oxidized burnish to allow for greater contrast and give the impression of depth. The creme colored plastic grip added to the contrast. The oxidized finish was carried over to the plated steel scabbard as well. The throat of the scabbard was usually stamped with the same serial number as found on the blade. The leader's dagger was worn on the left side, either attached directly to the outer belt, or with the suspension straps passed through the lower left pocket and attached to an inner buckle. A choice of two different double strap hangers was available to the wearer.... probably to distinguish between dress and service wear. While the metal fittings of these two hangers were identical.... predominately a round buckle with oxidized finish bearing the cogged insigne.... the straps were totally dissimilar. One set was made of unadorned black leather, while the second set.... ...probably the set designated for dress wear.... was made of fabric having silver stripes on black sewn to a black velvet backing. The hanger fasteners attached to the swivel rings on the two scabbard suspension bands. A 23cms aluminum portepee wound about the ferrule was normally worn on the leader's dagger for additional ornamentation.

The only similarity between the leader's dagger and the subordinate's hewer was the insigne on the crossguard and pommel. While the name would indicate the hewer was fully intended for use during the many emergencies that confronted the members in pursuit of their duties, the construction and the materials used would not permit any sustained heavy use as a working implement. The hewer was the most massive of the blade sidearms, but for the purpose of projecting the image of the Technical Corps rather than for intended use. The piece had an overall length of 40cm, and was worn (as prescribed by regulations) suspended over the left hip by means of a black leather harness with metal gate fastener that clipped to a suspension bar on the reverse of the upper scabbard fitting. All metal fittings of the hewer were nickel plated, with the hilt fittings having a black oxidized burnish. The two-piece grips were retained in place by two screws, and were finished in either ivory colored or dark orange plastic. The main body of the scabbard was finished in black lacquer, and had two externally mounted nickel plated fittings held in place by screws. The scabbard throat bore the same serial number as was found on the obverse of the blade, under the langet. The bolo-shaped blade did not bear a motto, but did have a groove on each side near the top of the blade. Depending on the service, a series of portepees were available for wear on the hewer. The TeNo hewer is a relatively scarce piece since not all members were authorized to wear it. The hewer was only

TeNo HEWER

TeNo SUBORDINATE WEARING HIS PRIZED HEWER SUPERVISES A TeNo LABOR DETAIL.

awarded to selected full-time subordinate members of the Technical Emergency Corps.

As with any general rule, there is always the exception. There exists, in the collection of Mr. Howard Bayliss, a hewer made by the Eickhorn firm which is approximately one-third larger than the standard hewer. While one is prone to classify such a piece as a "prototype", no reason can be attributed to this variation.

A RAILWAY OFFICIAL ASSISTING THE ARMY ON MANEUVERS.

THE GERMAN RAILWAY SYSTEM — NATIONAL RAILWAYS
[DEUTSCHE REICHSBAHN]

The condition of the German Railway System under the Weimar Republic was just one of many cause-celebre that Hitler and his Nazi Party tied to their political platform in their drive for power in 1933. While governmental controls were in the hands of a corporation, certain administrative rights had been parcelled out to the state government bodies. Obviously, this tended to conflict with the smooth and economical functioning of the entire railway system. This rather haphazard way of doing business stemmed from constraints imposed by the provisions of the Versailles Treaty. These provisions all but placed the railroads in a state of mortgage by designating the system as securities to be held by the League of Nations pending payment of reparations imposed on the German government.

While this condition was partially nullified by the Young Plan in 1930, which returned the railroads to the German government, state governments vied for control of the system that fell within their state's domain. Railway officials soon found they were confronted with both internal and external attempts at determining the future of the railroads. Among the heavy losers under these conditions was the struggling military. Logistics and troop movements between military concerns were unpredictable at best.

Hitler promised to right the situation if his party was elected to power. After grabbing the reigns of power from the Weimar Republic in 1933, it took Hitler until January 30, 1937, to bring the German Railway System under complete national control.

True centralized control was placed in the hands of **Dr.** Julius Dorp-Müller, Minister of Transport and Director-General of the German Railway. The ministry drew its security force from the employees of the National Railways rather than the regular police. This security force, or Sonderpolizei, was in effect an extension of the regular police. Railway security was specifically charged to the Bahnpolizei (Railway Police), with responsibility for the maintenance of law and order in railway stations, on platforms and bridges, in freight yards and at grade crossings. The National Railways also maintained additional security forces in the Bahn-schutzpolizei, a security patrol on trains and in stations. There also existed the Reichsbahnfahndungsdienst, a Railway Criminal Investigation Service formed to handle all aspects of criminal acts pertaining to the railroad, and the Reichsbahn-Wasserschutzpolizei, or Railway Water Protection Police, which was charged with railway police functions in all facilities directly associated with harbors, canals and inland waterways. These security forces comprised only a small percentage of the 670,000 railway employees on the rolls as of February 4, 1938.

MODEL 1935 RAILWAY DAGGER SHOWING TWO DIFFERENT HANDLE VARIATIONS.

A great deal of conjecture exists as to the first pattern daggers adopted by the Bahnschutzpolizei. While there is currently no evidence available to confirm or deny the designation, a Model 1935 Army officer's dagger is attributed to being the first authorized dagger sidearm for leaders of the Bahnschutzpolizei. The dagger was distinguishable from the standard Army in that it had a black colored handle. Two handle variations have been observed....the basic handle with seven rings and a thinner handle with nine rings. Because of the lack of distinctiveness between this and the standard Model 1935 Army, a stylistic and distinctively designed Bahnschutz-Führerdolch was authorized for wear in 1938 by leaders of Oberzugführer and up. There could be no confusion with this design since the obverse of the crossguard bore the winged railway wheel insigne of the National Railway. Metal fittings of the hilt were either dull finished cast aluminum or silver plate. A raised curved arm swastika adorned the top of the pommel. The handle was made of dark purple plastic (giving the appearance of being black). While the handle was similar to the handle of the Army dagger, it was slightly wider. The scabbard was constructed either of dull polished chrome over steel or silver plated. Two suspension hanger bands with swivel rings were provided for the double strap hanger. Metal fittings of the hanger were identical to the Army. The straps were a combination of metallic facing of silver with black stripes on a black velvet backing. The blade was identical in length and shape to the Army dagger. The overall length of the dagger was 40cms.

The piece that gives some credance to the Model 1935 is the Reichsbahn-Wasserschutzpolizei-Führerdolch, which combines the crossguard of the Army with the pommel of the Bahnschutz. This piece is considered to be one of the rarest of the production daggers. Its scarcity can probably be attributed to the extremely limited number of personnel bearing leader rank in the Railway-Water Protection Police.

Yet another regulation dress dagger is attributed to the National Railway....the Reichsbahn-Führerdolch or Railway Leader's Dagger (see illustration) worn by officials within the Railway Service with the rank of Oberzugführer and above. The specifications for this dagger were enumerated in the March 1, 1941, issue of Uniformen-Markt. A sketch, identical to the one shown, was submitted for approval to coincide with the prescribed uniform changes within the Railway Service which were taking place at that time. The dagger, according to the drawing and specifications, called for the pommel to bear the "sun-wheel" swastika and a wreath of oak leaves about the outer edge of the pommel. The raised insigne, making up the face of the crossguard, was the drafted winged wheel,

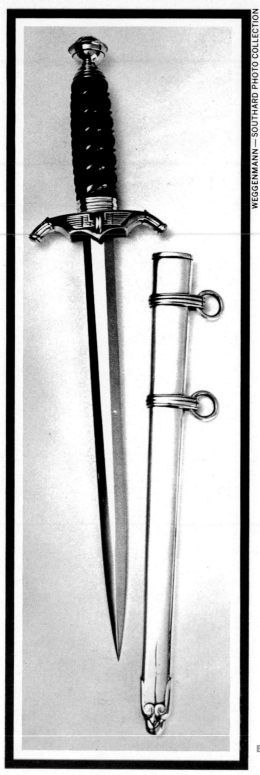

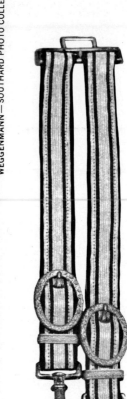

BAHNSCHUTZ LEADER'S DAGGER

**RAILWAY-WATER PROTECTION
POLICE DAGGER**

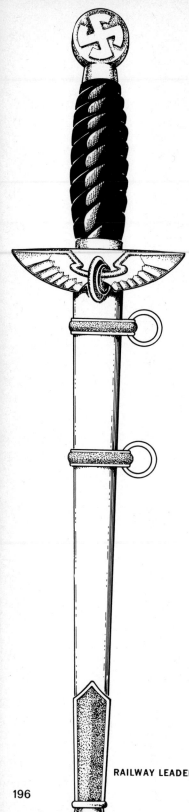

symbolic of the Railway Service. The grip was dark blue, but its construction was not specified. The scabbard tip was formed from a short "shoe" with small knob. This could possibly imply that the scabbard tip was externally mounted. All metal fittings were gold colored. Though the hangers were illustrated, no specifications were provided. It is possible that the base hangers were identical to the Railway Protection Service Leader's with the exception that the metal fittings were finished in gilt. Since the dagger was shown actually being worn in the referenced issue of <u>Uniformen-Markt</u>, it can only be assumed that the dagger did enter into limited production. Due to the reverses of the war, it is doubtful that this particular pattern ever entered into distribution....or at least in any quantity.

RAILWAY LEADER'S DAGGER

POSTSCHUTZ LEADER'S DAGGER

POSTAL PROTECTION FORCE
[POSTSCHUTZ]

The German communications media, to include the mail, radio, television, telephone and the press, fell under the administrative controls of the German Post Office following reforms instituted by the Nazis in 1933. An element of the Sonderpolizei, a small police force tasked with the mission of providing security to certain Reich Ministries exclusive of the Reich Ministry of the Interior, was simultaneously created. The purpose of this element, named Postschutz or Postal Protection Force, was to provide security to the extensive communications installations. The personnel of the Postschutz, which were drawn from the Sonderpolizei, were on a salaried payroll, and were under the overall supervision of the Postmaster-General, Dr. Ohnesorge. As installations grew and requirements expanded, volunteers were drawn from the SA/SS, as well as from the veterans of the armed forces.

A typical example of the expanding responsibilities of the security force was the laying of a cable on March 1, 1936, providing television and telephone service between Berlin and Leipzig. Mail service increased 14.78% between 1932 and 1937, while parcel post increased 30.39% during the same period. In 1937, telephone lines were spread over the country at an increase of 11.4%. Television service was introduced to the German public the previous year. [1] By 1942, the strength of the Postschutz had increased to 45,000 personnel to meet the demands of these increasing security requirements.

---

[1]Paul Schmidt, Statistisches Jahrbuch für das Deutsche Reich, (Berlin: 1939).

Supervisory responsibility for the Postschutz was taken from the German Post Office when it was absorbed as a part of the Ordnungspolizei (Regular Police) into the greater organization of the SS. From March of 1942 the organization bore the designation of SS-Postschutz.

From the time of its formation in 1933 to early 1939, personnel within the ranks of the Postschutz did not wear a dagger sidearm. However, in the early months of 1939, authority was granted for the wear of a distinctive dagger sidearm by selected supervisory personnel. The inclusion of the initials "DRP" (Deutsches Reichs Post) and a serial number on the underside of the crossguard would indicate that the daggers were rigidly controlled issue items rather than purchased independently by the wearer.

STANDARD MARKINGS ON THE UNDERSIDE OF THE REICHSPOST LEADER DAGGER. THE SERIAL NUMBER AND THE DEUTSCHES REICHS POST (DRP) MARKINGS WOULD INDICATE THAT THIS DAGGER WAS ORGANIZATIONAL PROPERTY.

Postal Group Leaders, Section Leaders and District Leaders, as well as officials of the Postal Protection Force, were authorized to wear the Postschutz-Führerdolch with their dress or service uniform. The dagger was worn suspended on the left side by means of a nickel plated double suspension chain link, similar to that found on the 1934 Luftwaffe Flyer's Dagger. However, the suspension chains differed from those of the Luftwaffe in that the rings were smaller and varied in number, with the upper chain having nine rings (not including the connecting swivel ring), and the lower chain twelve. The heavy nickel-silver metal fittings of the dagger and scabbard provided excellent contrast with the black ebony grip, and black painted steel base scabbard. While the pommel was virtually unadorned, the crossguard was stylistically designed in the shape of an eagle with an enamel swastika inset on the chest. The silver insigne of the Postal Service, an eagle/swastika/sparks design, was fitted on the surface center of the grip. The double edged blade was without motto. The scabbard had externally mounted fittings, with the upper and center bands serving as suspension bands for the chain hanger. The overall length of the piece was 38.5cms.

While the Postschutz-Führerdolch is considered relatively rare, it is the Postschutz-Dolch, or Service Dagger, that is the rarer of the two

patterns. The Postschutz Service Dagger was worn by subordinates up

to the rank of Meister (Senior Non-Commissioned Officer). This piece
was a design mixture of the NSFK knife and the Postschutz Leader's Dagger. The design of the hilt was basically the same as the leader's dagger, but mounted on a blade with exact specifications as that of the NSFK.
The black painted scabbard had externally mounted nickel-silver fittings.
The dagger was worn suspended from an outer belt by means of a single
leather suspension strap riveted to a swivel ring on the upper scabbard
band. The overall length of the service dagger was 35cms. This dagger
also appeared to be an issue item.

Subordinates often wore the standard Mauser service bayonet, especially as the war progressed. Those bayonets issued directly by the
Postal Service often bore the stamping "DRP".

No portepee was worn on the subordinates service dagger, however,
those leaders with the rank of Zugführer
and above were authorized to wear a
42cms aluminum portepee with inter-
mittent red thread throughout the cord
portion.

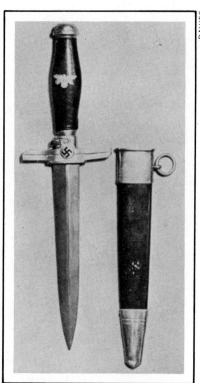

DAVIES

POSTSCHUTZ SUBORDINATE'S SERVICE
DAGGER

DETAIL OF
POSTSCHUTZ LEADER'S
DAGGER

REICHSMINISTER OF FINANCE, COUNT LUTZ SCWERIN VON KROSIGK, WITH HIGH
OFFICIALS OF THE CUSTOMS POLICE, TAKE A TOUR OF FACILITIES IN WIESBADEN.

CUSTOMS
[ZOLL]

Reparations imposed on Germany by the Versailles Treaty caused export trade to decline to one-third its former value....an economic fact that stirred inflation and brought about the economic collapse of the Weimar Republic. In an attempt to stabilize the economy, Hitler charged the German Minister of Trade with the responsibility of achieving a proper balance between foreign and domestic trade. Such a demand brought about an interplay between various ministries of which the Ministry of Finance was but one. Count Lutz Schwerin von Krosigk, Minister of Finance, levied a requirement on the Sonderpolizei responsible to his ministry....the Land and Water Customs elements. Their mission was the securing of the borders, ports and waterways from illicit traffic of incoming and outgoing trade goods. As with most treasury elements, the import-export taxes they collected contributed to the financial stabilization of the government. As security reigns tightened, especially after the outbreak of hostilities, added emphasis was placed on persons crossing the border. Since they, in effect, were themselves an element of the Regular Police, close cooperation was maintained between the members of Customs and the Police. By 1937, Germany was slowly on the road to financial recovery with an export surplus of 443 million Reichsmarks.

Since the Customs (Zoll) personnel were uniformed officials, it is not surprising that a request for a distinctive dagger to replace the sword as the basic sidearm was approved.

The Land Customs Official's Dagger (Landzollbeamten Dolch) was introduced in August 1937, as the standard sidearm for officials in the Ministry of Finance with the rank of Oberzollsekretär and above. Those officials of the Land Customs in the four highest ranks, to include the Minister of Finance, were entitled to wear the dagger with gold plated fittings rather than the white metal that was basic to the Customs Dagger. Officials were authorized to wear the dagger with their green or olive green service uniform. Hilt fittings resembled those of the Army except for the up-turned wing tips of the eagle crossguard, which was the design of the national emblem that was adopted by the Customs. Metal fittings of the very early production pieces were constructed of silver plated steel, however, this was soon changed to cast aluminum. A green leather or imitation leather covered the wood handle. An aluminum or

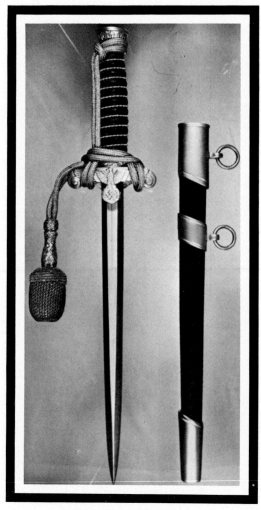

LAND CUSTOMS DAGGER

copper twist wire encircled the handle in a diagonal fashion, running from low left to upper right. The blade was identical in length and configuration to the Army dagger blade. Metal fittings of the scabbard were first silver plated steel. After going through a brief transition of being nickel plated, fittings were normally produced and finished in polished aluminum. Running edges of the scabbard fittings were at a diagonal. The steel bodied scabbard was covered with green leather or imitation leather. The upper and middle scabbard bands had a swivel ring to accomodate the hanger fastener. Two very minor variations in the suspension rings did exist, and were distinguished primarily by their width. The wider of the two are found on those patterns with aluminum scabbard fittings. The overall length of the dagger was 40.5cms. It was suspended by means of a double strap hanger, with each suspension strap having an

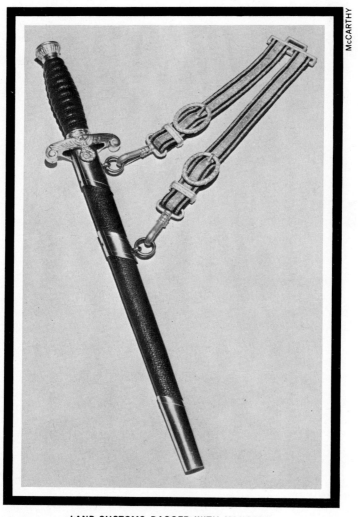

LAND CUSTOMS DAGGER WITH HANGERS

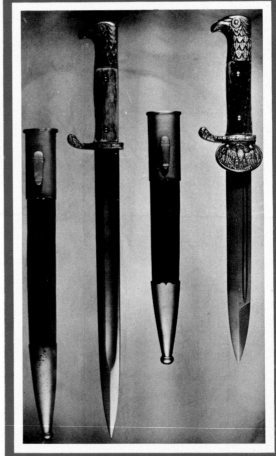

(LEFT) STANDARD 40cm DRESS BAY-
ONET WITH ALUMINUM FITTING
(RIGHT) CLAMSHELL DRESS BAYO-
NET, 34cms, WITH NICKEL PLATED
HILT FITTINGS.

aluminum facing with green stripes, and sewn to a green velvet or wool backing. The metal hanger fittings were made of aluminum (except for those ranks authorized gold plate), and were identical to the fittings of the Army hangers.

The Wasserzollbeamten-Dolch, or Water Customs Official's Dagger, was introduced at the same time as its Land Customs counterpart. Because the piece was restricted in wear to a very limited group of Waterway Customs officials on ocean-going customs vessels, this piece is considered to be one of the rarest of the basic issue daggers. The dagger was of the same configuration and length as the Land Customs, however, the metal fittings of the hilt and scabbard were gold plated, and the leather covering was dark blue. Unlike the hilt fittings of the Land Customs, the Water Customs Dagger fittings were not constructed of aluminum. As a result, the relief and detail were far superior. It is not known just exactly what the hangers for this particular dagger looked like.

Both daggers were normally worn with a 42cms aluminum portepee.

Subordinate personnel not holding official's rank were authorized to wear the service or dress bayonet sidearm. During the early Nazi government, Customs bayonets retained the clamshell guard that was characteristic of the Weimar period police bayonets. This clamshell was later deleted when the police patterns made the transition away from the clamshell guard. Bayonets of the Customs were basically identical to those of the police with the exception that the grip was void of any insigne. Original Customs bayonets would not show any trace of the three holes in the stag-horn grip as would be found on a modified police bayonet when the insigne was removed. The bayonet scabbard was normally brown leather with nickel plated scabbard fittings. The bayonet was worn in the same fashion as the police bayonet, suspended by means of a frog.

Dress pattern sidearms without ornamentation, as utilized by the Army (illustrated on page 289) were also authorized for wear by subordinate personnel.

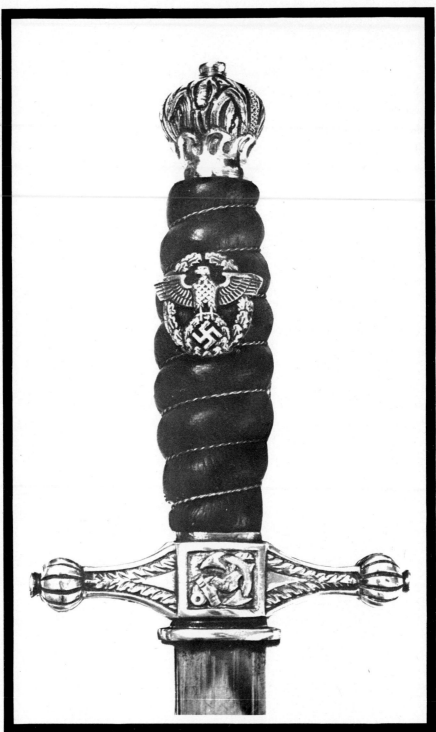

WATER PROTECTION POLICE LEADER'S DAGGER WITH POLICE EMBLEM IN HANDLE.

WATERWAYS PROTECTION POLICE
[WASSERSCHUTZPOLIZEI (WS)]

The Wasserschutzpolizei (WS) was initially established as the Reichs Waterways Protection on October 1, 1919, and was responsible to each of the individual state governments that they served. This status lasted until August 29, 1921, when control was turned over to the Reich government by the states. The states did, however, retain the authority to maintain jurisdiction over the legal aspects evolving from arrests, etc. This dual control presented a conflict of authority between the Reich and the states. The conflict was resolved in April 1931, when the Reich was given absolute control over the River and Ship Police. The individual states immediately undertook development of their own state-controlled waterways police. Even after full control reverted to the Reich government, a clearly defined organizational structure was not to follow. For example, the Rhine police were subordinate to the Gendarmerie, while the Bremen police were subordinate to the Orpo. This decentralized status was corrected with a final organizational order in 1937. On July 26, 1937, the river, lakes and ship police were amalgemated into the Wasserschutzpolizei, and placed under the authority of the Schutzpolizei. Even though the Waterways Protection Police were within the structure of the Schutzpolizei, it was afforded equal status.

Failure to arrive at a clear delineation of control resulted in continuous uniform changes with each reorganization. Up until 1934, the uniforms had been identical to the Schutzpolizei or Gendarmerie. On May 30, 1934, members of the river, lakes and ship police adopted a new uniform, and another organizational change. The organization that evolved, the Wasserschutzpolizei, drew its recruits from members of the Schupo who **209**

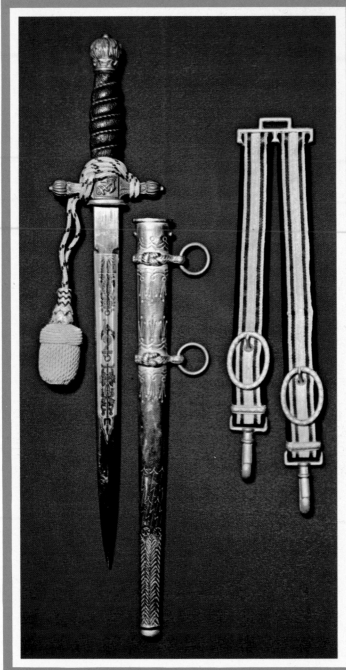

KNOTTED
ROPE
SUSPENSION
BANDS.

WATER PROTECTION
POLICE LEADER'S
DAGGER WITH 42cms
PORTEPEE AND
HANGERS.

had previous experience on rivers or at sea.   Due to the limited size of
the element, recruiting was highly selective.   The organization underwent its final uniform change on June 25, 1936.   It was not surprising that
the basic Navy uniform was adopted since it was more oriented to the Navy
and its traditions than to the Schupo to which it belonged.

The following year a dagger, which conformed to the Navy **motif,** was specifically designed and approved for the Wasserschutzpolizei. The dagger was officially adopted early in 1938 for wear by officers and administrative officials of the WS. Prior to the introduction of the dagger, the Navy officer's sword had been the primary dress sidearm of the WS. Police uniform regulations dealt specifically with the wear of the sword as pertains to the Waterways Protection Police:

With the Service Dress and Dress Uniforms:

(a) Officers were authorized to wear the Navy sword with portepee. It was worn suspended from under the tunic, or when the overcoat was worn, thru the slit in the pocket on the left side.

(b) Administrative Officers and Officer Candidates were given the option of wearing the sword as prescribed for officers, or the short police dress bayonet worn on the belt.

The S. 98/05 bayonet was authorized only by special order.

With the Parade Dress Uniform:

(a) For Officer personnel same as Service Dress.

(b) For Administrative Officials, Officer Candidates, and personnel with the rank of Zugsführer, same as Service Dress.

The portepee was worn attached to the sword, or to the bayonet frog when the bayonet was worn.

An added option was provided for officers and administrative officials following the introduction of the Waterways Protection Police Dagger in 1938. The dagger was worn interchangeably with the Navy sword with both the Service and Dress uniforms. It would appear that WS personnel preferred the sword rather than the dagger.

The dagger resembled the pre-1938 Navy dagger in every respect except that the wood grip was covered with blue leather rather than a white celluloid. When the Navy underwent a pommel transition in 1938, the WS retained the "flaming ball" pommel. While most scabbards were of the standard Navy design, some were made with the two suspension bands having a knotted rope design. This knotted rope was found in both the single and double rope patterns. The standard Navy etched pattern of the fouled anchor was common with the WS blade. The major departure was in the hangers and portepee. The 42 cms portepee was gold with blue thread, and was wrapped about the ricasso. The double strap hangers had gold metal fittings identical in design to the Army hangers. The straps were a gold base with blue stripes sewn to a dark blue velvet base.

Late in 1938, the Navy sword was replaced with the Police Officer's sword. The Waterways Protection Police dagger was worn until the early years of the war when it was phased out.

Daggers, Bayonets & Fighting Knives of the Military Arms

HERMANN GÖRING

HERMANN GÖRING

"Not Guilty!" was the matter-of-fact reply by Hermann Göring as he stood in the prisoner's box at Nuremburg when asked his plea against the numerous charges levied at him for crimes perpetrated against humanity. "Guilty!" was the verdict of the four power tribunal. Göring was subsequently sentenced to death by hanging. Slightly more than an hour before his appointed execution time, he bit into a concealed vial of poison. His early morning cremation at the former Dachau Concentration Camp, on October 16, 1946, came as an anti-climax in the thirty-two year career of Germany's number two Nazi.

Göring's career began as a young officer in Germany's infant air arm. He was propelled to national fame when he became an air ace. Germany recognized Göring's heroic feats by bestowing upon him its highest decoration, the Pour le Merite. His abilities as a leader earned him command of the famed Richthofen fighter squadron. By this time his egocentric personality had been formed, and he began to demonstrate the individual flair that was to become his trait. The considerable public notoriety fed his ego. By the time World War I came to an end, the pattern of his existence had already been established. Forced into the role of a civilian, Göring was at a loss as what to do with his life. Fame and glory had been his, but now he was just one of the millions of returning veterans forced to compete with the ever declining economic condition that was overtaking the defeated country.

The mood of the German people turned to dissatisfaction, followed by a general hostile attitude toward the Weimar government. Frustrated war veterans were displeased with the terms of the armistice that Germany was compelled to sign, and were of the opinion that the war effort had been undermined. They had returned from war only to be faced with growing unemployment and staggering inflation. Men, such as Göring, felt that the Bruning government was not sympathetic with their plight, and felt a sense of abandonment. It was only natural that they would look elsewhere for a solution to their problems. A young firebrand named Hitler, who had shared their experiences, appeared to be sympathetic to their problems, and led them to believe that his infant Nazi Party could provide the solution to all their ills. Hitler had a personal magnetism which appealed to Göring. Göring in turn had the financial and business connections that Hitler needed. The Nazi Party was struggling, and with the recruitment of each new member of Göring's stature, the Party and its coffers were bolstered. Hitler had determined Göring's character weakness early.... the need for personal acclaim and prestige. Göring became one of Hitler's most trusted and energetic lieutenants. Hitler had made a wise decision in his appointment of Göring as he took up the Nazi

(ABOVE) AS COMMANDER OF THE RICHTHOFEN FIGHTER SQUADRON. (RIGHT) GÖRING IN 1931.

banner with considerable zeal. On November 8, 1923, Hitler undertook one of the greatest political gambles of his career when he attempted the forcible establishment of the Nazi Party at the head of the Bavarian State. When he brandished a pistol in the faces of government and political representatives, Göring was at his side. Initially, the gamble appeared to be a success, but when Hitler withdrew feeling he had succeeded in his coup, the Munich "Beer Hall Putsch" crumbled into a complete failure. Göring was forced to flee to avoid arrest. He stayed out of the country just long enough for the immediate interest in the incident to subside, and returned to enter into Hitler's political intrigues.

Göring's ego was such that he was not satisfied with the routine existence of his civilian capacity. The former captain of the air arm was especially drawn to the appeal of a uniform and all it's trappings. President Hindenburg attempted to appease Göring, and at the same time, capitolize on his personal magnetism and varied contacts, when he elevated him to the rank of General of Infantry in August 1933. It is possible that the ranking officers of the Army had a great deal to do with influencing Hindenburg's decision since they may have been seeking a powerful ally against the growing threat of Röhm's SA. Regardless of the intent, his appointment earned considerable support for Hitler.... especially from those members of the military aristocracy.

Göring became one of the three most powerful men in the Nazi Party. He knew all too well not to oppose Hitler, which was one of the secrets to his long lasting career. He was not overly concerned with the opposition from Rudolf Hess, Hitler's dedicated but not too effective secretary. The close relationship between Göring and Hitler, and the increased powers that he was able to amass, made him second only to Hitler in the NSDAP. Thus, Göring was named to the cabinet as minister without portfolio when the Nazis became the minority party in the Reichstag following the 1933 elections. The 230 elected Nazis in the Reichstag formed a coalition with the center party, naming Göring as President of the Reichstag. This political maneuver added considerable power and prestige to the surging Nazi Party. Hitler used this growing strength to great advantage by forcing President Hindenburg to name him Chancellor. This move was to sound the death knoll for the Reichstag as that governing body was to convene only twice after Hitler legally assumed his new position of power. This was brought about largely through the efforts of Göring, who had entered into a secret conspiracy with a few selected members of Himmler's SS. It was not until after the war that the exact extent of Göring's participation in this conspiracy to overpower the German governing body was known. As Hitler looked from the upper window of his Chancellory, he could see the flames leaping from the building that housed the Reichstag. . . . flames that had been started by Göring's order. Hitler immediately proclaimed a Communist conspiracy, which eventually led to that party being, in effect, indicted for starting the fire. Göring used the much publicized trial of a half-wit Dutch Communist, conveniently found at the site of the fire, to expound the merits of the Nazi Party and the dangers to the German nation which would follow from similar radical political parties. Hitler hit upon this "cause celebre" to gain the eventual vote that outlawed opposition political parties, and allowed him to obtain virtual and eventual dictatorial powers. The emergency powers voted to Hitler allowed him to suspend all elections. With these acts, the Nazis became the dominant. . . the only. . . political party within Germany, and Hitler became the master. Hitler was not to forget the significant role that Göring had played in his becoming the sole leader.. . . . the Führer of Germany.

As the Minister of Interior of Prussia, one of Göring's most influential posts, he succeeded in undermining the Prussian police, which resulted in the eventual total Nazification of that law-keeping force. He used the newly created State Secret Police (Geheime-Staatspolizei - Gestapo) to great effect in suppressing or eliminating his personal or political enemies. . . . first in Prussia, then in the whole of Germany, when the organization was transferred under the control of the Minister of Interior.

Not all of Hitler's potential opposition came from outside the Nazi Party. The real or imagined threat of Röhm forced an alliance of intrigue between Göring and Himmler to eliminate the SA-Stabschef, and subjugate the massive SA. Hitler was convinced that the man who had been so responsible for winning a Nazi victory in the streets was only interested in gaining total power for himself. Hitler worked himself into a frenzy, and ordered the elimination of Röhm and other members of the SA believed to be supporting him. Himmler's SS was very effective and methodical in the round-up of these political "turncoats". The outcome of that night in June 1934, was the murder of Röhm and any other political or personal enemy that had the misfortune of being available. Göring's proven loyalty to Hitler brought him even closer to the Leader. The trust that Hitler had for Göring earned him the right of succession when Hitler officially designated his successor five years later. This distinctive honor brought Göring added fame and fortune, but also sealed his fate.

GÖRING AND THE BLADE TRADITION

Hermann Göring, without question, did more than any other person in the Nazi hierarchy to influence the design, production and wear of the dress dagger. Göring was an avid wearer of blades, dating back to the time when, as a tenacious eagle of the skies, he climbed into the cockpit of his aircraft armed with a stag handled hunting knife. It was from this beginning that he was associated with many specially designed daggers made either for him or the Nazi organizations which he was associated with. Many of the pieces specifically worn by Göring will be discussed in the chapters relating to the organizational blades.

When World War I ended, Göring was far better off than most of his comrades. He had the admiration of his countrymen, and the limited wealth to live like a nobleman. While others were desperately trying to scratch a living, Göring's favorite pastime was tracking down and scoring a kill on a wild boar or laying in wait for a deer with a prize antler. In these activities, he outfitted himself in a series of hunting costumes. He either purchased or was given a large selection of knives or daggers which he wore with the costumes.

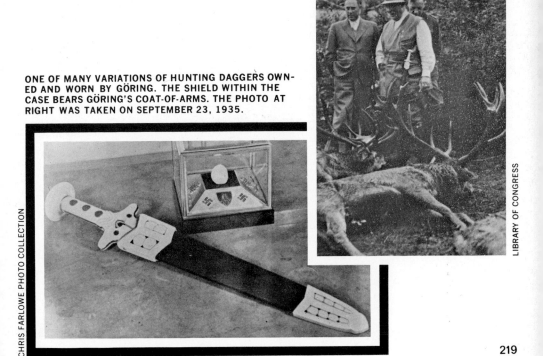

ONE OF MANY VARIATIONS OF HUNTING DAGGERS OWNED AND WORN BY GÖRING. THE SHIELD WITHIN THE CASE BEARS GÖRING'S COAT-OF-ARMS. THE PHOTO AT RIGHT WAS TAKEN ON SEPTEMBER 23, 1935.

Most of the daggers Göring wore mirrored the organizations which he headed. His love for hunting, and his position as National Hunting Master, resulted in a great number of variations in daggers reflecting the hunting theme.

His favorite was one of a pair given to him by Count Eric von Rosen, his brother-in-law by his first wife. The piece was made to order, and it reflected the craftsmanship that went into its construction. The hilt was bronze with silver highlites. The runic inscription which spanned the lower crossguard translated to read, "A knife from Eric to Hermann". The etched gold swastika on the front ricasso of the double-edged blade did not signify Göring's involvement with the Nazi Party, but was the Count's own heraldic symbol. The decorated upper and lower scabbard fittings were also made of bronze as were the sides. Between the scabbard fittings was a deep red grain leather. The Reichsmarschall surrendered this dagger to Colonel W.W. Quinn, G-2, Seventh US Army, on May 9, 1945. Colonel Quinn eventually donated this and the Reichsmarschall baton to the West Point Museum where it is located today.

The second piece worn extensively by Göring was also a gift from his brother-in-law. Count von Rosen had his symbol etched into the ricasso, but this time utilized the swastika in the design of the upper portion of the scabbard to signify Göring's political inclinations. The

LIBRARY OF CONGRESS

OCTOBER 10, 1937 AT CARINHALL.   JUNE 7, 1939 AT CARINHALL.

GÖRING'S FAVORITE DAGGER, PRESENTED TO HIM BY HIS BROTHER-IN-LAW.

ENTERTAINING PARTY LEADERS AT CARINHALL.

THIS DAGGER, ALSO A GIFT FROM COUNT VON ROSEN, WAS WORN EXCLUSIVELY WITH THE MANY HUNTING OUTFITS OWNED BY GÖRING. THE HANDLE AND POMMEL BEAR A RESEMBLANCE TO THE REICHSMARSCHALL DAGGER THAT FOLLOWED IN 1940.

dagger was richly decorated with precious stones, and had a fluted (elongated) ivory, handle. The handle and pommel of this dagger bear a remarkable resemblance to the hilt section of the Reichsmarschall Dagger which was to be designed for Göring in 1940. The piece was worn in the vertical position suspended by a short double chain hanger that joined at a snap-fastener.

GÖRING HOSTS A GROUP OF HUNTING MEMBERS AT A PARTY AT CARINHALL, 16 JANUARY 1938. HE WEARS THE DAGGER, ONE OF TWO, GIVEN TO HIM BY COUNT VON ROSEN.

On July 19, 1940, Hitler appointed twelve general rank officers to the rank of Feldmarschall. To soothe Göring's deflated ego, Hitler appointed him to the newly created rank of Reichsmarschall. The singular honor was bestowed upon Göring, thus making him the highest ranking military man in the German armed forces. The popularity-conscious Göring was thus able to maintain his image in the eyes of the German public. As befitted a man who craved the glitter of awards, decorations and uniforms, an entirely new style uniform was created bearing the unique insignia of his exclusive rank. To complete this striking ensemble, a beautifully designed and unique dagger was created. The Reichsmarschall dagger was hand-made by students of the Berlin Technical

**NEWLY DESIGNED
REICHSMARSCHALL EMBLEM**

Academy from a design submitted by professor Herbert Zeitner. Upon its completion in 1940, it was presented to Göring to be worn when fulfilling obligations as Reichsmarschall of the Greater German Reich. All metal fittings of the hilt and scabbard were finished in gold plate. The pommel was inset with diamonds and rubies with a very large precious stone crowning the pommel. The grip was made of ivory, fluted along the length. The grip ferrule was also inset with rubies about its circumference. The gold crossguard had a squared langet. . . . the entire piece composing a design of the national emblem with crossed Marschall's batons. The upper face of the crossguard bore the design of the Iron Cross engraved at each end. Information is not readily available as to the specifications of the blade. The scabbard was squared off rather than being the typical oval. It was fluted in design, terminating in a stylized oak leaf pattern. Unlike the standard scabbards, this piece had no scabbard bands, but was fitted with swivel rings affixed directly to the flat upper side of the scabbard. The dagger was suspended by means of a fabric double strap hanger with gilt fittings. The basic design was very similar to the hangers for the 1937 Pattern Luftwaffe Officer's Dagger. The rectangular buckles bore the relief design of a single oak leaf at each

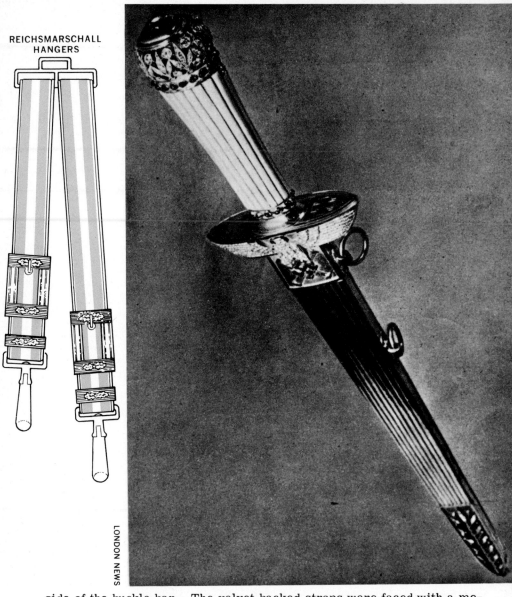

side of the buckle bar. The velvet backed straps were faced with a metallic braid with stripes running down each side. The dagger was illustrated and described in the 1940 issue of the Uniformen-Markt, but no photograph has ever been found of the dagger actually being worn by Göring. The dagger was discovered among an extensive selection of Göring's possessions, which were retrieved from a cave at Königsee by advancing US forces in 1945. The contents of that cave, to include this piece, were inventoried and photographed. Since that occassion, the dagger has not been heard of, nor has there been any indication of what happened to

it.

THE REICHSMARSCHALL DOLCH WAS SPECIFICALLY
DESIGNED FOR GÖRING AS A BADGE OF HIS SINGULAR
POSITION AS RANKING MILITARY OFFICER IN GERMANY.
CREATED IN 1940, IT DISAPPEARED IN 1945 AFTER BE-
ING INVENTORIED AMONG A LARGE CACHE OF MATE-
RIAL BELONGING TO GÖRING.

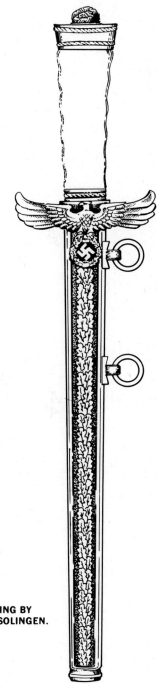

DAGGER PRESENTED TO GÖRING BY
INDUSTRIAL LEADERS FROM SOLINGEN.

GENERAL CHRISTIANSEN, WEARING THE 1937 PATTERN LUFTWAFFE OFFIZIERDOLCH WITH PORTEPEE, ESCORTS FIELD MARSHAL SPERRLE.

THE AIR FORCE
[LUFTWAFFE]

One of the most recognized and feared developments of WWI was aerial warfare. The aeroplane was employed with great effectiveness, both defensively and offensively. Aerial reconnaissance, bombing, strafing and interception of other aircraft were pioneered during this period. At a time when great numbers of men were being killed in the trenches, aerial combat was looked upon as a meeting of chivalrous knights engaged in "friendly", albeit deadly, combat. Few who took part in or were aware of the effects of aerial combat doubted the significance of air power in future conflicts.

When Germany capitulated, European powers did not wish to see a resurgence of power similar to that which had been mustered against them. In an effort to cripple Germany's future war-making capability, harsh limitations were imposed on that country. The Versailles Treaty called for the dissolution of the German air arm, and forbade the Germans to form any new military air organizations. Anything connected with air combat was struck from the books, and strict limitations on the construction and use of all aircraft were imposed. Contrary to these restrictions, there were those in Germany who wished to preserve the valuable experience gained during the War and continued to plan and develop covertly for the day when Germany would once again have an air arm. This group, headed by General Hans von Seeckt, Chief of the General Staff and acknowledged molder of the Wehrmacht, resisted opposition from the Army and Navy as to the formation of an independent air arm.

227

Highly talented personnel were earmarked for the Luftwaffe once it became a reality. Research was conducted at home in conjunction with civil air projects, and abroad under secret agreements. Civilian air sport organizations served as a reservoir for personnel who were later to be used, and as a means to introduce the youth to flying skills.

One of the early rewards that Hitler bestowed upon Göring was the establishment of the Air Ministry in 1933 with Göring being named as its head. The establishment of the Air Ministry had long been a dream of Göring's, and in affect, it became the supreme command echelon of the embryo Luftwaffe. Since both the Army and Navy were also secretly working on the development of their own independent air arms, they looked with disfavor upon Göring's influential surge. At Hitler's direction, they grudgingly gave up pilot-trained personnel to serve in the ministry.

Göring commenced to gather about him the most talented persons available. Many of the general officers who were to become leaders in the Luftwaffe during the Second World War were drawn from the ranks of Göring's wartime flying associates. He actively recruited from civilian sources, utilizing Lufthansa for the more capable personnel. He was able to draw such persons as Milch, Udet, von Greim, Loerzer, Christiansen, Keller and other equally talented civilians into his fold. Göring possessed a skilled staff from which to form the various departments required at Oberkommando level when Hitler repudiated the Treaty in 1935. With this act, the Air Ministry was redesignated Oberkommando der Luftwaffe (OKL), and was placed on equal footing with the other two services.

Research and development was in full swing, with most of the secrecy being lifted. Aircraft that had been secretly developed and then tested in Russia, made a sudden appearance. It wasn't long before these aircraft and their pilots received combat testing as Germany willingly provided men and material to take part in Spain's Civil War during the period 1936 to 1939.

The United States sent an emissary, Charles Lindbergh, to Germany in 1936 to evaluate the threat of the growing air arm. With Göring playing host to the world famous aviator, Lindbergh was escorted to manufacturing and test sites for equipment designated for the Luftwaffe. He was greatly impressed with the air developments that he witnessed.. ...especially with the design and speed of the record-holding ME-109 fighter. Lindbergh returned to the United States fully convinced that Germany's desires did not pose a threat to world peace.

A great deal of Germany's military budget was poured into Göring's Luftwaffe. When plans were readied to undertake expansion, Göring boasted that his Luftwaffe alone could bring Germany's enemies to their knees. When war did break out, the Luftwaffe was not able to live up to the expectations when confronted with the test of combat. During the early stages, aircraft provided close support to ground combat troops. In the air, bombers hit with devastating effect, and fighter-pilots pressed the Royal Air Force to the limit during the Battle of Britain. However, as Hitler over-extended himself, Luftwaffe resources, along with those of the other services, were parcelled away piecemeal until the realization came that the war was lost.

THE DAGGER TRADITION

While the German Navy had a tradition of carrying a dagger sidearm that dated back to 1849, the Luftwaffe could not boast of any such tradition.... save for Göring's own love for blades. It was because of his interest and the growing number of organizations that armed themselves with the dagger that Göring authorized his Luftwaffe officer personnel to wear a dagger. A dagger designed for the Deutsches Luftsportverband (DLV) in 1934 especially appealed to Göring, and it was this piece which was selected for wear. Another organization's dagger was selected because it met the requirement by its design, and largely because of the haste involved in outfitting the Luftwaffe with a dagger. Once selected, the DLV dagger was introduced early in 1935 for wear by all officers, non-commissioned officers and officer candidates. The dagger was officially redesignated the Luftwaffe Fliegerdolch, or Flyer's Dagger, though it continued to be worn for a short time by the DLV until a new dagger was designated for their organization.

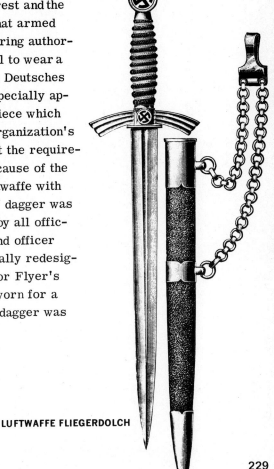

LUFTWAFFE FLIEGERDOLCH

230 **THE LUFTWAFFE FLIEGERDOLCH**

The Fliegerdolch, measuring 48cms, was suspended by a double chain link hanger which attached to the outer waist belt or a hook under the tunic. Hilt and scabbard fittings were initially produced of nickel silver, while later production pieces turned to natural polished aluminum. The round pommel screwed to the blade tang, and served to secure the hilt to the blade. A gold colored swastika "sunwheel" decorated both sides of the pommel, while an oak leaf pattern was engraved into the flat outer circumference. In the first patterns, the swastika design was engraved, but this was soon changed by the adding of stamped side-plates. It was not uncommon for the oak leaf pattern to be omitted from the pommel. The same swastika design used in the pommel was carried over to the front and back of the center section of the crossguard. The crossguard extensions were in the form of stylistic down-swept wings. The grooved wooden handle was covered with blue morocco leather with silver or gold colored wire wrapping running in a diagonal from low right to high left. The double edge blade normally bore no other marking than the manufacturer's trademark and the possibility of the ordnance inspection mark. The steel bodied scabbard was also covered with a blue morocco leather. The upper and center scabbard fittings accommodated a swivel ring to which the chain hangers were attached. The chain, which was made of nickel silver or aluminum, normally consisted of nine rings in the upper chain, and fourteen in the lower chain. The metal finish of the hanger remained consistent with the finish of the dagger.

Flying personnel had the distinction of wearing an aluminum portepee wrapped about the crossguard. Officer personnel were authorized to substitute a sword of similar design when the service dress uniform was prescribed for wear.

1937 PATTERN LUFTWAFFE OFFICER'S DAGGER

A rash of newly designed daggers were introduced in 1936 to provide a greater deliniation between organizations and rank structure. In 1937, the Luftwaffe followed suit by introducing a totally new dagger of its officers. Effective October 1, 1937, a dagger designated Luftwaffe Offizierdolch (officer's dagger) was authorized for wear by all officers and officer candidates upon successful completion of officer examinations. After March 12, 1940, qualified NCO's were also extended the authorization to wear the 1937 pattern dagger. Prior to this time, flight NCO's were permitted to wear the 1934 pattern dagger.

The pommel and crossguard were made from cast aluminum. The pommel was decorated with a swastika front and back, usually finished in gold, and surrounded by oak leaves. It is often the case that this gold

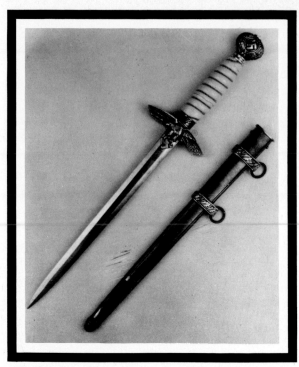

THE BLADE OF THIS ORIGINAL PROTOTYPE OF THE 1937 PATTERN LUFTWAFFE OFFIZIER-DOLCH HAS THE WORDS "ORIGINAL EICKHORN BLANKE WAFFEN URBILD." THE LAST WORD DESIGNATES THE PIECE AS A PROTOTYPE.

plate or finish has been removed over the years. Construction of the grip ranged from genuine ivory, solid plastic, or wood covered with a celluloid shell. Grip colors, which had no significance, ranged from white to dark orange. A single strand aluminum or bronze wire wrap followed the diagonal grooves in the grip, running from low right to high left. A nickel or silver plate ferrule with oakleaf design added to the appearance of the grip. The crossguard was cast in the design of an eagle in flight, symbolic of the Luftwaffe. In its talons was clutched a swastika. The reverse of the guard simply bore an outlined pebbled surface which was often used for engraving the owner's name. The upper portion of the guard was decorated by having an oak leaf design cast into it, or engraved into the flat surface. The double-edged blade was normally plain with the exception of the manufacturer's trademark. However, the purchaser did have the option of getting a blade with a specially designed or standard etched pattern at extra cost. The steel scabbard was normally nickel or zinc plated, while a few of the higher quality pieces were silver plated. The scabbard, which was basically pebbled, had an oak leaf pattern near the tip. Two scabbard suspension bands with swivel rings were also decorated with an oak leaf pattern. Overall length of the dagger measured 41.5cms.

McCARTHY

NOTE DETAIL OF THIS 1937 PAT-
TERN LUFTWAFFE OFFICER'S DAG-
GER WITH DAMASCUS BLADE.

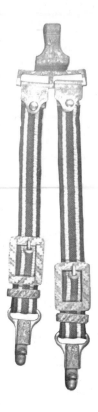

ON 1 OCTOBER 1937 A
TOTALLY NEW PATTERN
DAGGER, THE LUFTWAFFE
OFFIZIERDOLCH, WAS
INTRODUCED. (NOTE
DAMASCUS BLADE).

TWO LUFTWAFFE NCO's ON THE ITALIAN RIVIERA ON 29 NOVEMBER 1940 EMPLOY THEIR OWN INTERPRETATION OF THE REGULATION CONCERNING WEAR OF THE DAGGER. THE ONE TO THE LEFT WEARS THE FLIEGERDOLCH, WHILE THE ONE TO THE RIGHT WEARS THE OFFIZIERDOLCH WITH PORTEPEE. (ABOVE RIGHT) THE BUYER HAD THE OPTION OF GETTING A STANDARD PATTERN OR A SPECIALLY DESIGNED PATTERN ETCHED BLADE. THIS TYPE BLADE WAS HEAVILY PLATED, WITH THE PATTERN ACID ETCHED DEEPLY FRONT AND BACK.

Removable double strap hangers were used to suspend the dagger diagonally on the wearer's left side. A blue/gray facing with two aluminum stripes was sewn to a blue/gray velvet backing. Metal fittings were dull finished aluminum cast with an oak leaf design, with a rectangular buckle fitted to each strap. After May 31, 1942, general officers were given the authority to wear hangers with gold finished metal fittings to distinguish their rank.

Officers and authorized NCO's (Feldwebel and above on flight status) wore the 1937 pattern Luftwaffe Offizierdolch with a 23cms aluminum portepee wrapped about the ferrule.

MAJOR VON HEYDEBRECK GREETS MEMBERS OF THE BERLIN PHILHARMONIC AT COPEN-
HAGEN RAILWAY STATION IN 1940.

THE ARMY
[HEER]

Origins, if traced, of the military force within a state which has fostered militarism from the time of its inception, or even of that period of time when the military leaders made their alliance with Hitler, would swell this chapter to book length. The selected historical events are intended to show that the Army leaders had the capability of altering the course of German (and world) history on many occasions, prior to their overt act of attempted assassination on July 20, 1944.

Conditions in the German Army tended to pave the way for Hitler's rise to power. Germany had lost a world war and the morale of the Army was at its lowest possible ebb. Splinter groups, within the Army itself, were formed in an attempt to find a solution to the politico-socio-economic ills of Germany. Under normal conditions, the Army would not have given a second thought to the political precepts espoused by Hitler. However, the Army felt its position to be hopeless, and was grasping at any opportunity to regain its former glory. The German General Staff had been outlawed by the Versailles Treaty of 1919, and restrictions were imposed on the Army as to size and equipment. Officers and men were drastically reduced to 4,000 and 96,000 respectively to meet the maximum 100,000 limitation which was to be fully effective by March 31, 1920. An additional clause of the Treaty required that enlistments be of a twelve year duration, while commissions ran for twenty-five years. This prevented the establishment of a "shadow" army - a trained army of reservists created by short-term enlistments, capable of meeting any emergency, but not counted on the active roles of the military. The cream of the **237** professional soldiers were selected to fill the limited positions, and the remainder were dispersed throughout police forces, border guards and veterans' organizations.... all of which were trained and structured along military lines. The SA played an active role in placing skilled professional soldiers who were unable to be absorbed into the legitimate ranks of the Reichsheer. This activity was to last until 1935, when Hitler no longer saw fit to abide by the Versailles Treaty limitations. The SA was to gain considerable influence with the Army during the period they were able to fill selected positions in the newly organized Grenzschutz (Border Guards).... not to mention the large number of converts to Nazism within the Army. In affect, the Army and its aristocratic officer corps were struggling for survival. Hitler capitalized on this favorable situation by drawing men of high rank and noteworthy deed into his political command echelon. More important, he offered a place for the veteran in the growing Nazi Party.

The military forces of the Weimar Republic and the various Freikorps and veterans' organizations, much to their later dismay, joined forces with the quasi-military/political force of the Nazi movement to stave off the communist threat, which was believed to exist. Preparations were made late in 1932 to place the Reichswehr under the control of the police to put down the feared communist revolt. Hitler was able to successfully play off opposition groups among themselves, and used the pretext of a threatened civil war to force President von Hindenburg to appoint him Chancellor. With Hitler's political army greatly outnumbering the Reichswehr, he knew the Army had little or nothing to gain by a show of opposition. When the President made his decision to make Hitler Chancellor, barring relatively little opposition, the Army merely looked on with drawn tolerance. While much jest was made regarding the "Austrian Corporal", he did have empathy with the Army due to his war record. [1]

THE ARMY VERSUS THE SA

Immediately following Hitler's appointment, the Army High Command structure began a considerable reorganization that was to last until the following year. Considering the "silent" confrontation during the period of political inplay, the Army did not lose sight of the imposing threat of Hitler's Storm Troops. From a purely survival standpoint, it was to the best interests of the Army to court Hitler's favor, since only he could control his political army.

---

[1] Hitler was a genuine war hero having been awarded the Iron Cross Ist and IInd Classes.... awards not normally presented to men of his low rank.

The Army began their attempted supression of the Nazi armed formations as early as 1923 when Reichswehr Minister General Groener played a prominent role in the legal banning of the SA. Göring was finally able to cast off the ban on the SA in 1926. He relinquished his position as Stabschef of the SA to Captain Ernst Röhm in 1928 in order to devote his efforts to other areas. Röhm immediately set his sights for an all out confrontation with the Army High Command. It was no secret that he coveted the supreme position for himself, and meant to achieve that aim through his personal friendship with Hitler and the imposing strength of his SA. Through necessity, the Army was forced to make a series of agreements and concessions that in effect resulted in a stalemate between the two opposing elements. Since it was Röhm's policy to supplant the Army with the SA, a status quo was not to his liking. Demonstrating an outward show of loyalty to Hitler (assuming all the while that the Army could manipulate Hitler to their own end) General Blomberg, Minister of Defense, ordered that the eagle/swastika (the political symbol of Hitler's Party) insigne be added to all military uniforms effective February 1934. This act, coupled with others, marked the de facto recognition by the military of Nazi doctrine. The dissident ex-Army Captain Röhm attempted to counter this move by trying to convince Hitler that the SA should have the prominent role in internal security matters. Much to the surprise of both factions, Hitler came out in favor of the Army, designating the Reichswehr as the sole bearer of arms to be used in defense of the nation. This was a major victory for the Army, and a decided setback to the ambitious Röhm. Enemies of Röhm, the most prominent of which were Göring and Himmler, joined forces to eliminate the threat. The sub-rosa activities culminated in a bloody purge of Röhm and numerous other high leaders of the SA on June 30, 1934. This purge served as a catalyst to further eliminate political opponents of Hitler in the name of national security. While the SS (then a branch of the SA) was the primary tool in the purge, it was the Army that expected its own position to become more firm. To the contrary, they fell even further under the iron-willed control of the Führer. The Reichswehr itself was not without casualties. With the murder of two of its leading members, Generals von Schleicher and von Bredow, the Army's cooperation with the SS was to come back to haunt them.

THE ARMY AND THE WEHRMACHT

To cement his control, Hitler passed a law on August 20, 1934, requiring an oath of allegiance, but this time to himself, and not the Fatherland. The officers and men came forward to swear their oath as they had **239** done in the past, but with words that were considerably different, and their meaning more binding: "I swear by God this sacred oath, that I will render unconditional obedience to Adolf Hitler, the Führer of the German Reich and people, Supreme Commander of the Armed Forces, and will be ready as a brave soldier to risk my life at any time for this oath." This oath was to become the menacing "Sword of Damacles" that hung over the heads of the military. The last vestige of freedom and separatism had been relinquished to Hitler, who now assumed absolute power. The restraints imposed by the Versailles Treaty were arbitrarily relinquished by Hitler on March 16, 1935, and the Wehrmacht became a stark reality. A year later, the Army was to embark on the first of a series of gambles by marching unchecked into the demilitarized Rhineland. In a series of events designed to strengthen both his own position and that of the military, Hitler established the Armed Forces High Command (Oberkommando der Wehrmacht - OKW) with himself as Supreme Commander on February 1938. The OKW was rendered the equivalent status of other Reichsministries. This move, and the apparent aggressive bent of Hitler, had the full blessing of the German industrialists. They had long been pushing for rearmament so that they might reap the profits. They, like the Army, thought Hitler could be controlled. Little did they know....or possibly care.

GENERALFELDMARSCHALL BLOMBERG, WEARING THE ARMY OFFICER'S DAGGER, STANDS TO HITLER'S LEFT DURING A PRESENTATION AT NUREMBERG IN 1938 GIVEN BY GÖRING.

At the celebration of his forty-seventh birthday on April 20, 1936, Hitler announced the promotion of Blomberg to the rank of Generalfeldmarschall (making him the first to receive such recognition in peacetime, and the first to bear such rank during the Third Reich), and the subsequent promotion of Fritsch and Göring to the rank of Generaloberst, and Raeder to Generaladmiral. Hitler had intended to honor the Army and Blomberg by bestowing the newly devised rank of Reichsmarschall on Blomberg. However, it was Göring who eventually garnered this honor in July 1940, when, in an unprecedented act, Hitler conferred the rank of Generalfeldmarschall to twelve general officers of the Wehrmacht in a single day. This marked a considerable advance from the Reichswehr of 1920 that listed a total of 42 general officer ranks.

THE ARMY AND THE DAGGER

Paul Casberg, noted German designer, submitted designs to Hitler for an Army officer's dress dagger. After Hitler had interjected his own ideas, which caused considerable modification to the original design, the Heer Offiziersdolch, or Army Officer's Dagger, was officially approved by Hitler on May 4, 1935. The dagger gained immediate acceptance. The various retailers were provided the dagger for direct sale to authorized persons, or it was obtained directly from the quartermaster. The dagger was worn in lieu of the bayonet or sword by all officers up to and including field marshalls, medical and veterinary officer, officials having the equivalent rank of an officer and selected NCO's. Regulations prescribed that the dagger was to be worn with a 42cms silver portepee. It is from this that senior NCO's in the grade of Feldwebel upwards earned the distinction of "Portepeeunteroffizier".

The basic design of the Army dagger was to set the pattern for following daggers. It measured an overall length of 40cms. Initially, all metal fittings were silver plated, but as the war progressed, the quality of the dagger deteriorated considerably. The plastic grip ranged in color from white to dark orange. The variation in color had nothing to do with rank or branch of service. A genuine ivory grip could be purchased at the option of the buyer, although it nearly doubled the retail price of the dagger. Other options were available to the purchaser such as etched blades (either standard pattern or special order), damascus blades, or engraved crossguards. Each option executed simply added to the end price the buyer had to pay.

The dagger was suspended from a double-strap hanger with white metal fittings, except for general officer ranks, which were authorized

**SPLINTER PATTERN
DAMASCUS BLADE**

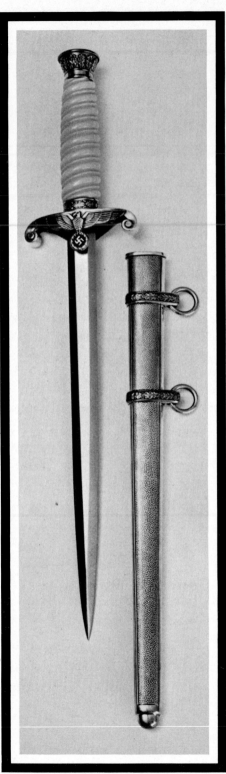

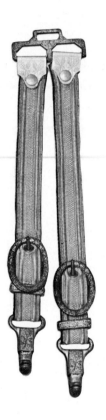

STANDARD PATTERN ARMY
OFFICER'S DAGGER AUTHOR-
IZED FOR WEAR IN 1935 BY
HITLER. THE HANGERS HAVE
AN ALUMINUM FACING ON
A GREEN OR GREY VELVET
BACKING. AFTER 1942,
GENERAL OFFICERS WERE
AUTHORIZED TO WEAR THEIR
HANGERS WITH GOLD COLOR-
ED METAL FITTINGS TO DIS-
TINGUISH THEIR SPECIAL
RANK. ALL OTHERS WERE
ALUMINUM, OR SILVER PLAT-
ED.

IN ADDITION TO NUMEROUS OTHER OPTIONS, THE WEARER COULD HAVE THE REVERSE OF THE CROSSGUARD ENGRAVED TO SUIT HIS LIKING. SHOWN ARE A COAT OF ARMS, OWNERS' NAMES, AND A MONOGRAM.

hangers with gold-colored metal fittings. While the metal fittings of the hangers did distinguish general officers from field and line officers, there was absolutely no deviation in the dagger itself to denote rank. A dagger specifically designed for field marshalls has been alluded to in other references, however, no such dagger ever existed.

An Ehrendolch des Heers (Honor Dagger of the Army) was, however, specially designed and presented. This piece is discussed in the chapter dealing with SA-Stabschef Victor Lutze.

Requirements of the war caused the dagger to be replaced by the pistol. The eminent possibility of self-defense overshadowed the existing regulations governing dagger wear. Wear of the Army Dress Dagger was forbidden after September 5, 1944.

The size of the Army brought about by rapid expansion, and the relatively long tenure of the dagger caused it to be one commonly available to the collector.

GRAND ADMIRAL RAEDER, COMMANDER-IN-CHIEF OF THE GERMAN NAVY

THE NAVY
[KRIEGSMARINE]

During the latter part of the ninteenth century, Germany made a concerted effort to rival Great Britain as a major sea power. The Navy had a long and honorable tradition, and its members were considered to be very stable in the face of political and international turmoil.

Despite its size and estimated effectiveness, the German Navy was no match for that of England and the Allied powers during the world's first major confrontation. As the position of Germany grew more hopeless in the eyes of the Kaiser, the High Seas Fleet was ordered scuttled at Scapa Flow to prevent its capture. The order by the German Naval Command carried with it great impact. Germany was now without an effective naval arm. When the Kaiser agreed to abdicate in the face of defeat and allow Germany to come to terms as the vanquished, it was members of the Navy that immediately reacted to the lack of support for the war effort on the home front. This reaction was so violent that it could actually be termed a revolt by the Navy.

The terms of the surrender announced on May 7, 1919, came as a blow to the professional military caste. The Versailles Treaty, signed on June 28, 1919, directed a greater part of its intent against the German Navy, which had introduced one of the most formidable fighting instruments of the war....the submarine. Part V of the Treaty imposed stringent arms limitations against the German military. This section of the Treaty restricted Germany's future Navy to six battleships (not to exceed 10,000 tons in weight) and six light cruisers, supported by twelve destroyers and twelve torpedo boats. More important, the total strength of the Navy was limited to 15,000 personnel, of which a total of only twelve admirals was authorized.

Admiral Paul Behnke, head of the post-war Navy, was determined not to let the naval arm lose the gains it had achieved earlier. His main concern was to continue submarine development. In 1922, Behnke gave his nod of approval to the Krupp arms firm to proceed with submarine development. Krupp set up a dummy Dutch firm (Ingenieur-Kantoor voor Scheepsbouw) at Kiel. This "Dutch subsidiary" of Krupp was successful in circumventing the Treaty limitations, and was able to provide Hitler with an effective submarine force when the terms of the Treaty were repudiated. Submarines were also manufactured for Germany in Finland. Hitler proclaimed the restoration of military sovereignty to Germany on March 16, 1935, and within seven months, Germany had a fleet of twelve submarines with fully trained crews in active service. Within a year, this number had grown to eighteen. The restriction of tonnage was put aside with the development of a series of "pocket" battleships and cruisers that made the renegade German Navy the most advanced of the European powers. Erich Raeder took the reigns of the Navy, and it was he who directed its expansion in spite of the imposed limitations. By 1934, personnel strength had grown to 25,000, followed by an increase of 9,000 the following year. Raeder remained as Chief of the Navy for fifteen years until he fell from Hitler's favor in 1943. He was replaced by Admiral Karl Dönitz, who had gained residual fame from Oberleutnant Prien's sinking of the British battleship "Royal Oak".

ADMIRAL DÖNITZ

Despite the considerable technical advances made by the Navy, its wartime role was a series of highs and lows, with the overall contribution considered insufficient. German fighting men were effectively transported by ship to execute the invasion of Norway. Submarine wolf packs took a great toll of merchant shipping until convoys and other defensive

measures brought about by the development of sonar imposed considerable losses on the submarines. The scuttling of the "Graf Spee" in the
mouth of the River Platt in Argentina was a major set-back for the Navy.
This act of combat avoidance was to set the standard for German Naval
line officers in the crisis that followed.   No major sea engagements
were initiated by the German High Seas Fleet. Though they attempted to
avoid contact, the battleships and cruisers too often were successfully
sought out and attacked by Allied aircraft.

The Naval officer, especially line officers, maintained a very high
esprit de corps. Few became deeply involved with the trappings that the
Nazi movement initiated because of their established tradition.

THE NAVAL BLADE TRADITION

The naval uniform, unlike that of the Army, remained relatively
unchanged over the years. It consisted basically of dark navy blue material with gold trim. A dagger sidearm was introduced for the Royal
Prussian Navy in 1849 for wear by its officers. This dagger, which was
to become the sidearm of naval personnel in the Hitler era following a
few modifications, was introduced for Imperial German Naval officer personnel in 1901. It was the dagger that had previously been worn by Naval
cadets only. The dagger was composed of gilt metal (normally brass)
scabbard, crossguard and pommel, which took the shape of the Imperial
crown. The grip was of solid yellow horn. On November 28, 1918, the
yellow grip was replaced by a black one. The brass scabbard with double suspension bands was replaced by a rather plain black-painted metal
scabbard with one suspension band. Since Imperial Germany had ceased
to exist with the defeat of its military arms, the Imperial crown pommel
was replaced by a brass flame-shaped pommel. This configuration was
rather short-lived. ... as of June 5, 1919, the black grip was discarded
for the previous yellow horn, and the gilt scabbard supplanted the newly
introduced black scabbard. This pattern dagger was retained until 1938,
when the German Navy ordered a modification intended to appease Hitler.

The Hitler Navy became a reality following Hitler's declaration of
restoration of military sovereignty in 1935. However, it was not until
April 20, 1938, that the Nazi-era Naval Dagger took its final form.

The dagger measured 36cms in overall length. The flame-shaped
pommel was replaced with a cast brass or bronze national emblem with
down-turned wings. The eagle was required by regulation to be worn
facing away from the wearer. A genuine ivory or a white celluloid covered wood grip with twisted wire replaced the yellow horn grip. The

crossguard, showing the fouled anchor insignia, underwent a minor design change. A lock button to secure the dagger in the scabbard was incorporated into the reverse side of the crossguard. The purchaser had the option of a plain blade or one with a double etched design. It was normal that the configuration of the double edged blade incorporate a double groove down the center. Another option available was the standard engraved design brass scabbard or one of a hammered pattern. In either case, the gilt scabbard had double suspension bands in the design of oak leaves, and affixed to the swivel rings. Design variations were to be encountered, especially in the wire grip wrapping, blade etching, scabbard suspension bands and sheath patterns.

The dagger was worn suspended from two separate strap hangers with snap fasteners at both ends. The straps themselves were of navy blue material with a dark blue velvet backing. The predominant feature was the oval buckle with lion's head found at each end. For line officers, all metal fittings on the hangers were gilt finished, while administrative officials had white metal (normally aluminum) finished fittings. A 42cms aluminum portepee, usually with a gilt hue, was worn wrapped in the traditional Naval style around the crossguard.

An extract of the regulations[1] concerning wear of Naval sidearms shows the alternatives available to Navy personnel, and the many exceptions causing alteration of the basic dagger:

VI. The Naval Sidearm and how they are worn.

1. Sidearms for all ranks from Petty Officer upwards are: (a) the dagger, and (b) the sword.
2. Midshipmen carry the Naval dagger with portepee. Naval cadets carry the dagger without portepee.
3. Non-commissioned officers and ratings on duty wear the bayonet on a black leather belt when so ordered.
4. The dagger is suspended from two dagger straps and the Naval sword from two sword straps; both will be worn as follows:

  (a) When the full dress belt is not worn:

   With undress coat: The dagger or sword is worn suspended from the inside belt.

   With frock-coat: The dagger or sword is worn suspended from the inside belt.

   With greatcoat: The dagger is worn outside the coat, either through an opening under the left-hand pocket flap or fastened to two short slings sewn to the underside of the left-hand pocket flap. The sword is suspended from the inside belt.

---

[1] Bekleidungs und Anzugsbestimmungen für die Kriegsmarine. M. Dv. Nr. 260 - Berlin, 1935. (Clothing and Dress Regulations for the Navy, Naval Service Regulation 260, Berlin 1935 - Revised 1937.)

NAVAL OFFICERS ACCOMPANYING SA STABSCHEF LUTZE IN FRANCE ON AN INSPECTION TOUR.

With tropical dress: The dagger or sword is suspended from the inside belt.

With mess dress: The dagger is suspended from the inside belt. (Wear of the dagger with the mess dress is optional.) The sword is not worn with the mess dress.

(b) When the full dress belt is worn:

With undress coat: The dagger or sword is worn suspended from the inside belt.

With frock-coat: The dagger fastens directly to the full dress belt. The sword is worn suspended from the inside belt.

With greatcoat: The dagger is worn outside the coat either suspended through an opening under the left-hand pocket flap or fastened to two short slings sewn on the underside of the pocket flap. The sword is worn suspended from the inside belt.

With tropical dress: The dagger or sword is suspended from the inside belt.

The dagger is always suspended from the dagger straps worn in the unregained position (diagonally), on all occasions applicable for the wear of a dress sidearm.

When reporting, the Naval sword will be unhooked from the regain-hook and held beneath the basket with the left hand, fore and index fingers extended. The position of the sword must be perpendicular with the drag, approximately two inches above the ground.

If the greatcoat is worn, the lower left flap will be drawn back. When the sword is drawn, the left hand remains in position holding the scabbard.

On all other occasions, the sword may be worn in the regained (vertical) or unregained (diagonal) position. On occasions when military honors are to be rendered, the sword shall be worn in unregained position and held in the prescribed manner. If worn suspended from the outside belt, the sword is worn in the regained position but is still held by the scabbard in the above prescribed manner.

5. The dress bayonet is worn on parades for the Führer and Chancellor, the Commander-in-Chief of the Navy, the Commander-in-Chief of the Army and the Commander-in-Chief of the Airforce. Honor companies wear the bayonet fixed.

6. Those who served prior to November 11, 1918, in the War and were entitled to wear the sword or dagger with portepee, are permitted to wear the same Naval sidearm worn with honor during that period. These weapons may be worn unaltered, on or off duty, providing the present rank held corresponds to the weapon concerned, and that the occasion is appropriate for the wear of such pieces.

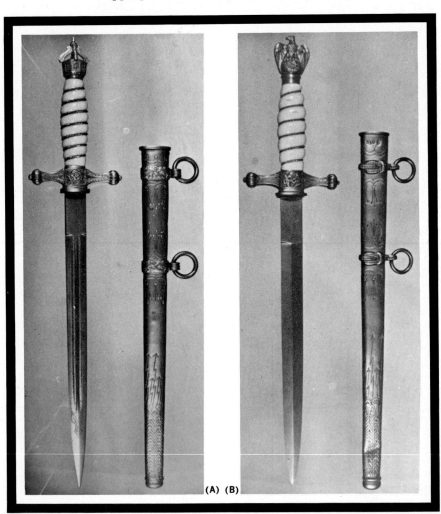

(A) (B)

7. Permission must be obtained from the Ministry of War (Commander-in-Chief of the Navy) for wear of Naval arms differing from prescribed patterns. Application may be made only if the weapon concerned has been worn by the applicant with distinction in the War or by his direct forebears. Those forebears must no longer be on active duty.

8. Officers, non-commissioned officers and midshipmen wear the Army-type short bayonets when marching in infantry formations or on landing drills. The bayonet is worn on the outer leather belt with portepee.

9. In foreign countries the senior Naval officer afloat will establish the necessary restrictions regarding the wear of arms.

10. The dagger (except for Naval Cadets) is worn with portepee as is the sword. The portepee for the dagger is tied to the grip and crossguard of the dagger in the manner known as the weave stitch. The sword portepee is strung around the upper part of the sword and then laced around the grip in a weave over the guard.

Dress Regulations for the Naval Field-Gray Uniform.

XXVIII. <u>Sidearms</u>:

1. The Army-type short bayonet is prescribed for all ranks. The Naval sword may be worn by personnel with the rank of Sergeant or Cadet and upward. With this type of uniform, the sword may be worn with an Army-type black all metal scabbard instead of the usual leather scabbard.

2. The bayonet is worn with a leather frog suspended from the outer belt. The sword is worn suspended from the outside belt on two carrying straps when battledress or greatcoat is worn.

3. Naval Cadets and other ranks entitled to wear the portepee with their sword or dagger will also wear the portepee with their bayonet.

4. The leather belt is worn by all ranks wearing the bayonet. Officers wear a solid round buckle of field-gray finish and brown leather frog; non-commissioned officers and ratings wear the field-gray rectangular buckle and black leather frog.

(A) THIS 1938 PATTERN DAGGER HAS THE IMPERIAL CROWN POMMEL WHICH WAS USED DURING THE PERIOD 1890-1919. HOWEVER, THOSE OFFICERS WHO SERVED PRIOR TO NOVEMBER 11, 1918 WERE PERMITTED TO RETAIN THE POMMEL. (B) THIS NAVAL ISSUE DAGGER BEARS A NAVY SERIAL NUMBER N306 ON THE SCABBARD AND BLADE RICASSO. THE BLADE IS OF A STELLETO PATTERN AND IS UNETCHED. THE STANDARD PATTERN ENGRAVED SCABBARD HAS THE KNOTTED SINGLE ROPE SUSPENSION BANDS.

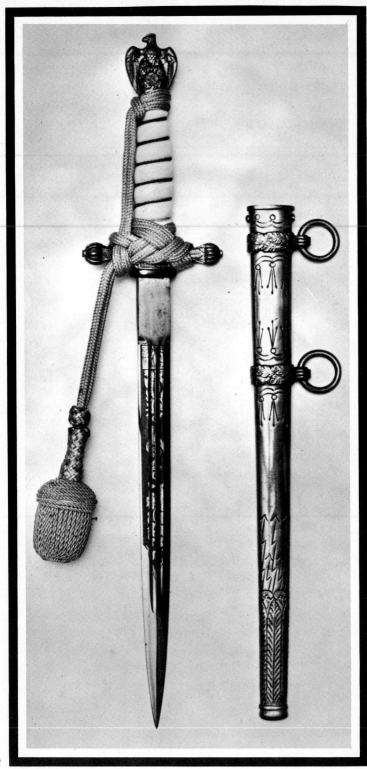

A STANDARD PATTERN NAVY DAGGER WITH HAMMERED SCABBARD.

BASIC PATTERN 1938 NAVY DAGGER WITH FOULED ANCHOR ETCHED BLADE DESIGN AND GILT PORTE-PEE.

Naval personnel were among the most ardent of the combat services in wearing the sidearm. However, when the tide of war turned against
Germany, wear of the dagger was greatly curtailed. An order issued by
the German Naval High Command on November 5, 1943, required that all
non-privately owned daggers in the clothing storage depots be shipped to
the naval central clothing issue warehouse at Kiel. Daggers were then
issued from this central location to meet specific needs as they arose.
By February 1944, daggers had been supplanted by pistols.

During the period 1942 to 1944, a great deterioration in the quality
of manufacture could be observed in the Navy dagger. Substitute material, especially in metals, were used. It was not uncommon to use a mixture of parts, both brass and pot-metal, in assembling a single dagger.

The war years produced no new dagger patterns per se for the
Navy. This precludes the existence of any daggers attributed to the Navy
that did not conform to the basic pattern or authorized forebears. No
satisfactory evidence has been made available to this author that would
substantiate the manufacture of an alleged "Naval Assault Dagger", even
though the date of manufacture has been given as prior to 1939.

THE NAVAL HONOR DAGGER

The Commander-in-Chief of the Navy, Grossadmiral Erich Raeder,
created a special Navy Honor Dagger which he awarded personally in recognition of exceptional, normally heroic, deeds. The first of the "Ehren-
dolches" was bestowed upon Admiral Albrecht on December 31, 1939. It

PHOTO BY DAVIS

THE POMMEL OF THE ALBRECHT DAGGER HAS 17 BRILLIANTS.

**KAPITÄNLEUTNANT
GUNTHER PRIEN**

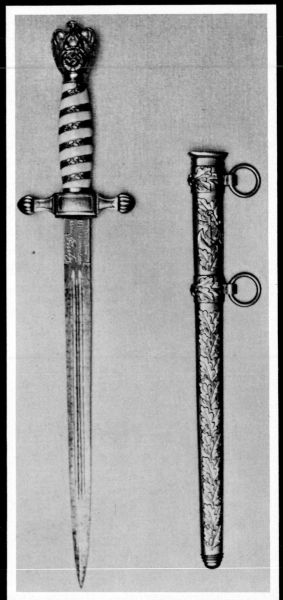

STEPHENS

**EHRENDOLCH DES KRIEGSMARINE
PRESENTED BY GROSSADMIRAL
KARL DÖNITZ.**

254

was almost a year later before the second award was made. Kapitänleutnant Gunther Prien, Commander of U 47, became Germany's hero overnight by sinking the battleship "Royal Oak" at a cost to the British Admiralty of over 780 lives. Prien was personally awarded the Knight's Cross of the Iron Cross by Hitler, and Raeder in turn recognized his gallantry by awarding him the Honor Dagger on October 20, 1940. Successive awards of the Honor Dagger were made on August 17, 1942, to Kapitänleutnant Erich Topp, Commander of U 552 and winner of the Knight's Cross with Oak Leaves and Swords; on September 1, 1942, to Kapitänleutnant Reinhard Suhren, Commander of U 564; on September 30, 1942, to Generaladmiral Carl Witzell; and in December 1942 to Generaladmiral Alfred Saalwächter. After his appointment in 1943, Grossadmiral Dönitz presented at least one Navy Honor Dagger to a U-Boat commander.

While the basic design of the Honor Dagger was identical in every respect to the normal Navy dagger, there was no set pattern for the presentation inscription (if any) placed on the damascus blade. Seventeen brilliants (usually real diamonds) were set in the swastika on the pommel, and a gold band of oak leaves wound around the genuine ivory grip. The gold plated scabbard was designed with a series of raised oak leaves. Each Honor Dagger was ceremoniously presented in a blue leather presentation case with white satin lining. When the dagger was worn, it was suspended in the same manner as the standard dagger.

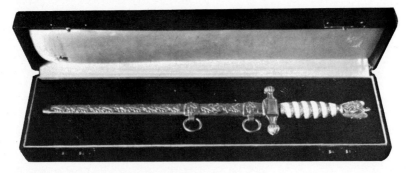

PHOTO BY DAVIS

NAVY HONOR DAGGER AWARDED TO ADMIRAL ALBRECHT ON 31 DECEMBER 1939. THIS WAS THE FIRST OF THE HONOR DAGGERS TO BE AWARDED, AND IS SHOWN IN THE ORIGINAL PRESENTATION CASE.

Other special award daggers, not falling into the category of true honor daggers, were produced and awarded to individuals and units in recognition of special acts, deeds or service. The basic difference lay in the scabbard design, which varied considerably. The grip, in most cases, was genuine ivory. Many of these special daggers, especially the grip, blade and scabbard had their origin during WWI.

GENERAL DIETL, COMMANDER OF THE ASSAULT ON NARVIK, IS AWARDED A SPECIAL NAVY HONOR DAGGER ON WHICH ARE ENGRAVED THE NAMES OF THE TEN DESTROYERS OF THE NARVIK GROUP.

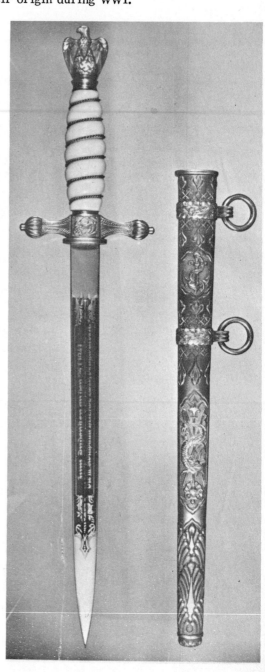

SPECIAL PRESENTATION NAVY DAGGER WITH IVORY GRIP AND RICHLY ETCHED BLADE WITH BLUED BACKING. THE INSCRIPTION READS "IN MEMORY OF 15 JANUARY 1941, 3rd COMPANY M.N., GROUP-NORTH, ORDNANCE." THE CENTRAL DESIGN OF THE REVERSE OF THE SCABBARD IS A PADDLE-WHEEL STEAMER.

SPECIAL PRESENTATION NAVY
DAGGER. NOTE THAT THE SWIVEL
RINGS ARE ENGRAVED.

SPECIAL PRESENTATION NAVY DAGGER

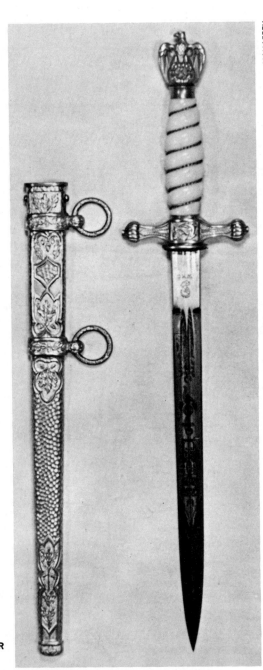

MAHAFFEY

NOTE HUNTING ASSOCIATION OFFICIAL WEARING A HUNTING KNIFE.

GERMAN NATIONAL HUNTING ASSOCIATION
[REICHSBUND DEUTSCHE JÄGERSCHAFT]

Göring's interest in hunting dated back prior to the time of his deep involvement with the Nazi movement. His income was more than sufficient to allow him his favorite pursuit.... hunting. This was at a time when the vast majority of the German people were in dire economic straits. His kills were added to the trophies in his hunting lodge, not to put food on the table in order to subsist. Göring cultivated many friends through his hunting activities and his newly acquired political contacts, all of which he used to great advantage. He was voted National Hunting Master of the German National Hunting Association. The honor added to his prestige and allowed him to add another series of uniforms to his already bulging closet.

Germany was a nation of hunting-conscious people. It had been their tradition for centuries to stalk the game of the forests. A great many poachers illegally earned their livelihood by killing game from the national reserves. The Association attempted to stem the poaching that threatened the indiscriminate killing of game, and to regulate in general the hunting practices through strict controls. It was the main objective of the Association to advance game conservation through the enforcement of its own and national regulations. Göring was very effective in consolidating the independent regulations of the various German states into a series of nationally recognized regulations.

Prospective members of the Association were required to undergo rigid field testing. If successful, they were given their hunting permit

SIR NEVILLE HENDERSON AND GÖRING (NOTE HIS NATIONAL HUNTING MASTER'S UNIFORM).

and membership in the Association. The more members that were taken into the Association allowed for greater ease in enforcement of reglations from within. Membership automatically authorized them to wear the distinctive green uniform and the hunting knife.

German hunters had been carrying a hunting knife for a great many years. It was a working tool, and not one designed solely for ornamentation. The knife was always designed with a sharp point, and often had the edge sharpened as well. The knife was used to bleed the fallen prey in preparation for skinning. No single pattern of knife existed for hunters even though they all assumed the same basic configuration. Due to the lack of distinctiveness over the years, about the only way to distinguish a hunting knife contemporary to the Nazi era is by the manufacturer's trademark, which often serves to date a piece.

Two different pattern hunting knives were designed especially for the German National Hunting Association, and were authorized for wear by its members from March 22, 1936. The pattern to be worn was left to the individual's personal taste and financial condition as he could purchase either of the two. The two patterns were classified as regulation and deluxe. The regulation knife should not be misconstrued to mean that this was the only approved design to be worn by members of the Association, as there were minor variations which existed between manufacturers. The knives of the Association each had a single identifying feature....a silver plated Association emblem affixed to the stag-horn grip by means of two pins. The insigne was the head of a deer with a swastika centered between the antlers. Below the head were the initials of the Deutsche Jägerschaft (DJ).

REGULATION NATIONAL HUNTING ASSOCIATION KNIFE

The regulation hunting knife, often erroneously referred to as a cutlass, was worn at all times when the member was in uniform. It was worn suspended from a green leather outer belt by means of a green leather frog, or from a cross-strap worn under the tunic when no belt was worn. A silver and gold knot was introduced on January 29, 1937, for all professional hunters (Berufsjäger) as a mark of distinction. This was worn normally wrapped about the frog rather than the knife itself. The hunting knife was of very ornate construction even in its simplicity. A tang nut, often in the shape of an acorn, secured the piece. Depending on the design established by a particular manufacturer, the grip cap was either fluted or heavily ornated with oak leaves. The stag-horn grip was especially cut to fit the tang extension of the blade and recesses of

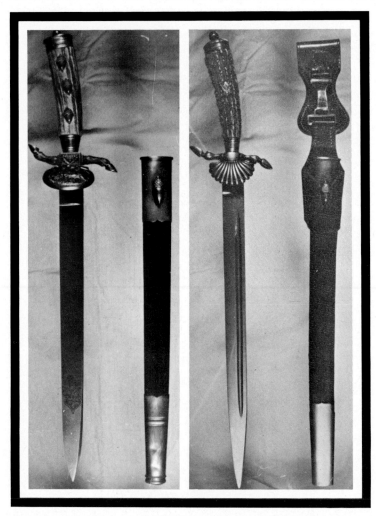

(LEFT) BASIC PATTERN HUNTING KNIFE. THIS SPECIMEN HAS BRASS HILT AND SCABBARD FITTINGS. (RIGHT) THIS REGULATION PIECE HAS THE UNETCHED BLADE AND A GROOVE, BOTH OF WHICH ARE NOT NORMALLY FOUND ON MOST REPRESENTATIVE PIECES.

the hilt fittings. The recurved crossguard was designed in the form of two deer legs. A fluted "clamshell" served to act as a stop when the blade was thrust into the dying animal....usually a wild boar or deer. The purchaser had the option of getting a plain blade or one etched on both sides with the hunting motif. Again depending on the manufacturer, the blade came with or without a fuller or "blood gutter". All metal fittings of the hilt were either nickel silver or nickel plated. The scabbard was dyed green leather with nickel plated, **externally** mounted fittings. The upper scabbard fitting had a button, often in the shape of an acorn, to allow the knife to be supported from a frog.

The deluxe hunting knife was basically the same as the regulation piece save for its length (34cms vs 49cms for the regulation) and the increased use of deluxe fittings. The cap, almost without exception, was heavily cast with a heavy concentration of oak leaves in relief. The crossguard had an oak leaf pattern added as well. The clamshell was the major point of departure, being a smooth convex with an Auerhahn decorating its face. The blade, which had a fuller, was normally etched on both sides with hunting scenes. The scabbard was green dyed leather with a

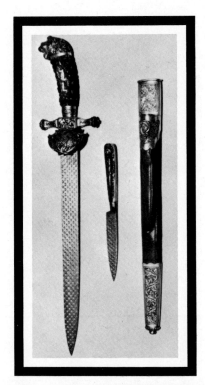

VERY ORNATE PRESENTATION HUNTING ASSOCIATION KNIFE WITH DAMASCUS BLADE. SUCH PIECES WERE SPECIFICALLY MADE FOR PRESENTATION TO HIGH RANKING MEMBERS OF THE ASSOCIATION, AND IN RECOGNITION OF SPECIAL DEEDS.

GÖRING, IN HIS CAPACITY AS NATIONAL HUNTING MASTER, DEVOTED A GREAT DEAL OF TIME TO ITS RELATED TASKS. THIS PIECE IS OF PRESENTATION QUALITY WITH AN INDIVIDUAL DESIGN WHICH CONFORMS TO THE BASIC PATTERN.

DELUXE NATIONAL HUNTING ASSOCIATION KNIFE MANUFACTURED BY THE EICKHORN FIRM.

A WIDE VARIETY OF UNOFFICIAL HUNTING KNIVES WERE USED BY WOODSMEN. BOTH OF THESE SPECIMENS HAVE A SWASTIKA INSIGNIA INLAID IN THE GRIP. THE PIECE TO THE RIGHT WAS MANUFACTURED BY THE BOKER FIRM.

pebbled grain finish. The externally mounted nickel plated scabbard fittings were deeply engraved with a hunting scene. The manner and conditions for wear were the same as for the regulation hunting knife.

Specially designed pieces, deviating somewhat from the basic pattern, were produced on order for presentation to members within the Association. Göring took an active hand in the designing of these, and he was the recipient of at least one beautifully designed hunting knife.

The Association continues to exist in Germany today performing the same functions that were performed during the Hitler regime. Members continue to carry the regulation hunting knife.... identical in design, but with a slight modification to the grip insigne. These postwar knives have been passed off as original Nazi era pieces by removing the insignia, and gluing a reproduction replacement insigne to the surface of the stag-horn grip. This also applies to the deluxe pattern hunting knife. It is very difficult to discern an original hunting knife from one of relatively current manufacture.

A GATHERING AT STATE FOREST SERVICE HEADQUARTERS.

STATE FOREST SERVICE
[STAATSFORSTDIENST]

The State Forestry Service consisted of civilian and military, state and private offices working toward a single aim. Its principal concern was the administration of all matters concerning conservation of the nation's timberland and wildlife. The state game laws and regulations which were imposed on the German Hunter's Association were prescribed by this organization. Hermann Göring enjoyed a dual status in this connection since he was the National Hunting Master, and was also responsible for the supervisory control of the State Forestry Service.

An administrative branch of the Army and Air Force was charged with the independent responsibilities for Forestry Service within their respective arms. The members of the Luftwaffe wore the official state uniform, a forest green with rich green velvet collar, with insignia having a green backing. A series of distinctive rank insignia was designed to distinguish the qualifications of the members. For members of the military who had been accustomed to the recognized military rank insignia, the new pattern of oak leaves took some getting used to. Instead of the members having a military designation, ranks were distinguished by the classifications as applied by the Forestry Service....trainees, assistant forester, senior forester and forester administrative officials. It would seem that the Luftwaffe exercised the greatest degree of control, with Göring responsible for the Service, and the highest ranking official being a Luftwaffe general officer.

The most powerful man in the wald or forest of Germany was the professional forester. He carried the recognized badge of his position, **267** and was considered the last word in matters of wildlife and conservation. The more wealthy landowner often hired a private highly trained forester to maintain the woods and guard against poachers on the expansive estate. There was a great deal of mutual cooperation between the private and state forestry official.... to the point of sharing a similar uniform and forestry knife.

As with the knives of the German Hunting Association, the knives of the State Forestry Service had been in existence for many years prior to the Hitler era. Some degree of standardization was achieved after 1933, but the pattern remained basically the same as the one which had come before. All foresters, regardless of affiliation, were authorized to wear the forestry knife. Slight variations in the quality were used as the feature to distinguish rank or position. Low ranking officials and assistant foresters qualified to wear the knife with the stag-horn grip only,

FORESTERS SOUND THE TRUMPET AT A BIRTHDAY GATHERING FOR THE HEAD OF THEIR SERVICE, HERMANN GÖRING.

while the ivory or white celluloid handles were reserved for the senior officials and foresters. Three grades of knots also served to distinguish the rank of the individual. The solid green knot was for the rank of Forstanwärter and above; silver with green stripes for the Förster and above; gold with green stripes for officials in the grade of Oberlandförster. The knot was normally tied about the guard, however, it could also be tied about the suspension frog.

Specifications were not flexible in the manner of wear since the piece was worn most of the time. It was worn suspended by either a brown or black leather frog. When an outer belt was not worn, a narrow green waist belt was normally worn under the tunic to be used in place of the cumbersome cross-strap. At no time could the knife be covered.

Forester officials of the military were also authorized to wear the Forestry knife. They customarily purchased a pattern of simple design to meet the basic needs of their position.

VARIATION KNIVES FOR LOW RANKING OFFICIALS AND ASSISTANT FORESTERS.

Within the limitations of their rank, forestry personnel could purchase the style of knife which suited their taste and finances.

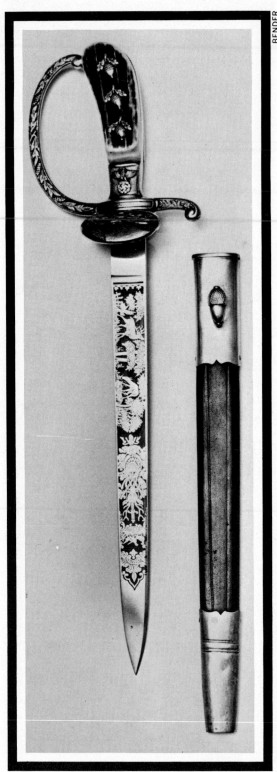

**FORESTRY KNIFE FOR LOW RANK-
ING OFFICIALS AND ASSISTANT
FORESTERS.**

No single knife can be singled out as descriptive of the State Forestry Service knife since there was no regulation design. Manufacturers provided a wide range of variations and options to be offered to the prospective customer. There were some similar points in the design which were characteristic of the Forestry knife.... all were finished in a gold colored metal (either brass base metal or gold plate), had a knuckle bow, a clamshell and an etched pattern on both sides of the blade. While there was no grip insigne for the Service, each handle was adorned with three fittings in the form of an acorn and leaves. The presence of a swastika in any form is extremely rare, but they did exist. The scabbards were leather base with externally mounted fittings. The higher quality pieces had a design either cast or engraved in the lower scabbard fitting. No set length can be attributed to the Forestry knife due to the wide range of variations available to the purchaser.

STATE FOREST SERVICE KNIVES AUTHORIZED FOR WEAR BY FORESTERS AND SENIOR OFFICIALS.

GÖRING IN COMPETITION TRAPSHOOTING.

GERMAN RIFLE ASSOCIATION
[DEUTSCHER SCHÜTZEN-VERBAND]

$\mathcal{S}$hooting clubs increased throughout Germany over a period of five centuries, but it was not until the 19th century that the sport became firmly entrenched. Shooting competition provided an outlet from the hard working routines of the farmers and villagers. It was not uncommon that a club from one town would challenge a club of another. At the meeting of the two clubs in friendly competition, a festival spirit would prevail. The trophies ranged from handmade plaques to very ornate silver cups. Regardless of the trophy, it was looked upon with pride and honor by the winning town.

When the shooting clubs became formalized throughout Germany, the German Rifle Association was formed with a president at its head. As an association, it was neither military nor political in nature. Gatherings, such as those generated by the shooting competitions, came to the attention of the Nazi leaders who wished to gain more votes for their party. Control, even partial, of an association claiming such wide-spread membership as the Rifle Association became the immediate concern of the Nazi leaders. The association was well, though loosely organized and leaned heavily toward uniform trappings and ceremonies. This made it a perfect vehicle for Nazi infiltration. After 1933, clubs throughout Germany underwent intensified Nazification.

The primary purpose of the association was to form a social alliance among persons interested in shooting, and to provide an outlet for competitive shooters in the form of rifle and pistol matches. It also served to foster interest in marksmanship and safe handling of weapons among the general populous. Non-competitive gatherings were largely social in nature. However, after the association became infiltrated by the Nazis, the gatherings took on an atmosphere of small political rallies.

A select regulation hanger was designed and approved in 1938 specifically for the Rifle Association. Heretofore, members were permitted to wear a wide variety of blades which were in keeping with the association uniform. When a standardized uniform was proposed, it was only natural that a standard blade design would follow. Wear of the newly designed hanger was authorized in the spring of 1939 as sufficient quantities were produced and made available. Requirements of the war soon reduced the number of shooting competitions until they all but disappeared. Membership was drawn off to serve in the military, ammunition was less available, and the efforts of the people were directed at something more constructive to support the war effort. As the association dwindled, demand for the hanger was thereby drastically reduced. Not long after its introduction, manufacture of the marksmanship hanger was either considerably reduced or curtailed. By 1943, the hanger was totally out of production.

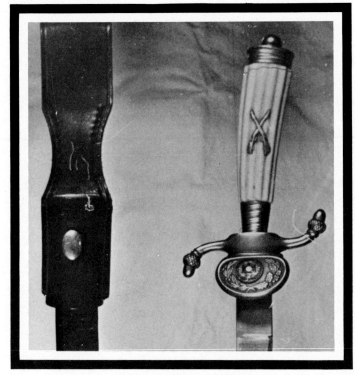

RIFLE ASSOCIATION HANGER

The hanger was authorized for all members of the German Rifle Association. Numerous blade manufacturers produced this piece during its brief life. It was purchased directly from a retailer. It became a standard part of the green uniform that was worn by association members at semi-official gatherings and other functions related to shooting ceremonies.

The regulation hanger normally measured an overall length of 54cms and was worn suspended externally from an outer belt by means of a bayonet-type leather frog, or from under the tunic by means of a cross-strap. The pommel, tang nut, ferrule, recurve crossguard and clamshell were either nickel or gold plate. The crossed rifle insigne which was fitted to the center front of the ribbed white celluloid handle was made from gold wash aluminum or brass. The clamshell bore the silver emblem of the Schützen Verband, which was retained by means of two pins through the shell. It is only on this organizational insigne that a swastika is found. The long single edged blade was etched with an elaborate pattern commemorating shooting and hunting. The scabbard was constructed of black leather with externally mounted nickel or gold plated metal fittings. There was no metal underbody to give structure to the scabbard body.

In spite of the number of representative pieces found in collections, a genuine specimen of the Regulation Rifle Association hanger remains a rather scarce item.

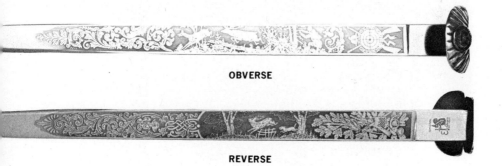

OBVERSE

REVERSE

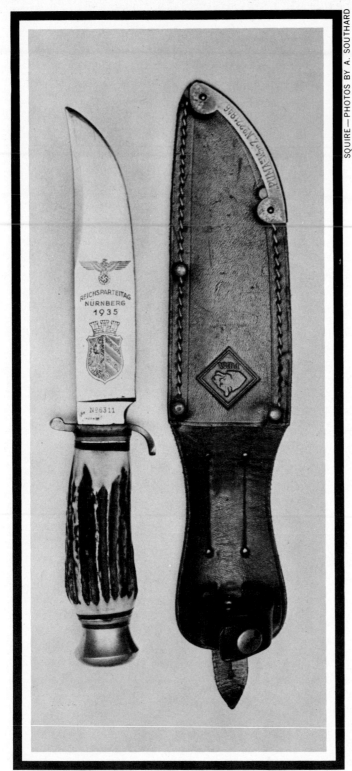

A HUNTING KNIFE
TOKEN FROM THE
1935 PARTY DAY
RALLY.

MINIATURE DAGGERS, LETTER OPENERS
AND TOKENS

The subject of miniature daggers is one that generates as many questions as answers. Due to the scarcity of individual pieces and the lack of original period data, many of the comments attributed to miniature daggers stem from observation rather than qualified knowledge. Miniature daggers have largely been classified as "salesman samples" or an advertising media. For those who classify these pieces as "salesman samples", the first question which comes to mind is, "Why isn't there a representative sample for each basic dagger produced by a firm .... or is there?" For those who might classify these solely as advertising media, the next question is, "Why doesn't each piece have a name or slogan on the blade or elsewhere?" The concluding assumption is they served both these purposes and more.

It is quite probable that a firm provided its salesmen with daggers in reduced scale to be shown to prospective customers. This allowed for ease of handling, and still provided the customer with a representative example of the firm's craftsmanship. The Alcoso firm, which had the widest range of scale pieces, is one such firm which may have employed this practice, while E & F Horster is but another.

The most common use of a miniature was to advertise the name of a commercial firm. The name and address of the firm was usually engraved on the blade, and given to the firm's select customer or prospective customer for use as a letter opener or decorative desk ornament. The name of the firm was drawn to the attention of the user with each use.

Lesser quality pieces, to be given as "favors", could be obtained from a Solingen blade firm in quantity and at a relatively low price. These low quality items normally did not bear the firm's name. About the only use these pieces could have had was for opening letters. These quantity favors did not have a scabbard and often did not bear any blade markings whatsoever. They were crudely cast with stamped blades, and were not the exact scale of the pieces they resembled.

Larger miniatures of very high quality were produced to exact scale. It was probably this pattern which served as the salesman sample. These could also be obtained through special order to be used as a presentation piece in recognition of any special achievement. A dedication was sometimes engraved on the blade and even the scabbard. It was not unusual for these scale miniatures to be mounted on a stand of some design, and be used as a desk weight or similar ornamentation. Speciments of these pieces have thus far been accounted for: Luftwaffe 1934 Model, Luftwaffe 1937 Model, Heer, Kriegsmarine (pre-1938), Kriegsmarine (1938 pattern),

 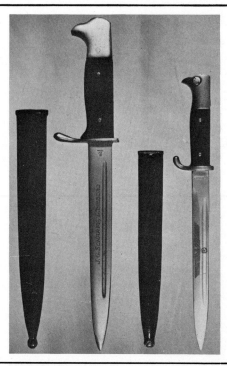

THE BASIC ARMY SERIES. L to R: PRESENTATION PATTERN MEASURING 23.5cms PRODUCED BY ALCOSO. THE SMALLEST OF MINIATURES PRODUCED BY E & F HORSTER, WITH WHITE HANDLE AND SILVER PLATED METAL FITTINGS MEASURES 19cms.

TWO DIFFERENT VERSIONS OF THE 84/98 DRESS BAYONET. THE ONE TO THE LEFT IS 23cms AND WAS PRODUCED BY SOLINGEN METALLWARENFABRIK STOCKER & CO. AS AN ADVERTISING GIFT, WHILE THE ONE ON THE RIGHT IS 18.5cms AND BEARS THE NATIONAL EMBLEM ON THE FRONT AND A FIRM'S ADDRESS ON THE REVERSE RICASSO.

Regulation Hunting Knife, RAD Leader, and 84/98 Dress Bayonet. This listing excludes any miniature swords which were also produced during the period. Other pieces have been alluded to but never encountered, while additional specimens have been recently produced.

No miniature hangers are known to have been produced, however, a portepee could be purchased in two sizes....one for the smallest of miniature daggers, and one for the scaled pieces normally used for presentation purposes.

The area which adds the greatest range of blades for which there was no standardization were the tokens given or sold at the numerous political rallies to raise funds for the Party treasury. A wide assortment of blades were made available....from the crude inexpensive letter opener to the very ornately etched or engraved hunting knife. One of the favorite tokens of the times was the pocket knife. This served a functional purpose as well as carrying a message for the Nazi Party.

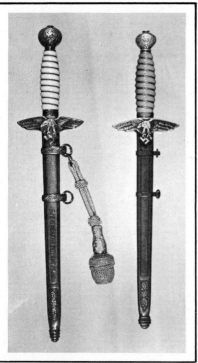

THE BASIC LUFTWAFFE SERIES. L to R: PRESENTATION PATTERN 1937 MODEL MEASURING 25.5cms PRODUCED BY ALCOSO. THE SCABBARD IS ENGRAVED "R.O.A. LEHRGANG 1939." SMALL SIZE MINIATURE MEASURING 23.5cms PRODUCED BY SMF.

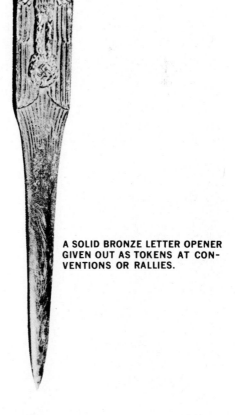

A SOLID BRONZE LETTER OPENER GIVEN OUT AS TOKENS AT CONVENTIONS OR RALLIES.

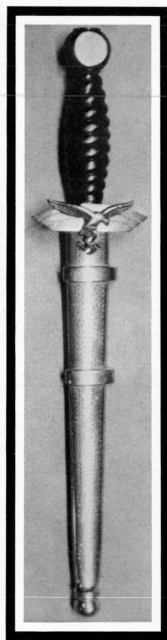

GEORGE LAMBERTSON

DAVIS

PEN KNIFE GIVEN AS A TOKEN DURING HITLER'S STRUGGLE FOR POWER. THE CAST HANDLES ARE MADE OF BRONZE WITH DETAIL IN RELIEF. THIS SPECIMEN WAS MADE BY HUGO LINDER DELTAWERK, SOLINGEN.

KEN WARD

McCARTHY

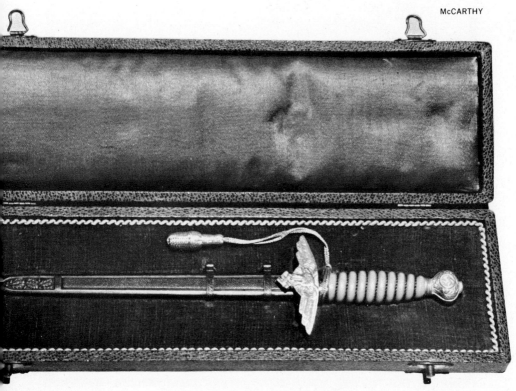

CASED MINIATURE LUFTWAFFE DAGGER

THIS SS MAN PLACES HIS "TRENCH KNIFE" WHERE IT IS READILY ACCESSIBLE.

BAYONETS AND FIGHTING KNIVES

German military men were steeped in the tradition of self defense, and the ability to defend their homeland was well learned. Because of this professional attitude, wartime regulations required that personnel be armed at all times when in a uniformed status, and not in a secure, closed building. When not armed with a rifle, pistol, or similar weapon, active duty personnel were required to be armed with the blade sidearm. Under other than combat conditions, that sidearm was either the service or dress bayonet Model 84/98. The soldier in combat was often armed with a fighting knife....either issued or of his own selection, in addition to the bayonet.

The purpose of the sidearm was for use as a close combat weapon. In the case of the 84/98 bayonet, it served as an extension to the Mauser rifle, and was used as a thrusting weapon. The philosophy of the bayonet was a very real one to the foot soldier engaged in close combat. His ability to use the bayonet often meant the difference between life and death.

BAYONET 84/98

The following is the size and weight data of the 84/98 bayonet:

Length with sheath ....15.9 inches
Length without sheath ....15.2 inches
Weight with sheath .... 1.3 lbs.
Weight without sheath .... .9 lbs.

The bayonet was worn at all times when the individual was in uniform. It was worn suspended from the waist belt by means of a black

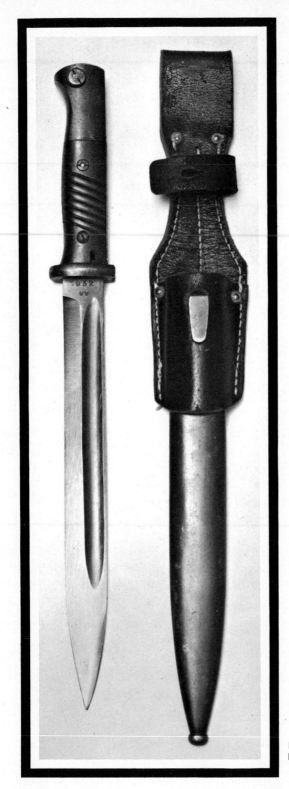

NOTE BAYONET MARKINGS
ON REVERSE OF SIDEARM.

MODEL 84/98
MAUSER BAYONET

leather frog, and was strapped to the entrenching tool when the full field equipment was worn.

The actual bayonet consists of the blade, grip section and pommel. The blade, constructed of blued tempered steel, is straight, ending in a double-edged point. The back of the blade is flat. A groove and cutting-edge bevel are milled into each side. The groove is often referred to as a "blood gutter". The cutting-edge of the bayonet was an exception to the regulation (A.H.M. 37, Sec. 8, Para. 164) that stated a sidearm would only be sharpened at the time of mobilization.

The upper portion of the back of the grip has a length-wise cutout for the rifle's stacking rod when the bayonet is fitted to the rifle. Moisture, dust, etc., that enters the grip is removed through the matching notches in the grip plates. The upper end of the grip forms the pommel. Its front is a blunted beak, and on the back are two mounting surfaces for the bayonet lug. In the pommel are the hole for the cylindrical part of the catch pin, the milling and cutout for the engagement part of the catch pin, the socket for the bayonet lug spigot and the hole for the rifle's stacking rod. The grip section also includes the upward extension of the blade, referred to as the tang (the original German refers to this portion as the hilt).

The handle consists of the grip section with pommel, crossguard, guard plate, both grip plates and grip screws with slotted nuts. The blued steel crossguard has a cutout to slide it on over the blade, two holes for rivets and a rounded notch in its back side for the barrel of the firearm when the bayonet is in fixed position. Two holes are bored through the tang above the groove and cutting-edge bevel of the blade, and the crossguard is then joined to the blade with two counter-sunk rivets.

The guard plate, a blued steel stamping, has two spring flaps with two holes for the grip screws that slide over the grip section. The folds protect the grips from sideward blows. It is secured in position by the grip screws and slotted nuts.

The grooved grip plates made of bakelite or walnut are for holding the bayonet. Each has two holes for the grip screws that are countersunk for the screw heads and slotted nuts. At the lower end of the grip plates are notches so that moisture can escape, and dust, etc., be removed. The grip plates, along with the guard plate, are affixed to the grip section by two grip screws (with tapered threads) with blued steel slotted nuts. The grip screws are installed so that the slotted nuts are on the left (outer) side. There was no particular time when the grip plates

285

MORTAR CREW IN POLAND, 1939.

changed from wood to plastic as both were utilized during the duration of
the war.

A catch pin with retainer spring and catch pin nut is housed in the
seat and hole in the pommel, and serve to secure the bayonet to the bayonet lug of the rifle when the lug is engaged in the bayonet notch. The
blued steel catch pin consists of a cylindrical section threaded for the
catch pin nut and a perpendicular four-faced catch, which is housed in
the catch pin cut-out in the pommel channel. A coil steel spring retainer slides over the cylindrical portion of the catch pin, and seats on one
side in the hole in the pommel and on the other against the catch pin nut.
The catch pin nut joins the catch pin to the pommel under tension from
the compressed retainer spring.

The bayonet sheath is constructed of blued seamless drawn steel
tubing or rolled and welded sheet steel. It is straight, fitted with a hard-
soldered-on button at its lower tapered end. A carrying hook is riveted
and hard-soldered to the left (outer) side. The carrying hook may be of
one piece, or consist of an upper plate hard-soldered to a pin with a lower plate. At the upper rear edge of the sheath's narrow side is the threaded hole for the mouth-piece screw. The blued steel screw with tapered
threads secures the mouth-piece in the sheath. Early production 84/98's
have a hard-soldered-on threaded reinforcement for the mouth-piece screw
on the rear narrow side.

The mouth-piece consists of the mouth-piece ring, and a pair of steel spring strips each riveted to a wide side of the mouth-piece ring with a rivet. The steel spring strips serve to retain the bayonet in the scabbard.

A comment is necessary at this point concerning service and dress bayonets that appear to be the same as the basic configuration of those pieces used during the second war era, but in fact are not. Pioneer personnel during the First World War made extensive use of bayonets with a sawtooth back. This sawtooth backing was used to saw down stakes holding barbed wire, in preparation for assaults into the trenches. However, the sawtooth edge did not have an application in the second war, and was not carried over in the manufacture of Nazi era military service bayonets. Dress bayonets having three grip retaining pins instead of two, or with hilts painted black, are of pre-1933 manufacture, and were not normally carried over for use after that time.

CARE AND MAINTENANCE

Care of the bayonet was prescribed by regulations.[1] Sidearms could only be disassembled by trained ordnance personnel at the direction of the responsible ordnance officer or ordnance non-commissioned officer. They were to be cleaned each time they were used, being sure to remove perspiration, moisture and dirt. The blued portions were to be carefully cleaned to avoid damage to the protective blue coating. All parts were to be lightly oiled, with the wood grips being treated with linseed oil. Rust spots could not be removed from the blued areas or unfinished steel parts, but were repeatedly oiled. Cleaning was not to begin until the sheath had reached the surrounding temperature. Removal of the catch pin and sheath mouth-piece for cleaning was forbidden. Pulling and hammering nails with the pommel or guard plate of the bayonet, wood splitting, opening containers and the like with the blade were also forbidden. Since a soldier in the field uses those utensils at his disposal to get the job done, it was obvious that this latter restriction was ignored.

Issued bayonets were the responsibility of the individual, to be stored in his wall locker, whereas unissued bayonets were secured in the unit arms room as prescribed in H. Dv. 498, Annex 2.

---

[1] Die Seitenwaffen, (Manual for Ordnance and Supply Personnel; as of April 12, 1940), (Berlin: 1941).

Privately purchased sidearms were the responsibility of the individual, but also conformed to existing regulations as pertained to the bayonet.

Unusable bayonet parts or those declared a loss were replaced from authorized stock. However, it was necessary that replacement parts were authenticated with a fault slip. Unserviceable bayonets were replaced through service channels.

BAYONET MARKINGS

The principal marking on a service bayonet is the serial number. The Army and Air Force utilized the same numbering system for accountability. On January 1 of each year, the serial numbers reverted back to one. A production series was numbered from 1 to 9,999. The 10,000th item started with 1a to 9,999a; 20,000th item started with 1b to 9,999b, etc., going through the alphabet until such time a production series was completed. At no time did production ever reach a point where a given series exceeded the entire alphabet, as production rarely exceeded 260,000 units of a given item. The serial number was stamped in the ricasso immediately next to the crossguard, and on the sheath near the mouthpiece. Navy bayonets carry two numbers. . . . the standard Army style accountability number, not exceeding four digits, and a Navy accountability number stamped into the guard. This number is preceded by a "N" and usually followed by a letter of the alphabet. The date of manufacture was normally stamped into the flat edge of the blade near the guard regardless of service. A wappen-amt was stamped into the pommel and the sheath button. The design of the wappen-amt underwent a change in approximately 1937 from the old style to the Nazi style mark. Periodically, manufacturers' trademarks are found on the reverse of the ricasso, but this mark was normally reserved for bayonets designated for export.

MODEL 98 PATTERN DRESS SIDEARM

An optional dress sidearm was introduced for the military forces to be worn following normal duty hours. It was worn with the walking-out dress uniform, suspended from the outer belt by means of a black leather frog (brown in the case of the Luftwaffe personnel, and white for SS personnel on parade). The shorter blade length (20cms) was worn by NCO personnel, while the longer blade (25cms) was worn by enlisted men. In both cases, a distinctive colored portepee could be worn attached to the suspension frog by members of the Army and Air Force.

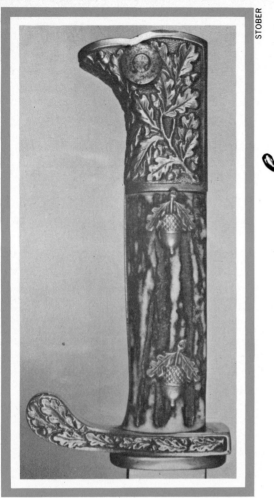

THIS EXCEPTIONALLY FINE QUALITY DRESS SIDE-
ARM WAS MANUFACTURED BY THE FIRM OF PAUL
WEYERSBERG. THE CROSSGUARD AND POMMEL ARE
SCULPTURED WITH AN OAK LEAF PATTERN. BRASS
ACORNS AND OAK LEAVES DISGUISE THE GRIP RIV-
ETS RETAINING THE GENUINE STAG HORN GRIPS.

20cms
DRESS SIDEARM

25cms
DRESS SIDEARM

While the sidearm resembled a bayonet in every respect, it could not be classified as such since it could not be attached to a rifle. The bayonet lug groove would indicate that it could. However, the groove was not large enough to fit the standard Mauser rifle.

Even though the hilt and blade were nickel plated (in some cases, blades were chrome plated), there existed other major differences between the sidearm and the service bayonet. The checkered plastic grip plates were normally riveted rather than screwed on. An exception to this were the patterns produced by the firm of E. Pack & Söhne. The major identifiable difference was the single upward curved extension of the crossguard on the dress sidearm.

Many options were left to the purchaser when it came time to procure a dress sidearm. Grip plates were offered in plastic, leather, wood and genuine or imitation stag-horn. The scabbard could be either the standard black sheet steel, or a brown or black leather with externally mounted nickel plated fittings. The blade could be purchased with a saw-tooth back at added cost. One option that was particularly appealing to the soldier was the wide range of blade etchings that were made available to him. These patterns were developed around the basic dedication "Zur Erinnerung an meine Dienstzeit" (To the memory of my service time). The design of the etching often reflected the brance of service of the wearer. Designs were often purchased for both sides of the blade, usually with the second reflecting the wearer's unit. An insignia of branch of service could also be placed on the face of the pommel as well. Depending on the pattern or manufacturer, etched designs were finished in either a plain backing, or a backing in blue or black to accentuate the design.

THIS OTHERWISE STANDARD (20cms) NCO DRESS BAYONET BEARS THE ETCHED DEDICATION "EHRE, KRAFT, FREIHEIT" (HONOR, STRENGTH, FREEDOM), WHICH IS THE SECONDARY MOTTO OF THE SA. IT IS POSSIBLE THAT THIS BAYONET WAS CARRIED BY MEMBERS OF THE 271st INFANTRY REGIMENT "FELDHERRN-HALLE."

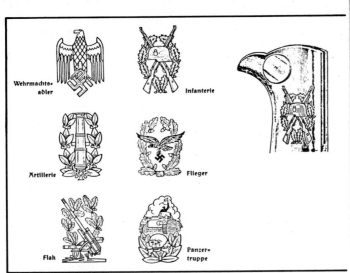

A VARIETY OF BRANCH INSIGNIA COULD BE ENGRAVED IN THE POMMEL OF THE DRESS SIDEARM.

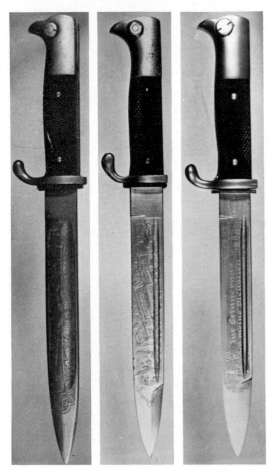

SPECIMENS OF THE SHORT BLADED ETCHED DRESS SIDEARMS. WHEN A FALSE EDGE IS EMPLOYED, A NARROW FULLER IS INCORPORATED INTO THE BLADE DESIGN.

BAYONET KNOTS (TRODDELN)

These knots constitute those worn by enlisted men of infantry and artillery regiments. The top designation (company) is for infantry and the lower designation (battery) is for artillery.

1st BATTALION

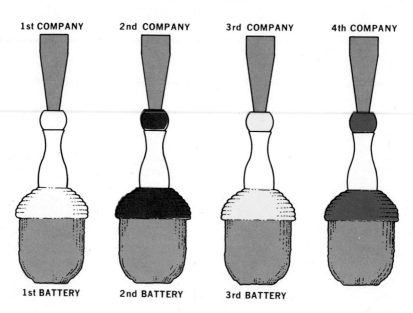

1st COMPANY   2nd COMPANY   3rd COMPANY   4th COMPANY

1st BATTERY   2nd BATTERY   3rd BATTERY

2nd BATTALION

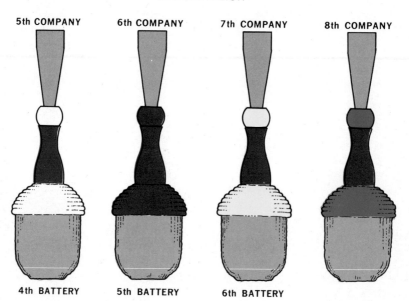

5th COMPANY   6th COMPANY   7th COMPANY   8th COMPANY

4th BATTERY   5th BATTERY   6th BATTERY

3rd BATTALION

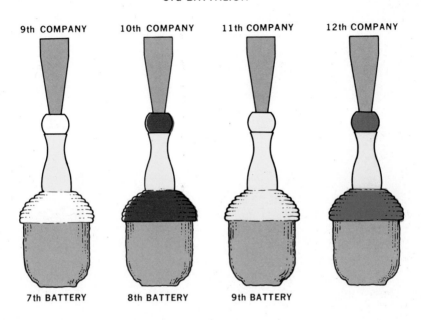

9th COMPANY 10th COMPANY 11th COMPANY 12th COMPANY

7th BATTERY 8th BATTERY 9th BATTERY

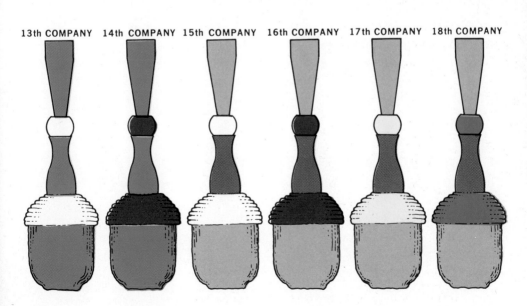

13th COMPANY 14th COMPANY 15th COMPANY 16th COMPANY 17th COMPANY 18th COMPANY

A green or red felt pad, placed in the cutout portion of the pommel, served only to decorate the dress sidearm. It also amplified the
fact that the piece was for dress purposes only, and not intended to fit
on a rifle.

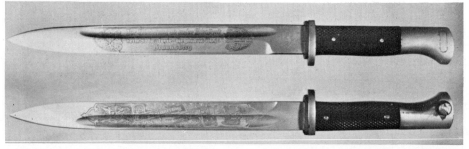

THE M 84/98 DRESS SIDEARM ON TOP INDICATES THAT THIS PATTERN WAS NOT RESTRICT-
ED TO PIONEER UNITS SINCE THE ETCHED UNIT DESIGNATION ON THE REVERSE SIDE OF THE
BLADE IS FOR THAT OF THE INFANTRY REGIMENT No. 24 STATIONED AT BRAUNSBERG.

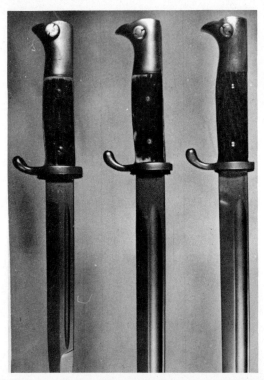

NICKEL PLATED DRESS SIDEARMS WERE USED BY MEMBERS OF THE ARMY, AIR FORCE, POLICE, AND FIRE DEPARTMENT. GRIPS MADE OF GENUINE OR ARTIFICIAL STAG-HORN WERE AN OPTION MADE AVAILABLE TO THE PURCHASER. THE GRIP TO THE RIGHT IS MADE OF WOOD GROOVED TO SIMULATE STAG HORN.

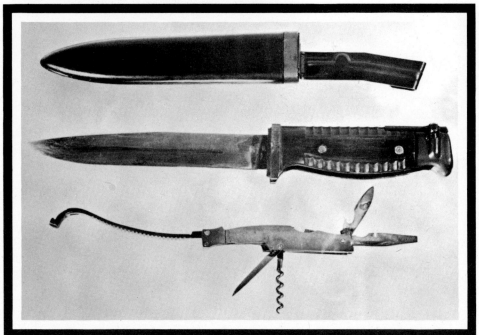

THIS GERMAN CARBINE BAYONET WAS DEVELOPED IN 1942 FOR USE AS A COMBINATION BAYONET FOR THE KAR 98 AND AS A CLOSE COMBAT AND UTILITY KNIFE. MANUFACTURED BY THE EICKHORN FIRM, IT SAW EXTREMELY LIMITED DISTRIBUTION. THE COMBINATION TOOL FIT INTO AND BECAME AN INTEGRAL PART OF THE GRIP ASSEMBLY. ON JULY 1, 1943, THE BAYONET WAS GIVEN THE DESIGNATION S(SEITENGEWEHR)42.

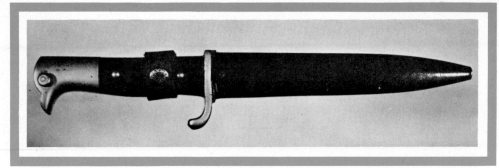

PIECES OF THIS DESIGN ARE OFTEN ERRONEOUSLY ATTRIBUTED TO BE THE YOUTH HONOR BAY-
ONET. HOWEVER, THIS DESIGN WAS DEVELOPED FOR AND WORN BY OFFICER PERSONNEL DUR-
ING WWI. IT WAS CARRIED OVER FOR GENERAL USE AS A FIGHTING KNIFE DURING THE SECOND
WAR.

(LEFT) THIS WWI PATTERN CLOSE COMBAT KNIFE WAS CARRIED OVER FOR USE DURING THE SECOND
WORLD WAR. THE BASIC DESIGN WAS RELATIVELY UNCHANGED, AND ONLY THE TRADEMARK DATES
THE PIECE. THE GRIP WITH THE DIAGONAL GROOVES IS NORMALLY CHARACTERISTIC OF THOSE USED
IN WWI. (RIGHT) TWO PATTERNS OF CLOSE COMBAT KNIVES CARRIED OVER FROM THE FIRST WORLD
WAR.

CLOSE COMBAT KNIVES

In hand-to-hand combat, the edge went to the combatant who was better trained and adequately armed. The well trained professional soldier saw to it that he had the edge by carrying a close combat knife (also referred to as a trench knife, which was a name given to it during the trench warfare of World War I). Close combat knives were a basic item in the unit's stock, and were issued to the individual. In some cases, the individual preferred to select his own fighting knife. The basic issue knife was constructed of a one piece blade and tang, fitted with two wood grips normally riveted in three places for added strength. The blade was double edged, with the second edge running halfway up the top portion of the blade. A short metal guard provided the necessary weight in arriving at a closely balanced knife. The sheath was constructed of seamless

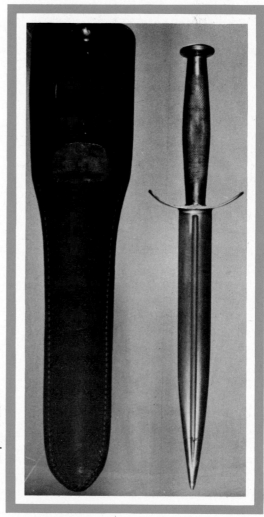

THOUGH EXPERTLY MACHINED, THIS FIGHTING KNIFE GIVES THE APPEARANCE OF BEING HAND-MADE. THE ONLY INDICATION THAT THIS IS NOT A MADE UP SPECIMEN IS THE ORDNANCE WAPPEN-AMP STAMPED INTO THE LEATHER OF THE SCABBARD.

drawn steel tubing or rolled and welded sheet steel painted black. A
spring clip was normally riveted to the back, allowing the wearer to fit
it to his belt, clip it to his boot, or some other portion of his uniform
which would allow for ready access. It was not unusual for combat knives
to be handmade or converted from some other blade. Since the piece
was a working tool, the blade was normally honed to a fine cutting edge.
Many of the close combat knives used in World War II were blades which
were designed and manufactured for use in the preceding war.

THESE WERE THE BASIC ISSUE ORDNANCE FIGHTING KNIVES OF THE WEHRMACHT.

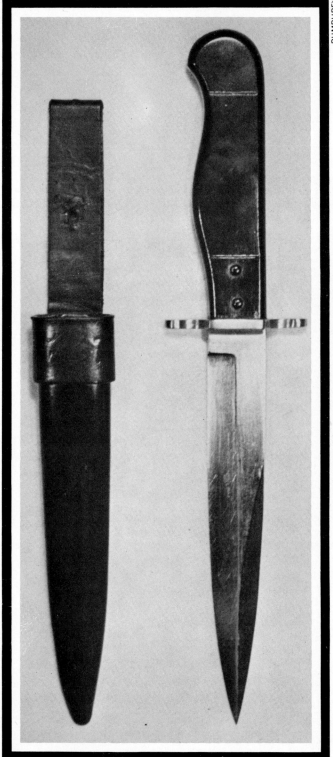

THIS PIECE HAS THE DESIGNA
TION "NAHKÄMPFER-D.R.G.M."
(CLOSE FIGHTING KNIFE) ON
THE RICASSO. FITTED FOR A
RIFLE, IT ACTUALLY FIXES TO
A RIFLE.

VARIATION
CLOSE COMBAT KNIFE

299

GERMAN PARACHUTISTS ON CRETE, 1941

UTILITY KNIFE

Germany's last major airborne assault during the Ardennes Offensive in 1944, was a night operation to secure bridges for the advancing armor. This was the first night operation attempted by German airborne troops. The aircraft became so separated during their flight to the designated drop zones that the descending paratroopers were scattered over five countries. The operation, born of desperation, ended in total failure, with many of these elite troops either killed or captured. It was a poor final showing for the nation which had pioneered the art of vertical envelopment.

The German paratrooper was a respected fighter, and his equipment was a prized trophy for the infantryman who opposed him on the ground. The Utility Knife, a distinctive piece of the paratrooper's gear, was especially prized.

This general purpose Utility Knife was introduced in the Summer of 1937 for issue to Luftwaffe and Army paratroops, [1] and to Luftwaffe air crewmen. For air crews it was part of the survival equipment issued in case the aircraft was forced down. To the paratrooper, who put his life of the line every time he jumped, the knife had greater significance. With it he might have to cut a fouled suspension line to make his 'chute open, or sever the riser if he found himself hanging from a tree. To him, his "gravity knife" could mean the difference between life and death.

---

[1] The Army airborne troops were transferred to the Luftwaffe in 1938.

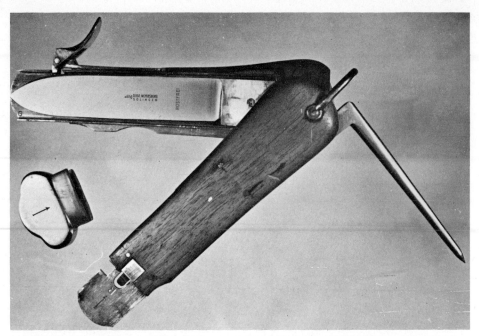

DISASSEMBLED NICKEL PLATED UTILITY KNIFE MADE BY WEYERSBERG. THE BLADE MAY BE LIFTED OUT OF THE TRAY WHEN THE HANDLE IS OPENED. "ROSTFREI" MARKING MEANS THE BLADE IS MADE OF STAINLESS STEEL.

The knives were produced under military contract by various Solingen blade firms. Variations in the knives, such as blue or bright nickel exterior finishes, and whether they were takedown or non-takedown patterns, apparently stem from the source of manufacture. The knife remained basically the same in all cases.

The knife was designed for use with one hand so it could meet any emergency requirements. To extend the blade, the locking lever is unfolded and depressed to release spring tension from the blade. Turning the knife downward allows the blade to slide out of the handle, where it is locked in position by releasing the locking lever. The way the blade slid into position earned it its classification and common name of "gravity knife". Its official designation was, however, Kappmesser (Cap Knife) ....deriving its name from the protective cap at the end.

With blade extended, the knife measured 25.5cms. It had a swivel ring at the rear for attaching a lanyard, to prevent loss of the knife in case it was dropped. Folded into the handle was a pick used to splice the single riser from which the paratrooper was suspended after his parachute opened. A pair of plain wooden handles were pinned to each side of the metal blade tray. The locking lever simply cammed the lock spring

NICKEL PLATED UTILITY KNIFE AT LEFT IN COMPARISON WITH THE BLUED VERSION AT RIGHT. NOTE LUFTWAFFE EAGLE IN WREATH NEAR RICASSO OF BLUED VERSION; THE SUPPLY PURCHASE CODE "RB Nr. 0/0561/0020" IS ON THE OTHER SIDE OF THE BLADE.

out of engagement with the blade when depressed. This leaf-type lock spring is easily broken, and continuous use should be avoided. The takedown version has a small square button in the handle next to the front cap. When depressed, blade unextended, the cap may be pulled off, handle swung to the side, and the blade lifted out of the tray. When reassembling, align the arrow on the cap with the arrow on the side of the blade tray. Blades bear various markings, ranging from the maker's trademark to only the supply contract number.

Since the Utility Knife was worn every time an aircraft crewman made a flight, or a paratrooper put on his field gear, mint specimens are difficult to find. As indicated by its name, this knife was designed for use, not appearance.

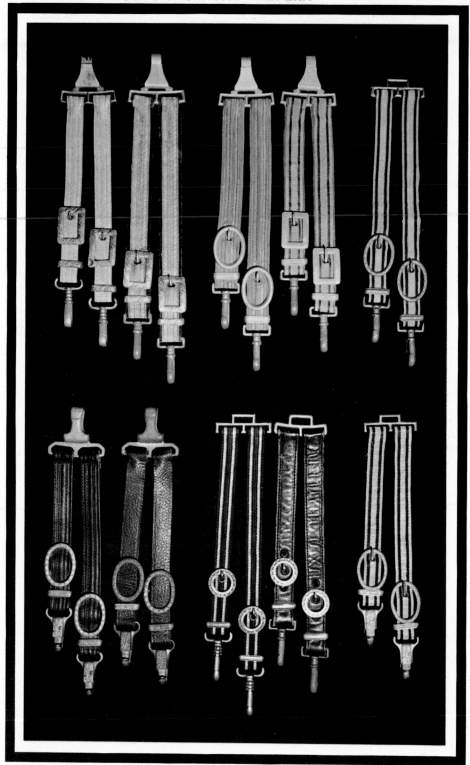

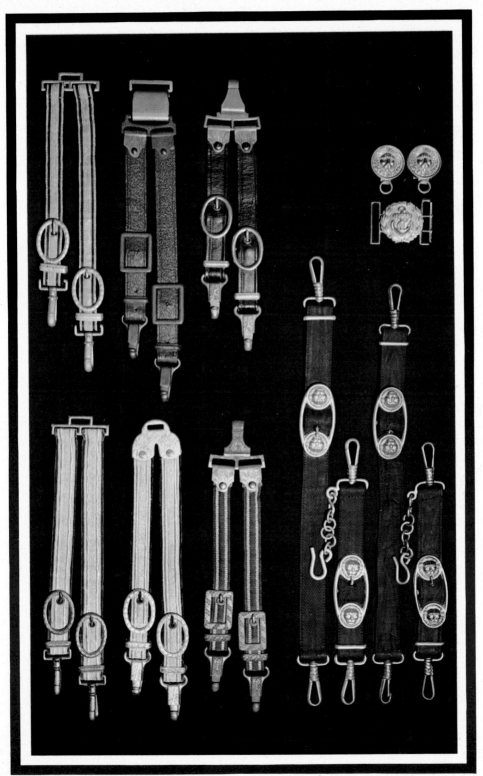

305

(Hanger descriptions on next page)

DAGGER HANGERS

(A) GOLD DIPLOMATIC/GOVERNMENT OFFICIAL
(B) SILVER DIPLOMATIC/GOVERNMENT OFFICIAL
(C) RED CROSS LEADER
(D) SOCIAL WELFARE LEADER
(E) WATER PROTECTION POLICE LEADER
(F) LUFTSCHUTZ PRESIDENT/VICE PRESIDENT
(G) LUFTSCHUTZ LEADER
(H) TeNo LEADER (DRESS)
(I) TeNo LEADER (SERVICE)
(J) RAILWAY POLICE LEADER
(K) LAND CUSTOMS OFFICIAL
(L) LABOR CORPS LEADER
(M) HITLER YOUTH LEADER
(N) ARMY GENERAL OFFICER
(O) ARMY OFFICER
(P) LUFTWAFFE OFFICER
(Q) NAVY ADMINISTRATION OFFICER (ALUMINUM)
(R) NAVY LINE OFFICER (GOLD)

Miscellaneous

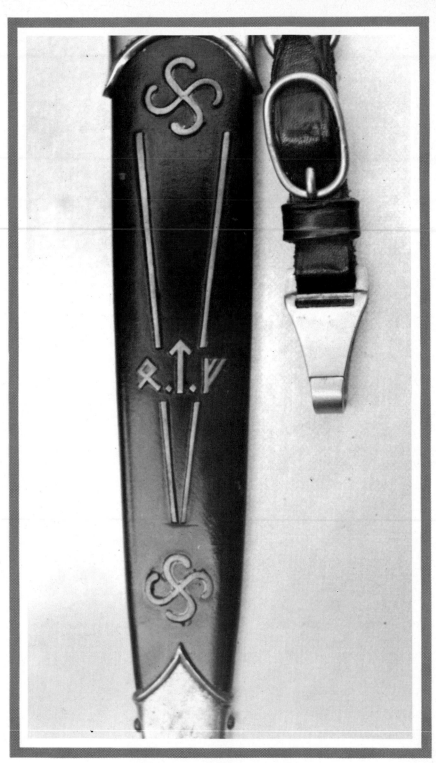

NOTE RUNIC SYMBOLS ON SS SCABBARD.

NAZI PAGANISM AND THE RUNIC SYMBOL

Thule was believed to be a continent.... another world to which only the select few were admitted. It shares a place in history parallel to another of the great undiscovered realms of the world, Atlantis, the lost continent. The belief in the existence of this strange domain of Thule is recorded as early as the second century BC. The precise whereabouts of this lost land are not known, but it was believed to lie in the area that is bordered by Norway, Iceland and the North of Scotland. The only present day references to this strange land are to be found in two towns, one on the East coast of Norway, and the other on the South side of Iceland, both bearing the name, Thule. The important point to note is that Thule represents the home of the spirit of Valhalla, the traditional Viking "Other World" of legend to which the spirits of the great went when they died. When the Viking races lost their power, and other nations became dominant, the beliefs in Thule were still carried on. In the twentieth century, new followers of this belief rose to the acceptance of this world where only the superior were admitted. Adolf Hitler and his followers felt they were among those who were predestined to this fate.

There is no doubt that the Nazis held a belief in Valhalla, astrology and occultism. It was belief of astrology that prompted Rudolf Hess to fly to England in 1940 with the intention of halting the war with Britain for, as he believed, it was favored in the stars that Germany and England keep peace. The obsession of the Nazi mind with astrology was more than just a passing whim. They made use of a special department within Goebbles' Ministry of Propaganda called AMO... Astrology, Metaphysics and Occultism... to further their beliefs. The purpose of this propaganda department was to issue proclamations stating the greatness of the Führer's future as promised by the stars. These statements were presented all over the world through the media of astrological magazines. Millions of people beyond the boundries of the Greater German Reich came to believe that it was Hitler's destiny to rule the world. It was the astute Dr. Goebbles who knew that once people had read the written word, they would believe, and having people believe in their system was more than winning half the battle.

Having formed reasonable grounds for acceptance by the Nazis of Thule, the next step in the belief of occultism is logical. It must be recognized that the symbolic practices of Freemasons take on the pattern not unlike occult practices. In both cases, the use of symbols, signs and mystic regalia is prominent. When the Nazi Party acceded to power in 1933, one of the first proclamations issued by the new government was the abolition of Freemason Societies within the Reich. The motive behind this was to prevent the formation of secret society meetings which, if politically inclined, could plot against the governing power. Distrust of Freemasons by official bodies was not unique to the Nazis, as for centuries the Catholic Church had waged an unceasing war against the society. The Nazi Government succeeded in terminating the activities of the Freemasons during the entire Hitler era. In its stead, a more bizarre and clandestine organization rose up....the Thule Society.

The origin of the Thule Society extends as far back as 1917, when it was formed in Munich by a Rudolf Freiherr von Sebbottendorf, a German of Turkish extraction. Among the activities of the Thule Society, and apart from pseudo-religious ones, was the condoning of anti-Semitic and racial practices. The society grew, and with financial aid managed to buy a newspaper, the "Münchener Beobachter", and through this medium expounded its manifesto of race hatred. Here was a society which kindled beliefs similar to those of Hitler and his followers. Understandably, the connection between the two organizations grew. The society was completely under the wing of Nazism when, in 1934, von Sebbottendorf fled from Germany. His exit is believed to have been precipitated by the June Purge. With von Sebbottendorf no longer in control, the Thule Society became the perfect organ for the Viking spirit revived under the sign of the swastika.

RUNIC SYMBOLS

The word rune is frequently associated with matters pertaining to secrecy or mysticism. In fact, the word is synonymous with the mystic arts. The basis for this comparison is that the use of runes was applied especially to dedications which could only be read by the person to whom it was intended, or by one conversant in the art of its application. Such was the complexity of the renderings to which runes applied themselves

that present-day students of the subject have a new name for it...crypto-
grams. This description of the subject is understandable when it is
understood that rune messages were frequently written backwards, and
formulated in riddles.

The use of runes goes as far back as the second century AD, and
quite possibly even further. The runic alphabet is based on three early
alphablets, which had a content ranging from 16 to 27 letters. All three
alphabets had a common feature, that being the first seven letters of each
were F, U, T, H, A, R. K. Because of this, the language of the runes
is frequently called Futhark. Usage of Futhark runes have been noted on
many items, the most common of which are stones and monuments. Because the art of rune writing was carried almost exclusively by the Vikings, the most common areas for the location of rune-stones are Germany and Scandinavia. Perhaps more incredible is the fact that rune-
stones have also been discovered in Scotland, the Orkneys, Iceland, Green-
land, Canada and the United States. This gives serious grounds as a basis for the thesis used by historians who subscribe to the belief that it was
the Vikings who first discovered the Americas. The common feature of
these discoveries is that in all cases the rune messages were written as
cryptograms.

A more interesting development in runic culture was the formulation of a numerical system, which was advanced enough to permit the
formation of figures containing up to four digits. This permitted the use
of such figures to be based on a common origin of four squares of eight
segments each, allowing the numerals from 1 to 9,999 to be incorporated into a design. The use of this numbering system was certainly used
by the Nazis, and it is reasonable to suppose that the application of this
and the Futhark alphabet was applied only to subjects which were intended to be either clandestine or further the Nazi myth.

DAGGERS AND THE RUNE
In the minds of the German designers, runes were incorporated into the design of virtually every Nazi dagger which was introduced for wear.
The symbol most often used was the swastika, which actually is not a
rune. However, since it received such prominence after being designated the official symbol of the Nazi movement, it readily fit into the Nordic
myth. Two very obvious runes, the sigrunen (⚡⚡) and the SA (Ⲁ) rune,
are found in the form of grip inlays on the daggers belonging to the two
largest formations of the NSDAP. The sunwheel (⊕) was used in the design of the 1934 Pattern Luftwaffe Fliegerdolch. On rare occassions,
entire blade inscriptions were made up from runic symbols.

NOTE TIGER TRADEMARK ON BLADE OF LABOR CORPS SUBORDINATE'S HEWER.

DAGGER MARKINGS

Periodically daggers are encountered without any external markings whatsoever. This is by no means rare, unless a dagger that is supposed to have a motto is found without one. ... such pieces void of markings are uncommon. Blades normally have, as a minimum, the manufacturer's trademark, but more often than not, there is a series of additional markings which will greatly assist the collector in making proper identification. Markings are like fingerprints as they relate to a given series or set of circumstances which aid in identification.

TRADEMARKS

There were over a hundred firms devoted to the manufacture of blades in Germany during the Nazi era. Most were located in or around the city of Solingen in the Wupper Valley. Part of the Ruhr complex, the raw materials such as iron, aluminum and lead, was abundantly available to support the blade industry. Firms normally set their trademark in the reverse of the blade near the tang to show pride of craftsmanship. Adding the trademark was accomplished by means of a die-strike or acid etching. Each firm had their own registered trademark, and sometimes a series of trademarks. Trademarks were expressed in the form of a name, abbreviation, number or insigne. It was not unusual for trademarks to change. For example, the firm of Carl Eickhorn had three different oval marks centered about the squirrel design during the period 1933-1934. This was changed to the upright squirrel with sword in 1936, followed by two more changes in 1941 and later.

313

PERIOD 1933-1934	PERIOD 1934-1935	PERIOD LATE 1935- LATE 1941	PERIOD LATE 1941 TO DISCONTINUATION OF DAGGER PRO- DUCTION IN 1944.

RZM CONTROL MARKS

By October, 1934, the Nazi Party Department of Ordnance or Reichs-zeugmeisterei (RZM) was established to exercise controls over the manu-facture and letting of contracts involving production of Party-related items From late 1934 to 1936, political form blades bore the RZM code mark, which eventually totally supplanted the manufacturer's trademark. Firms made application to the RZM for permission to manufacture controlled items. Upon acceptance, they were awarded a control number which re-lated to their individual firm. Inspectors were provided for periodic spot-checks in an effort to maintain quality control. The Munich-based central office of the RZM strictly regulated the manufacture, quantities, distribution and criteria for award of all political daggers.

In addition to the control number on the reverse of the blade, a control tag was attached to the handle of each newly produced dagger. Violations of RZM regulations could be traced back to the manufacturer through the control code. A listing, though not all inclusive, of the RZM awarded codes is provided to better assist the collector in making rapid identification:[*]

RZM MANUFACTURERS' CODE LISTING

M7/1   Gebr. Christians, Christianswerk, Solingen

M7/2   Emil Voos, Solingen

M7/3   Kuno Ritter, Solingen-Gräfrath

M7/5   Carl Julius Krebs, Solingen

M7/6   H & F Lauterjung, Solingen

M7/7   Herm. Konejung, Solingen

M7/8   Ed. Gembruch, Solingen-Gräfrath

---

*If the reader has access to a blade which bears both the RZM con-trol code and the manufacturer's trademark which is not included in this listing, it is requested that this information be provided to the author.

M7/9	Solingen Metallwaren-Fabrik Stocker & Co. (SMF), Solingen
M7/10	J. A. Henckels, Solingen
M7/11	E. Knecht & Co. , Solingen
M7/12	Waffenfabrik Max Weyersberg (WMW), Solingen
M7/13	Artur Schüttelhöfer & Co. , Solingen-Wald
M7/14	P. D. Lüneschloss, Solingen
M7/15	Carl & Robert Linder, Solingen
M7/18	Richard Abr. Herder, Solingen
M7/19	Ed. Wüsthof Dreizackwerk, Solingen
M7/22	Wilh. Weltersbach, Solingen
M7/23	Carl Halbach, Solingen
M7/25	Wilh. Wagner, Solingen- Merscheid
M7/26	Jacobs & Co. , Solingen-Gräfrath
M7/27	Puma Werk (Lauterjung & Sohn), Solingen
M7/29	Klittermann & Moog, Haan bei Solingen
M7/30	Gebr. Gräfrath, Solingen-Widdert
M7/31	August Merten Mw. , Solingen-Gräfrath
M7/33	F. W. Höller, Solingen
M7/34	C. Rud Jacobs, Solingen-Gräfrath
M7/35	Wilhelm Halback, Solingen
M7/36	E & F Hörster, Solingen
M7/37	Robert Klass, Solingen-Ohligs
M7/38	Paul Seilheimer, Solingen
M7/40	Hartkopf & Co. , Solingen
M7/41	Rudolf Schmidt, Solingen
M7/42	WKC-Waffenfabrik, Solingen-Wald
M7/43	Paul Weyersberg & Co. , Solingen
M7/45	Karl Böcker, Solingen
M7/46	Emil Gierling, Solingen
M7/49	Friedr. Herder A. S. , Solingen
M7/51	Anton Wingen Jr. , Solingen
M7/52	Herbertz & Meurer, Solingen-Gräfrath
M7/55	Robert Herder, Solingen-Ohligs
M7/56	C. D. Schaaff, Solingen
M7/57	Peter Lungstrass, Solingen-Ohligs
M7/59	C. Lütters & Co. , Solingen
M7/60	Gustav L. Köller, Solingen
M7/62	Friedr. Plücker Jr. , Solingen-Gräfrath
M7/64	Friedr. Geigis, Solingen-Foche
M7/66	Carl Eickhorn, Solingen
M7/67	Gottlieb Hammesfahr, Solingen-Foche
M7/68	Lauterjung & Co. , Tiger-Stahlwaren u. Waffenfabrik, Solingen

M7/71	Herm. Hahn, Solingen-Wald
M7/72	Karl Rob. Kaldenbach, Solingen-Gräfrath
M7/74	Friedrich Aug. Schmitz, Solingen
M7/78	Herm. Linder Söhne, Solingen
M7/80	C. Gustav Spitzer, Solingen
M7/81	Karl Tiegel, Riemberg Bej. Breslau
M7/82	Gebr. Born, Solingen
M7/84	Carl Schmidt Sohn, Solingen
M7/85	Arthur Evertz, Solingen
M7/86	Cuno Liemscheid & Co., Solingen-Aufderhöhe
M7/88	Juliuswerk-J. Schmidt & Söhne, Riemberg i. Schlefien
M7/92	Pet. Dan Krebs, Solingen
M7/94	Gebr. Bell, Solingen-Gräfrath
M7/95	D. A. Schmidt & Söhne, Solingen
M7/97	F. Koeller & Co., Solingen-Ohligs
M7/98	Ernst Erich Witte, Solingen
M7/103	Josef Hack, Steyr (Ober-Donau)
M7/111	H. Herder, Solingen
M7/112	Carl Wüsthof-Gladiatorwerk, Solingen
M7/114	Hugo Linder C. W. Sohn, Solingen-Weyer

While the normal control code is reflected as RZM M7/66, the complete control number may read RZM M7/66/38/SS. An analysis of the code will assist the collector in determining if the dagger is assembled from parts, historically correct (as in the case of the Röhm SA Honor Dagger), and to establish period of manufacture:

RZM: Reichszeugmeisterei
M   : Metal
7   : Duty dagger and hunting knife producer
66 : Code designating manufacturer (Eickhorn)
38 : Year of manufacture
SS : Political organization

In addition to the strict manufacturing controls imposed by the RZM, they also imposed rigid price-fixing to insure price uniformity. Considering the state of the economy, controls were necessary to insure the widest possible distribution of Party-related items. At first glance, the 9.00 Reich Marks* retail price of the SA Service Dagger does not appear to be exorbitant. Although when one considers that the average weekly wage in 1937 was 36 RM, from which 7.30 RM was deducted for taxes, the purchase of a dagger did place a financial burden on many buyers.

_____

*1 Reich Mark (RM) was the equivalent of .40¢ in 1939.

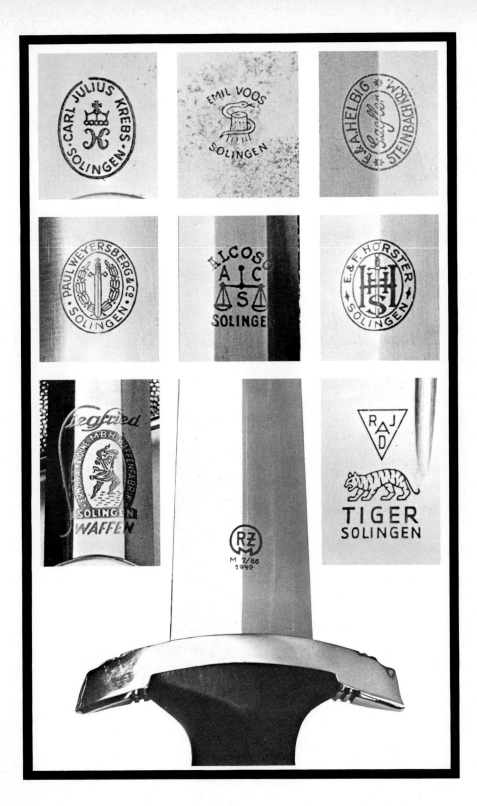

PATENT MARKS

Patents, as in any country, protect a unique design, invention, etc., for a firm, organization or individual. While trademarks were registered for protection, designs were patented for the same reason. The bulk of the daggers were not patented since they were designed under the specifications or guidance of a governmental agency. Some pieces, however, were designed at the initiative of a single firm, submitted for approval, and, upon acceptance, application for a patent was made. The blade was then designed with the Patent Pending mark....gesetzlich geschützt or Ges. Gesch. Daggers manufactured for the TeNo and DRK are prime examples of patented designs. Patents were even extended to design modifications of hangers.

NOTE PATENT PENDING MARKING ON REVERSE OF TeNo BLADES.

ORGANIZATIONAL MARKS

DRP: Deutsches Reichs Post (not to be confused with D. R. P. or Deutsches Reichs Patent)....found on the underside of the Postal Protection Leader's Dagger crossguard accompanied by a control serial number. This mark was also used to identify service bayonets used specifically by the DRP.

Z: Zoll (Customs)....normally found on bayonets used by Land Customs personnel.

D. R. K.: Deutsches Rotes Kreuz (German Red Cross)....sometimes found stamped or engraved on the reverse langet accompanied by a unit designation....B. G. 1 N. 4. (example).

NPEA: National-Politische Erziehungsanstalten....this mark, sometimes shown as N. P. E. A. , was normally stamped or engraved on the front face of the upper or lower crossguard. It was usually accompanied by the number designation of the school.

Musterschutz NSKK-Korpsführung: Trademark protection mark of the NSKK Headquarters....found on the reverse of the top link of either the upper or lower chain connecting with the snap fastener of the 1936 Pattern NSKK Service Dagger.

ORGANIZATIONAL MOTTOS

Blade mottos, found only on political form daggers, were acid etched into the obverse of the blade by means of a template, and the lettering darkened by an acid process or the addition of a black liquid substance which was dried in the recesses of the lettering. Scabbard wear and maintenance often caused this intentional darkening to be worn from the motto. Mottos found on damascus blades were normally executed in raised relief. With the exception of the HJ Fahrtenmesser, all mottos read from the blade tip to the hilt. The officially established mottos, which were the slogans of the organizations, were as follows:

A. Motto: Alles für Deutschland

Translation: Everything for Germany

Organization: SA and NSKK

Comment: The motto underwent a design change during the first year a Service Dagger was authorized. Standardization was achieved by early 1934, and remained unchanged after that time.

B. Motto: Meine Ehre heisst Treue

Translation: My honor is loyalty

Organization: SS

Comment: On rare occasions, an exclamation point will be found at the end of the motto. A rare variation of this motto is "Unser Ehre heisst Treue" or "Our honor is loyalty". This latter motto is sometimes found on high quality award or presentation Service Daggers.

C. Motto: Blut und Ehre!

Translation: Blood and honor!

Organization: Hitler Youth/German Youth

Comment: The HJ-Fahrtenmesser had its motto executed in bold script, while the HJ-Führerdolch utilized block lettering. The exclamation point was an integral part of the motto in both cases.

D. Motto: Arbeit adelt
   Translation: Labor ennobles
   Organization: Labor Corps

E. Motto: Mehr sein als scheinen
   Translation: Be more than you appear to be
   Organization: NPEA
   Comment: Blades are encountered with a variation in the formation of the "s".

SA/NSKK GROUP MARKS

Group marks, in the form of abbreviations, are found on the reverse face of the lower crossguard of SA and NSKK Service Daggers produced with the nickel silver fittings during the period 1933 to early 1935. Distribution of these daggers was strictly controlled, and the marking served as an additional control factor.

Abbreviation	SA Gruppe	NSKK*
A	Alpenland	-
BO	Bayerrische Ostmark	B
B	Berlin-Brandenburg	Berlin (B)
Do	Donau	-
Fr	Franken	B
Ha	Hansa	B
He	Hessen	G
Ho	Hochland	B
KP	Kurpfalz	Kurpf-Saar (B)
Mi	Mitte	B
Nrh	Niederrhein	B
Ns	Niedersachsen	B
Nm	Nordmark	B
No	Nordsee	B
NW (Special Unit)	Hilfswerk Nord-West	-
Ost	Ostland	G
Om	Ostmark	B
P	Pommern	B
S	Schlesien	G
Sa	Sachsen	B

*Name same as SA. Where name is different, the name is shown under the NSKK heading with the Brigade or Gruppe status shown in parenthesis following. B=Brigade; G=Gruppe with designations effective as of 1937.

Sm	Südmark	-
Sw	Südwest	B
Su	Sudeten	-
Th	Thüringen	B
Wm	Westmark	B
Wf	Westfalen	B
W (Special Unit)	"Feldherrnhalle"	-
L	-	Leipzig

SS GROUP MARKS

(Same comments as made for the SA/NSKK Group marks are applicable to the SS marks.)

Gruppe Designation	Gruppe Name
I	Nordost
II	Ostsee
III	Spree
IV	Elbe
V	Südwest
VI	West
VII	Süd
VIII	Südost
IX	Fulda Werra
X	Nordsee
XI	Mitte
XII	Rhein-Westmark
XIII	Main
XVII	Donau
XVIII	Alpenland
XX	Weichsel
XXI	Warthe

PERSONALIZED MARKINGS

On rare occasions, there are circumstances where a combination of the proper information is provided....name, rank, unit and possibly an event....which will allow for identification of a specific owner of historical note. Such personalized data was executed on order, at additional cost to the purchaser. Engraving was sometimes accomplished on the premises, but more often than not, engraving requests were sub-contracted. While additions to the pommel, crossguard, or scabbard were normally engraved, a dedication on the blade was normally accomplished by the blade manufacturer. Additions made after the time of purchase were easily accomplished by simply taking the dagger to a competent jeweler. The type of personalized additions which can be encountered are monograms, name, name and rank or dedication. There is no end to the varieties which can be found.

SERIALIZED MARKINGS

Daggers, owned by an organizational unit which required strict control on items of issue all bear a serial number which was executed on order at time of purchase. Where a piece was owned by an individual, identification may be determined providing the proper organization and event date are available. Owner serial numbers are normally restricted to the political form dagger, whereas accountability numbers can be found on any organization dagger owned and accounted for by that group. Serial and accountability numbers were either die-struck or engraved... ...normally at some point on the crossguard.

Daggers limited in production and distribution were strictly controlled from the onset of their production. This type of dagger was manufactured on order, serialized at time of assembly, and issued with the proviso that the piece be returned upon separation from the organization.

ORDNANCE MARKS

Ordnance inspection marks or wappen-amt are usually restricted to the military series of blades, and to the combat pieces in particular.

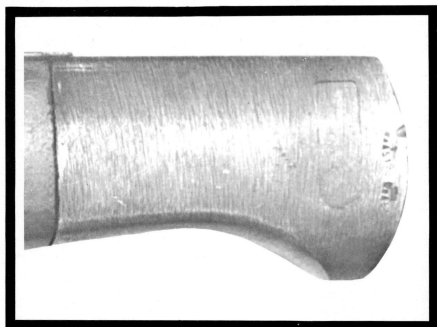

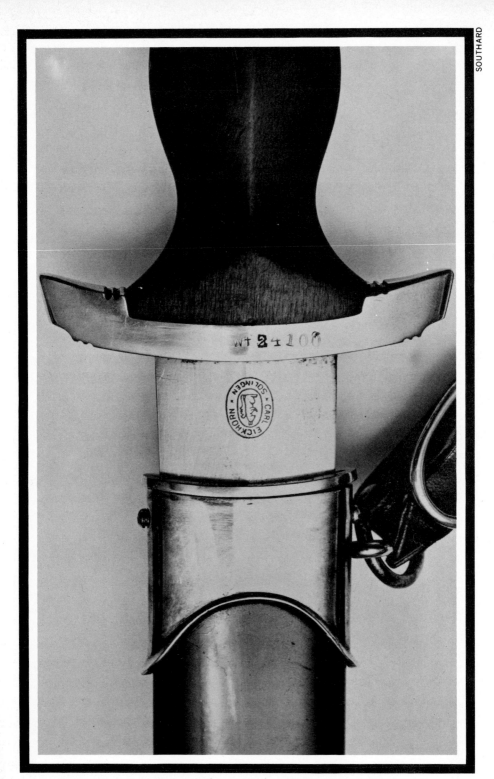

NOTE ACCOUNTABILITY NUMBER ON REAR OF CROSSGUARD (Wf-WESTFALEN).

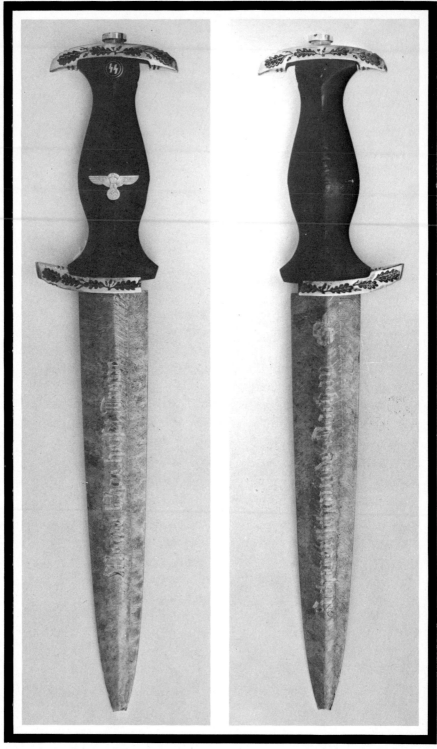

324   **HIGH QUALITY SS SERVICE DAGGER PRODUCED BY THE CRAFTSMEN AT DACHAU.**

PAUL MÜLLER AND THE DAMASCUS BLADE

The German blade industry was provided with an economic shot-in-the-arm when Hitler decided to employ the dagger sidearm as a badge of distinction within his Nazi Party. As the Party ranks grew, the demand for daggers which had been designated grew proportionately. Competition grew keen among manufacturers in vying for the wholesale and retail sales. Quality and craftsmanship were often the deciding factors in determining which firms were granted contracts.

Etched and engraved blades were a fairly common commodity to those who could afford the extra expenditure. Of particular interest were the beautifully handforged Damascus steel blades. The extremely high cost, usually in excess of ten times the basic blade, reflected the hours of labor on the part of the blade masters. Skilled craftsmen were few, and the process was one requiring a great deal of know-how. The blade artisan accomplished his end by spending many hours with the blade, alternating between the forge, water and his anvil. The finished Damascus blade was created by hammering layers of steel and iron into a very thin guage.... then rolling the metals, hammering until the two fused, and finally heating the piece to a very high temperature. The process was repeated over and over until the smithy was satisfied with the temper, weight and configuration of the blade. The blade was then treated in an acid bath and polished. The acid dissolved the softer of the two metals and a design was formed.

Artisans in Solingen found that the Damascus patterns could be artificially manufacturered at considerable less cost, in far less time and in greater volume. This was accomplished by means of a die or metal stamp that bore a specific pattern which was hammered into the heated steel. The dies reflected an art-form in themselves, taking on various patterns. The most common patterns commercially produced were rose, mosaic, ribbon, maidenhair and peacock feather. Still another technique was used to accomplish the artificial Damascus. A pattern was achieved through acid etching, giving a comparitively similar product to the original Damascus. However, these copies did not bear the mark of originality which sometimes was forged on the original Damascus blade. "Echt Damast" (Genuine Damascus) or "Damast" was reserved for those original Damascus blades which were so painstakingly produced by a select few.

One of the major factors in adding to the cost of a Damascus blade was the limited number of artisans capable of producing a worthwhile finished product. In 1938, only six smiths in all Germany were qualified to produce a Damascus blade: Paul Dingler, Robert Deus, Paul Hillman, Otto Kossler, Karl Wester and Paul Müller.

Oddly enough, Paul Müller was to become the center of controversy following his appointment as master smithy with the newly founded title of Reich Training Smithy, established in December 1938. Each firm protected their designs and artisans with a guarded jealousy. Rightfully so, considering the livelihood of many craftsmen relied on their continual ability to produce a saleable product. The Solingen firms considered their area to be the center of the German blade industry, and fully intended to keep it that way. Dr. Well, Geschäftsführer, representing the Chamber of Industry and Commerce in Solingen, complained bitterly at Müller's appointment. The basis of the complaint was two-fold: (1) That Müller simply was not a good smithy, and (2) his appointment would cost Solingen

PAUL MÜLLER

potential sales. Müller countered with a series of stiff accusations against the Solingen Chamber of Commerce and selected manufacturers in a letter addressed to SS-Gruppenführer Pohl. The controversy continued briefly and was brought to an abrupt end when the Solingen representatives were pointedly reminded that it was the Reichsführer-SS himself who desired the services of Müller. When the following contract was signed by Himmler, Müller's security in old age was assured.

CONTRACT
between

the Gesellschaft zur Förderung und Pflege Deutscher Kulturdenkmäler e. V. (an organization established to safeguard German cultural monuments) represented by SS-Gruppenführer Pohl in Berlin W 50, Geisbergstrasse 21

and

sword smith Paul Müller in Dachau

Par. 1

Sword smith Paul Müller pledges himself from the day of this contract to teach members of the SS designated by the RF-SS, who are masters in the smith handicraft, the art of making damascene swords, so that the traditional art is preserved and carried on by the SS.

Par. 2

In the training camp Dachau, the SS has set up a smithy for the forging of swords, the master of which is Paul Müller.

Par. 3

Herr Paul Müller is bound to comply with the directions of the RF-SS, or his deputy, and is responsible to the RF-SS for all his actions.

Par. 4

Herr Paul Müller receives a monthly payment of Reichsmark 450, and accomodation free.

Par. 5

This contract is negotiated for lifetime.

Par. 6

If Herr Paul Müller should be unable to work or be restructed in his work by way of an accident, also when working, before reaching his sixty-fifth year, he will receive his salary uncurtailed.

Par. 7

Herr Paul Müller, after completing his sixty-fifth year will receive a pension of 75% of his active salary, for life.

Par. 8

Both parties receive a copy of this contract. The Gesellschaft takes over payment of any document tax.

Berlin, June 24, 1939 | Dachau, June 24, 1939

Gesellschaft zur Förderung und Pflege Deutscher Kulturdenkmäler e.V.

Signed: Pohl | Signed: Müller

Accepted:

Berlin, July 6, 1939

Signed: Himmler
Reichsführer-SS

Müller began to practice his trade at Dachau, turning out expertly crafted Damascus blades, and also training the specially designated students in the state of the art. Himmler levied many requirements for production on Müller, and became greatly concerned if there was the slightest indication there might be an interruption to his work. Requirements of the war effort were the one problem Himmler could not circumvent. By 1943, pistol sidearms were rapidly replacing blades, and the demand for specialized blades was curtailed almost to the point of totality. Müller reflected his deteriorating status and the state of Damascus training and production in the following letter:

SS Reich Training Damascene Smithy | Dachau, 13.4.1943

Dachau
SS-Lager

Re: Convocation to the W-SS

SS-Hauptsturmführer Wiemann
Berlin-Lichterfelde-West 3
Unter den Eichen 127.

Herewith I inform you that both assistants Doll and Koth were drafted into the W-SS Panzergrenadierdivision "Leibstandarte Adolf Hitler" on April 14, 1943. Also the damascene specialist Sturmmann Flittner was drafted into the Kraftfahrer-Ersatzabteilung in Berlin-Lichterfelde as of April 15, 1943.

Heil Hitler!

Signed: Müller

The master artisan's complaints were to no avail. He continued on for a brief period producing Damascus pieces on order for the Reichsführer-SS, but even this was eventually curtailed. By the following year, Himmler made it known that he had little time to be concerned with the production of blades. The exercise on the part of the SS to carry on the art of damascene production came to an end a brief five years after it had begun.

SELECTED BIBLIOGRAPHY

Anders, Karl and Dr. Hans Eichelbaum: <u>Wörterbuch des Flug-wesens</u>, Verlag von Quelle & Mener, Leipzig, 1940.

Angolia, John R.: <u>Swords of Hitler's Third Reich</u>, England, 1969.

Atwood, James P.: <u>The Daggers and Edged Weapons of Hitler's Germany</u>, Omnium-Druck und Verlag, Germany, 1965.

<u>Basic Handbook....The SA of the Nazi Party</u>, MIRS, London, 1945.

<u>Bekleidungs....und Anzugsbestimmungen für die Kriegsmarine M.Dv. Nr. 260</u>, Berlin, 1935.

Bozich, Stanley J.: <u>Collector's Guide....German Relics 1929-1945</u>, 1967.

<u>C.I. Handbook, Germany</u>, April 1945.

Deakin, F.W.: <u>The Brutal Friendship</u>, New York, 1962.

Delarue, Jacques: <u>The History of the Gestapo</u>, The Chaucer Press Ltd., England, 1966.

Denckler, Heinz: <u>Pimpf, dein dienst im Deutschen Jungvolk in der Hitler-Jugend</u>, Berlin.

<u>Die Seitenwaffen</u>, Manual for Ordnance and Supply Personnel, as of April 12, 1940, Berlin, 1941.

<u>Eickhorn Kundendienst</u>, Sales catalogue for the Eickhorn Firm, 1939.

<u>German Military Uniforms and Insignia 1933-1945</u>, We Inc., Conn., 1967.

Gritzbach, Erich: <u>Hermann Göring, Werk und Mensch</u>, Zentral-verlag der NSDAP, 1943.

<u>Handbook on German Military Forces</u> - TM-E 30-451, US Army, 1945.

<u>Handbuch der SA</u>, Verlag "Offene Worte", Berlin 1939.

Höller, F.W.: Sales Catalogue for the F.W. Höller Firm, 1938.

Klietmann, Dr. Kurt-Gerhard: <u>German Daggers and Dress Sidearms of World War II</u>, Falls Church, Va., 1967.

Klietmann, Dr. Kurt-Gerhard: Selected Monographs.

Mollo, Andrew: <u>Daggers of the Third German Reich - 1933-1945</u>, London, 1967.

<u>Nationalsozialistisches Jahrbuch, 1944</u>, Zentralverlag der NSDAP, München, 1944.

O'Neill, Robert J.: <u>The German Army and the Nazi Party</u>, Gorgi Books, London, 1966.

<u>Organizationsbuch der NSDAP</u>, 1937-1943 editions.

Santoro, Cesare,: <u>Hitler Germany....as seen by a Foreigner</u>, Internationaler Verlag, Berlin, 1938.

Schmidt, Paul: <u>Statistisches Jahrbuch für das Deutsche Reich</u>, 1938, Berlin, 1939.

Seilheimer, Paul: Sales catalogue for the Paul Seilheimer Firm, 1938.

Shirer, William L.: <u>The Rise and Fall of the Third Reich....A History of Nazi Germany</u>, Simon and Schuster, New York, 1960.

<u>SS Dienstaltersliste der Schutzstaffel der NSDAP</u>, Organization list of SS Officer Personnel, Stand vom 1 Dezember 1937.

Taylor, Telford: <u>Sword & Swastika</u>, Quadrangle Books, Chicago, 1952.

Vagts, Alfred: <u>Hitler's Second Army</u>, Infantry Journal, Washington, D.C., 1943.

Wiers, Helke U.: <u>Der junge Reichsburger</u>, Berlin, 1937.

Wilkinson, Frederick: <u>Swords & Daggers</u>, The Chaucer Press Ltd., England, 1967.

FROM THE LIBRARY OF THE FÜHRER!

This volume of "The Hitler Albums" offers you a complete photographic study of Mussolini's state visit to Germany in September of 1937. It was compiled from Adolf Hitler's personal photograph album which was removed from his library at "Berghof Obersalzberg" on May 6, 1945. Many months of careful research have resulted in a scholarly and accurate presentation of the historical background, the personalities involved and the overall significance of the visit. As you turn the pages of this deep-grained, vinyl leather covered book, the minute-by-minute accounting of events plus the superb photographs makes you an eyewitness to history. You will see and experience the most dynamic spectacle of power ever witnessed in the Third Reich.... in its parades, maneuvers and demonstrations, just as the Duce did.... thirty-three years ago.

The Hitler Albums by R. JAMES BENDER

175 PHOTOS & ILLUSTRATIONS   8½ x 11 FORMAT

144 PAGES   GOLD EMBOSSED, DELUXE BINDING

$10.95